The Moche

The Peoples of America

General Editors
Alan Kolata and Dean Snow

This series is about the native peoples and civilizations of the Americas, from their origins in ancient times to the present day. Drawing on archaeological, historical, and anthropological evidence, each volume presents a fresh and absorbing account of a group's culture, society, and history.

Accessible and scholarly, and well illustrated with maps and photographs, the volumes of *The Peoples of America* will together provide a comprehensive and vivid picture of the character and variety of the societies of the American past.

Already published

The Moche
Garth Bawden

The Tiwanaku:
Portrait of an Andean Civilization
Alan Kolata

The Timucua
Jerald T. Milanich

The Aztecs
Michael E. Smith

The Iroquois
Dean Snow

The Cheyenne
John Moore

In preparation

The Nascas
*D. M. Brown and
Helaine Silverman*

The Incas
Terence N. D'Altroy

The Navajo
Alan Downer

The Sioux
Guy Gibbon

The Cherokee
Gerald F. Schroedl

The Mayas
Don S. Rice

The Moche

Garth Bawden

First published 1996
First published in paperback 1999

Blackwell Publishers Inc.
350 Main Street
Malden , Massachusetts 02148
USA

Blackwell Publishers Ltd
108 Cowley Road
Oxford OX4 1JF
UK

Library of Congress Cataloging-in-Publication Data
Bawden, Garth.
    The Moche / Garth Bawden.
        p. cm.—(The peoples of America)
    Includes bibliographical references and index.
    ISBN 1- 55786- 520–5 (hbk)
    ISBN 0- 631- 21863–7 (pbk)
    1. Mochica Indians. I. Title. II. Series.
F3430.1.M6B38   1996
985 ' .00498—dc20   96-11695
                                        CIP

British Library Cataloguing in Publication Data

A CIP catalogue record for this book is available from the British Library.

Typeset in 11 on 12½ pt Sabon
By Best-set Typsetter Ltd, Hong Kong

This book is printed on acid-free paper

Contents

Preface

In the late 1980s, our vision of the society we call the Moche was suddenly and irrevocably altered. A series of discoveries on the north coast of Peru at once revealed stunning artistic and technological achievements of Moche society and dramatically sharpened our awareness of the immense power wielded by its leaders. Curiously, the sites where these discoveries were made had long been familiar to local residents and scholars alike. But no-one suspected that they still held the potential to transform our understanding of the ancient Moche.

Today, Sipán consists of a group of mud brick pyramids which rise over the greenery of the huge Lambayeque Valley, whose lush fields extend east and west as far as the eye can see. These great structures tower over the modest cane and adobe houses of the nearby village, most of whose residents are farmers, like many generations of their ancestors. Originally Sipán was one of the many centers of Moche religion and government whose impressive remains still dominate the coastal landscape. Although these sites cannot fail to evoke admiration of the indigenous people of coastal Peru, they rarely generate the excitement of new discovery. Ironically, pillagers of Peru's rich archaeological heritage, working under cover of night in this obscure village, initiated the events that forced us to reassess our ideas of the Moche. In the smallest pyramid of the group, looters looking for treasures to sell on the illegal antiquities market stumbled on the most elaborate tombs ever found in the New World. In adobe chambers set into the core of the pyramid were the remains of the persons who wielded supreme power in the Lambayeque Valley almost two thousand years ago. Buried with them was the full panoply of authority, a rich profusion of artistic creations in precious metal and stones whose vivid iconography graphically portrayed the source and extent of their power. Unhappily, a portion of this unparalleled historical resource was removed before knowledge of its existence reached the authorities. However, in 1987 looting was stopped and a careful program of excavation was initiated whose results continue to astonish the world.

At about the same time, Peruvian archaeologists working in the Chicama Valley made other extraordinary discoveries. Here in sight of the Pacific and swept by the ever-present sea winds, stands an imposing group of Moche pyramids named the Huaca El Brujo complex. This location is especially meaningful because one of the earliest permanent villages of the Andean coast – Huaca Prieta – is visible from the top of the pyramids. Thus the visitor at a glance can span 4,000 years of Andean history. While clearing the face of one of these edifices the archaeologists encountered wonderfully preserved painted murals and sculptural friezes in high relief. Revealed to human sight for the first time in many centuries and frozen in time by the sculptural medium, a life-sized line of naked and bound captives march to their fate escorted by splendidly attired warriors. Elsewhere a row of dancers dressed in bright red costume participate in a long-forgotten Moche ceremony while nearby scenes of human sacrifice vividly depict a central event in Moche political ritual. While Moche murals had long been known from other sites, none matched the variety and drama of the Huaca El Brujo examples and none had ever before offered such access to the political structure of the Moche.

I could select other similar examples to illustrate the great advances in Moche archaeology that characterize the 1980s. Work by Peruvian, French, and North American scholars spans the entire North Coast and has immensely added to our knowledge of Moche history and culture. Today, more than ever before, we are able to look beyond the material remnants of the past to appreciate Moche society as a vibrant product of North Coast civilization. In this enterprise we are now meeting face-to-face the individuals whose ambitions motivated these achievements. Equally important, we can better observe the wider

North Coast populace that comprised the human foundations of their power. It is this enduring tier of society that outlasted the ultimate fall of Moche society and ensured the passage of many of its essential qualities to their present-day descendants in the continuum of the North Coast cultural tradition.

These major recent contributions make this an auspicious time in Moche archaeology. I therefore feel privileged to have the opportunity to tell the story of this fascinating society. In this book I draw on my own personal experience of Andean studies which span a quarter of a century and have generated abiding interest and affection for the region and its people, past and present. More importantly, I am heavily indebted to the work of the many contemporaries and distinguished predecessors who have provided the knowledge without which it would not be possible to study the social structure, cultural diversity, and complex history of Moche society.

I also owe much to the personal support of the colleagues who have willingly given me the benefit of their experience and ideas. Only a few can be singled out here for special thanks. Long ago Karl Lamberg-Karlovsky planted the seeds from which grew my interest in the structural meaning of Moche iconography. Luis Jaime Castillo, Michael Moseley, Jim Richardson, Izumi Shimada, and Santiago Uceda willingly shared their wealth of knowledge about archaeology of the Peruvian north coast and its social interpretation. They directed me to fieldwork and references of which I was unaware, and allowed my use of their documentation. Andrea Heckman and Douglas Sharon provided inspiration and practical help in the areas of shamanism and Andean social conception that they know so well. Alan Kolata provided the opportunity for me to write the book and throughout its preparation offered valuable suggestions and unreserved encouragement. Through the clarity of her perception and the precision of her editorial observations, Erica Hill is largely responsible for any literary coherence that I achieved. Finally, Pedro Asmat and the people of Moche who unstintingly welcomed me to their homes, gave me their practical assistance, and nurtured my interest in their culture, more than all others molded my awareness that Andean past and present are parts of an historical totality that transcends time and its fleeting succession of events.

Part I

The Moche World

1

Introduction: Encountering the Moche

A great civilization flourished in what is now northern Peru during the first centuries of the Christian era. Its craftsmen created the brilliant ceramics, textiles, and metallurgy that grace museums around the world. Its great flat-topped pyramid mounds still tower over the surrounding land, creating a dramatic visual link between their builders and the present. Extensive field systems in the desert bear mute witness to the effectiveness of its agriculture. These brilliant monuments to artistic, architectural, and economic accomplishment were created by a people we usually call the Moche. We know them almost entirely through their material remains. As a people they remain largely anonymous. A primary object of this book is to remove the Moche from their isolation and to see them both as the vital human possessors of a rich cultural heritage participating in the daily endeavors that are the domain of all humans beings, and as the creators of a rich and long-lasting civilization.

Who were the Moche? Everyone would agree that they were people who lived in the river valleys of the arid north coastal region of present-day Peru in the first few centuries of the Christian era. We do not know what they called themselves. The word "Moche" is the name of one of the rivers that flow through the northern desert of Peru. It was arbitrarily adopted by scholars to describe the architectural and artistic monuments of this early period. There is no reason to assume that the Moche were ethnically distinct from their coastal predecessors or that they migrated into the region from elsewhere. They were in all probability descendants of people who had regarded the area as home for many centuries. Their roots probably go back to the original settlers of the coastal valleys soon after 2,000 BC, perhaps even farther to the early maritime communities of the region. Nor did the Moche disappear around AD 750, the assigned end of Moche archaeological "culture," or at any definable subsequent date. Their descendants created the great Chimú state, the largest political unit ever seen in the Andes prior to the Inka Empire. Moreover, they represented the bulk of the North Coast subject population of this great fifteenth-century polity and its Spanish Colonial and Republican successors. Today many of the indigenous people who live in the north coastal area of Peru are in all likelihood the distant descendants of the people of the Moche period.

This knowledge, while placing the Moche in general historical context, does little to help us understand the people themselves or the human reality that lies behind the imposing remains of their civilization. In the absence of any written record to provide firsthand information of their ideas and aspirations, the task of illuminating the Moche must depend on less direct means. A consequence of this situation is one that is common to the study of all ancient societies. Because of this lack of cultural or historical continuity we unavoidably tend to alienate them from ourselves and regard them as we would units of analysis, frozen in time and space, only to be glimpsed through rigorous scientific study of limited material remains.

Archaeology often represents the only means of learning about ancient people and their accomplishments. However, in the modern era, the central themes of archaeology have hindered comprehensive study of human cultures. For much of the first half of this century research emphasized the isolation of geographically segregated archaeological patterns, largely through the medium of decorated ceramic styles. The spatial dimensions of these stylistic patterns were the so-called "archaeological cultures" that correlated people with the artifacts they made. Stylistic change through time represented "culture history." This endeavor, though vital for providing a means of ordering the wider archaeological record, overemphasized the material record and downplayed its underlying social structures and the dynamics of change.

More recently archaeology has moved into a phase where this

work was used as part of the data base for systemic studies of human societies. This intellectual current regards the interaction between environment and social systems as the central force driving organizational strategy. Economic motivations are primary in this relationship. Together with these rather general propositions comes acceptance that the determining factors in social integration and change are fundamentally similar across cultures, reflecting the action of universal processes. It follows that cross-cultural comparative methodology is a major interpretative vehicle for this archaeology, with its emphasis on cultural similarity rather than uniqueness.

Both of these major approaches, albeit differing in their theoretical viewpoints, place priority on material aspects of human society over the intangible, and interpret change in terms of broad universal trends rather than culturally distinct developments. While this is quite understandable given the nature of archaeological data, it has the unavoidable effect of giving priority in social organization and change to material aspects of economy, technology, and the physical environment. Conversely, ideational issues such as religious belief, social values, and innate cultural conceptions are downplayed. The intangible motivations that impel all human creativity are overlooked and the rich complexity of human social achievement and history are reduced to common denominators. More significantly, individuals and communities are equated with their material residue. The result is a generalized and unbalanced view of human society in which the actors who created the great cities and monuments of ancient civilization are lost in disembodied economic and subsistence systems which appear to compel society onward without human input. The person is lost in the machine.

So it is with the Moche. The splendid artistic and architectural creations ascribed to Moche civilization are too often pallidly treated as reflections of technology. Analytically, this information provides knowledge of prevailing production techniques and related issues regarding the nature of craft organization, specialization, and state control. Similarly, on a comparative level Moche society is most commonly interpreted by reference to a progressive sequence of social evolutionary stages derived from cross-cultural ethnographic study. By comparing its material remains with those believed to characterize such social stages as chiefdom and state, scholars strive to understand the society and its component systems. But these approaches describe Moche society only in as far as it fits universal patterns of technology and social organization. This approach looks outside for understanding of society rather than deriving it from observation of the distinctive cultural creation of a unique people and history.

Only recently, and to a limited degree, are the Moche people being viewed more broadly as the manifestation of all aspects of their culture, conceptual as well as material. Scholars are now beginning to look beyond materialist interpretations to discern the concepts that molded social behavior of a thriving human culture whose descendants are still with us. From this perspective art becomes the rich symbolism of vital religious belief and political ideology. Technology is the manifestation in the social world of deep cultural ideas which encompass the materials, techniques, and objectives of the product. The economic system is more than a description of the means used to obtain food and wealth and to control labor. It also is a reflection of the mental principles that direct the strategies employed to effect these goals. In this book I use this broader approach to the material record, viewing the Moche within the historical context of their own culture in order to reach a closer understanding of this most absorbing of indigenous Andean civilizations.

People, Culture, and Moche Archaeology

At the outset it is necessary to discuss briefly a major terminological issue associated with Moche studies. In reality the word "Moche" has no single, absolute meaning. The word has been variously used to describe a significant number of themes. In its most common use, Moche refers to a North Coast people of the period approximately AD 100–750 and the culture reflected by its distinctive artistic and architectural remains; for the sake of clarity I use this definition in my book. However, in this apparently simple definition, there is basis for confusion. The three components – people, culture, and material residue – are extremely difficult to correlate as expressions of a single entity. They need not, indeed usually do not, possess the same well-defined spatial and temporal boundaries.

Most permanent are people. People are the omnipresent and enduring agents who create culture and outlive any particular art style or technological innovation. There really is no problem here unless one attempts to equate changing archaeological expressions with transformation in the populations who made them, an approach that raises the potential of seeing major cultural change or demographic replacement where none existed. This is not a significant issue in current Andean north coastal study where most scholars would accept overall stability of population through time.

The relationship between the material record and culture is more problematic. On the most visible level culture is expressed through the distinctive material objects, styles, languages, and behavior that characterize a definable social group. But these tangible features are only manifestations of the shared values and beliefs of the group which, in turn, are formed by its long experiential history. While culture is the creation of human beings and, in the daily world, provides the accepted parameters for their purposeful thought, action, and identity, it functions at the subconscious structural level. Over time culture evolves through the constant interplay between the social action and innate structure of a group. However, given its grounding in deep social psychology, it is necessarily stable, resistant to short-term influence. On the other hand the material objects created by a culture, while deriving their specific forms and meaning from fundamental cultural concepts, respond to relatively transient influences. Thus, while fundamental cultural character persists through the generations, its material expressions necessarily change as a function of taste, technological modification, economic contingency, religious or political edict, and so on.

It follows that the very common practice in archaeology of assuming that a well-defined material assemblage corresponds to a discrete cultural entity is often mistaken. This is especially so in a situation like that of the Moche where the "culture" is traditionally defined by a very limited set of archaeological items. Its distinctive elite art style, elaborate iconography, and monumental architecture all relate to exclusive areas of social life. The broader social domain in which most people lived is not represented in this material. Specifically, as we shall see, the nature and context of distinctive Moche traits strongly suggest that they were symbols of dominant religious and political ideology, serving the interests of a ruling elite. Thus Moche "diagnostic" material indicators can reflect neither the total spectrum of cultural existence nor its longevity as is sometimes implied. As with historical accounts, so it is in archaeology. The records speak chiefly of the few who ruled society, and the bulk of the population remains hidden.

I believe that there was no distinctive Moche "culture" as such. The elaborate art and architecture that comprise the Moche archaeological record are actually the symbols of one particular successful system of power and its accompanying ideology. On a broader level, archaeologically-defined cultures like those of the Moche, and its Gallinazo and Chimú counterparts, were actually specialized and brilliant products of the persistent cultural tradition evolved by the people of the North Coast region. This vital tradition and the people who created it over millennia of history far antedated and outlived the various religious and political systems devised by the Moche and their counterparts. In this book I describe both the small part of this cultural tradition that was the Moche power structure and the people of the North Coast from which it emerged and who lived under its sway during the Moche period – in Western chronometry the interval from approximately AD 100 to AD 750. For simplicity's sake I shall call both of these rather different social categories "the Moche," while here stressing that they can carry separate historical and social connotations.

A final, less complicated source of terminological confusion comes from simple place names. The causes of this, however, are much more obvious and resolved with the help of a glance at the map in figure 1.1. Geographically the area occupied by Moche-affiliated society is that portion of the north coast of Peru extending from roughly 5 to 10 degrees south of the Equator, the area between the Piura Valley in the north and the Huarmey Valley in the south bounded by the Pacific Ocean and the Andes Mountains (figure 1.1). The habitable land of this region comprises a number of fertile river valleys running

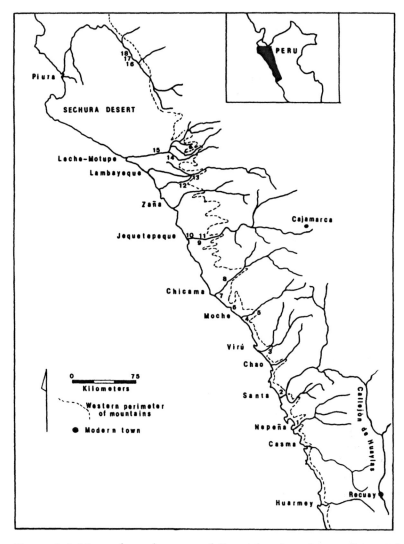

Figure 1.1 Map of north coast of Peru showing river valleys and principal Moche sites mentioned in text. (1) Pañamarca; (2) Pampa de los Incas; (3) Huancaco; (4) Cerro Blanco site; (5) Galindo; (6) Huanchaco; (7) Huaca El Brujo Complex; (8) Cerro Mayal/ Mocollope; (9) La Mina; (10) Pacatnamú; (11) San José de Moro; (12) Sipán; (13) Pampa Grande; (14) Huaca Latrada; (15) Huaca Lucía, Batan Grande; (16) Loma Negra; (17) Nima/Valverde; (18) Vicús.

through desert terrain. Although sometimes referred to as the Moche area in studies of this subject, for clarity I term this area the North Coast region, thus stressing its long-term ecological integrity, an important characteristic that would be obscured by linking it with any single social group. Fittingly, the North Coast region was the home of people whose archaeological remains similarly suggest general cultural integrity through time, although there were certainly local differences. Lastly, in the center of the region lies the Moche River Valley. This valley, prominent in archaeological history, contains the long-presumed focal settlement of Moche civilization, located at a contemporary village of the same name. Again to avoid unnecessary confusion I call this center the Cerro Blanco site after the hill that looms above its extensive architectural remains.

Current Issues in Moche Studies

While traditional emphasis on refinement of Moche "culture history" and ceramic style seriation continues, research focus has moved to issues concerning the nature of North Coast society. Current interests broadly fall into two general categories. These include social organization and social structure.

Today's interest in social organization derives largely from the emphasis on cultural evolution and its relationship to the physical environment that stemmed from earlier research in ecological evolution and comparative ethnographic research, and accompanied the "New Archaeology" of the 1960s and 1970s. In this approach the environment is seen as a system that, together with economic structures, determines the form of human society. This work assumes the existence of a series of universal patterns (stages) of social organization of ascending complexity, ranging from nomadic band to complex state, each stage with its own set of characteristics. A central premise of this model is that social evolution is progressive and, unless catastrophic events intrude, will move from simple to complex. This process is viewed as applicable to all human societies.

This branch of research has long been prominent in Moche studies and has focused on such issues as whether the ruling elite governed a chiefdom or a state and whether this was theocratic or secular (Haas, Pozorski, and Pozorski 1987; Isbell 1986, 1988:186–9; Schaedel 1985). Current research has largely moved from simple identification to deeper exploration of the strategies of social organization manifested in large-site settlement planning (Bawden 1982a, 1982b; Moseley and Day 1982; Shimada 1994b), of the wider economic connection of Moche rulers (Shimada 1987, 1994a), of social hierarchy as reflected in variation in burial elaboration (Alva and Donnan 1993; Castillo 1993; Donnan and Mackey 1978) and of the nature of social evolution through the Moche period (Bawden 1994a, 1995; Shimada 1994a, 1994b).

The other branch of Moche studies seeks to explore conceptual structure underlying the organizational forms. Although this approach also has antecedents, these were limited until comparatively recently due to the tendency, discussed above, to view the Moche as one example of a universal social stage whose dynamics could best be explained by reference to general patterns and processes. Largely within the last decade a number of scholars have initiated research that views people of the North Coast region as representative of peculiarly Andean culture. According to this approach, society of the Moche period was organized and motivated by distinctive structural principles arising from its own long history. It shared these principles only with its related societies in the Andean realm rather than obeying the dictates of universal laws and thus cannot be understood by simple comparison with cultures elsewhere in the world.

Structural studies take two forms. One uses archaeological materials of the Moche period, the other uses documents and ethnographic information from the wider Andean area as well as from the North Coast region. Included in the Moche archaeological record is a rich body of iconography, painted on fine pottery and corporate architecture, crafted in precious metal, and woven into textiles. Most of the portable works come from elite burials throughout the region. The patterned and representational nature of this iconography permits its characterization as the codified symbolism of an ideology of power. In this role it depicts the religious rituals and mythic events that supported the regional social order of the Moche period and linked it to deeper shared belief. Scholars study the specific iconographic themes and social contexts to gain knowledge of their significance in Andean terms.

Of vital help in this endeavor is the study of the structural principles underlying Andean society. These principles compose the conceptual context within which specific cultural construction occurs. Accordingly, iconography, as the symbolic manifestation of a cultural tradition, can only be understood as an outgrowth of social structure. Scholars are confronting this intellectual challenge in part by engaging in a dialogue with the Andean past. Historical documents of the early Spanish Colonial period contain detailed information of indigenous landholdings, residence patterns, and administration. This material provides valuable information on pre-European concepts of social organization and economic interaction on the north coast of Peru and in the Andean area generally. Finally, during the past few decades there has developed expanded awareness that modern Andean natives have preserved many aspects of their ancestral world-view. While constantly adjusting as it appropriates aspects of the wider Andean cultural mixture, traditional thought remains a vital and successful force for social integration in the modern world. By living and working in remote Andean communities, outsiders are increasingly learning the ways in which traditional world-view constitutes a unified and holistic vision of human physical and metaphysical experience and is a strong bond that has endured through many centuries of change.

By these means current students of Andean culture are progressively becoming aware of the strong sub-stratum of traditional structural principles which embrace all Andean peoples and unite them with their ancestors through the ages. In the specific instance of the Moche, this realization of continuity helps to remove the gulf which time and cultural ignorance has placed between them and the present. Moreover, it provides a broad intellectual framework within which the people of the North Coast region can be revisited and their forms of social organization understood as manifestations of the great sweep of New World conceptual creativity.

Time, Tradition, and Structure

As far as we know, pre-European Andean peoples did not use a writing system, so there is no direct communication to help us in our exploration of this period. The question thus arises as to how we can view Moche civilization in its own terms, separated as it is from the present by well over 1,000 years.

On the purely chronometric level the passage of time can be regarded as constituting a progressively expanding void between present and past. However, in the broad experience of any distinct human society, time represents an historical continuum within which a culture emerges and develops. Time is thus culturally transformed into tradition which embraces living members of a society and their forebears in a temporal unity. Moreover, the particular concepts that define their cultural tradition limit the possibilities for action and change open to the members of society. While culture is constantly adjusting according to the dictates of history, such change is not random but occurs within the structure of beliefs that are the heritage of all members of a society, past and present. These core principles are, of course, made explicit in the lifeways that comprise the vital living culture of contemporary members of the tradition. Thus the past becomes accessible and understandable in the context of persisting cultural belief. More importantly, the people who created the tradition through the centuries are no longer lost in time but become familiar as the ancestors of vital living cultures.

Following this reasoning, the Moche elite and the wider population whom they ruled were products of a strong cultural tradition that arose on the north coast of Peru and can be perceived in the strong continuities of the archaeological record that I shall discuss later in this book. However, we should not ignore the fact that the peoples of the Peruvian north coast were in close contact with their coastal and highland neighbors. The resulting interaction through many centuries greatly enriched the regional tradition through its incorporation of important features of material and conceptual culture. On the broader level the North Coast tradition was one among many in the world of the American Indian, sharing with all indigenous New

World peoples, past and present, a world-view that distinguishes this great family of peoples from later arrivals. At this point it is useful to examine this fundamental belief pattern, or structure, for it affected all aspects of social life and provided the broad psychological context within which all indigenous New World peoples, including the Moche, constructed their distinctive cultural traditions.

Social structure embodies the innate complex of shared values and rules which defines group psychology or "world-view," the relations between group members, and responsibilities associated with these relations. Of the numerous scholars who have explored this subject the ideas of two are especially relevant to my study. Victor Turner (1969) identifies two opposing and complementary forces present in all human societies. "Structure" promotes the formation of a differentiated and hierarchical system of legal, political, and economic institutions and positions which orders social life. By contrast "communitas" resists such order in fostering communal equality where individuals submit willingly to the informal authority of respected elders. These opposing forces are mediated through ritual to attain the complementary balance that defines a stable society and sets the parameters for the specific forms of social organization and action constructed in every human group.

Louis Dumont discusses this general structural variability from a somewhat different perspective through his constructs of holistic and individualizing ideology and applies his thinking to complex Oriental and Western civilizations (Dumont 1980, 1986). He defines holism as a social order that innately accepts society as collective Man (1980:8–11). It places the interests of the wider group above individual well-being. Thus the systems of social order accommodate the broad needs of the collectivity rather than any particular interest group. In this, holism resembles the structural tendency of Turner's communitas. Dumont contrasts this holistic concept of society with that of the modern West where in an individualistic setting the Human Being is regarded as the measure of all things (Dumont 1986), the end for whose happiness society was contrived. Of course, these two descriptions simplistically describe ideal and opposing structural forms. As Turner emphasizes, all real societies incorporate both qualities in different degrees. However, the dominant structure is usually apparent so that, while in the most egalitarian society there may be same tendency toward personal advancement, this must be developed within the conceptual limits set by the broader holistic context.

Andean social organization is embedded in an holistic structural fabric defined by principles whose origins are rooted in kinship relations, whether real or constructed. One's social position in such a setting is assigned by relationship within the community, not through personal aspiration and achievement. Kin-derived principles function on both spatial and temporal planes to subsume the individuality of each member of society within an ordered social universe. The character of the individual is merged with those of his or her lineage ancestors in a concept of time in which Western ideas of historical progression have little meaning and the accomplishments of the honored dead are the potent and omnipresent heritage of their descendants. Personal identity is submerged in a collective universe peopled by the entire group, past and present.

In today's Andean village the concept of duality embodies these holistic tenets and actively manifests them in the physical world. Though variable in nature (Moore 1995) duality is an organizing principle that is central to Andean social structure. The basic Andean social unit, the *ayllu* – a group of people recognizing common descent and communal control over natural resources – usually incorporates some form of dual social organization which affects important aspects of daily life (e.g. Urton 1981:40–3). The Andean *ayllu* often contains two chief social components, the "moieties" of anthropological writings, each with its own sub-segments. Customarily marriage partners are from different moieties within the *ayllu*. Mutual labor and ritual responsibilities between members of these social segments connect them in a network of reciprocal obligations that promotes group self-sufficiency and reinforces social solidarity. Dual organization is often reflected in a residential pattern in which settlements are divided into moiety-specific sectors. Fundamental to these practices is the belief that the health of the *ayllu* is achieved by the balance of opposing but complementary forces of both the natural and the supernatural world.

The role of leadership in such society is consequently only meaningful in the context of the wider relational system which embraces the entire society. At the community level authority is exercised by consensus rather than through exclusively political mechanisms. Where the modern nation has intruded into traditional Andean society, the tenures of local state officials are construed in historical terms as fulfilling the obligations owed by these persons to the wider community rather than as their achievement of superior power.

Even in the primary example of Andean political formation, the great fifteenth-century Inka Empire that so impressed the Spanish invaders, rulers masked their power with an ideology grounded in principles of genealogy, ancestry, and duality. The capital, Cuzco, was divided into two clearly demarcated sectors corresponding to the *hanan* (senior) and *hurin* (junior) Inka moieties (Zuidema 1990; also see Murra 1968 for a discussion of Aymara moiety structure in the sixteenth century). Moreover, by presenting themselves as a traditional, though senior, kinship line, descended directly from the supernatural founding ancestor of their group – the Sun – Inka emperors used basic holistic Andean precepts to obtain spiritual force and the authority to rule. This authority was constantly reaffirmed in ritual. Here, in the familiar everyday world, social order was reinforced by enactment of the timeless mythic events that ordered and explained the fundamental conceptual structure of group cohesion. In these ritual events, Inka rulers performed the role reserved in less complex societies for shamans, undergoing ritual transformation in order to mediate with the supernatural for the benefit of the community. Although acting in a very different political context they, like the local officials of today, acquired prestige and political authority through ceremonial roles performed within the domain of basic Andean social belief.

Thus, all aspects of life were shaped by this holistic social psychology. It provided the conceptual boundaries within which the many local communities evolved their culture, and made possible the great opportunities for political, economic, and religious creativity whose accomplishments are so evident in the archaeological and historical records of indigenous Andean peoples. We can assume that Moche society in its role as another, though earlier, member of the family of New World cultures equally manifested similar principles, while adapting them to the specific challenges of the Peruvian north coast through the rich regional tradition of which it formed part.

Sources and Interpretations

Archaeology

There are several sources of knowledge regarding the Moche, some more direct than others. The most widely used is the archaeological record. The extremely dry environment of the coastal desert preserves nearly every type of material, including those that normally perish such as cloth, basketry, and food. This inventory, together with more substantial remains of art and architecture, provides a rich and comprehensive material record of all aspects of life along the north coast of Peru that has drawn explorers and later archaeologists for many decades. Consequently, our knowledge of the material culture of the people of the region is probably unparalleled for any ancient Andean civilization. However, most archaeological research until recently was conducted in the central and southern part of the region, in the so-called "core area" of the Chicama, Moche, and Virú Valleys. This naturally led to the projection of results from this area to the entire region, a questionable practice whose implications for cultural interpretation I shall discuss later.

There are complementary sources of information. These consist of written observation by early Spanish chroniclers, and ethnographic study of modern coastal peoples and their highland neighbors. Although not as immediate as the material residue of ancient people, when viewed within the unifying framework of a long-term cultural tradition, these sources provide important information regarding the descendants of the Moche and help to fill the historical continuum which connects them to their predecessors. I summarize all of these sources in order to make clear the types of information available to scholars and some of the biases that they encourage.

The beginnings   Long before the inception of formal investigation along the Peruvian north coast, the region had been the target of less scientific probing. The Spanish from the outset condemned their predecessors' burial customs as pagan, hastened to supplant them with Christian ritual, and eagerly took advantage of these customs to enhance their own wealth. They immediately capitalized on the age-old Andean practice of burying finely crafted precious metal of religious and social significance with the dead. Interred in large cemeteries and burial mounds that were often quite visible in the desert, this vast quantity of symbolically precious gold and silver quickly became the target for treasure hunters, looters, and government-supported miners, all eager to turn it into bullion which then could be converted to negotiable currency. Concurrently, they culturally transformed the meaning of gold and silver from social symbol to financial token, a process that in itself illustrates the enormous cultural gulf that existed between Indian values and those of incipient Western capitalism.

Naturally, the chief targets of these mining enterprises were the most conspicuous indigenous sites. The Moche Valley settlements of Chan Chan, capital of the Chimú polity, and the Cerro Blanco site, believed to be the earlier Moche "capital," were the largest of these sources of treasure. Their profusion of plundered metal was converted to bullion in specially built smelters under government charter and used to sustain the emerging Colonial administration, to create private fortunes, and to swell the coffers of the Spanish Crown. So avid were Moche Valley looters that they diverted the river into the Huaca del Sol, the largest Moche edifice, so as to remove more easily its mud brick core and reach the treasure believed to have been buried inside. While we will never know exactly how much precious metal was removed from this great Moche center during the Colonial period, it seems clear that a vast quantity of gold and silver was irretrievably lost.

However, other items, also buried in great numbers, were not so valued by the treasure seekers and to a large extent remain intact today. Immense quantities of fine Moche pottery vessels embellished with exquisitely painted themes of the physical and supernatural world found their way into private hands and museum collections around the world. While their original places of manufacture and social contexts of use have been largely lost, they remain an invaluable source of information about the people, politics, and religion of the Moche period. In fact the availability of this pottery and, to a lesser extent, wooden and textile objects, played a decisive role in shaping the early direction of Moche and north coastal Peruvian archaeology.

Toward the end of the Colonial period the North Coast monuments began to attract attention of a more scholarly nature. Under the auspices of the late eighteenth-century Spanish Bishop of Trujillo, Martínez de Compañón ([1782–8] 1978–91), the great Moche platform mound, the Huaca del Sol, was carefully mapped. A succession of visitors continued this work, together comprising a rather colorful sample of nineteenth-century explorers. The Prussian Alexander von Humboldt set the stage with his reports of pre-European architectural remains in addition to his pioneering achievements in the natural science of the Andean and Amazonian areas (Humboldt 1814). He was followed by the Swiss Johann von Tschudi and the European-trained Peruvian Mariano Eduardo de Rivero who in the mid-century published the earliest comprehensive description of Andean ruins (Rivero and von Tschudi 1855).

It was the US diplomat and consummate explorer E. G. Squier, however, who did most to initiate the modern epoch of scientific inquiry in the Andes. His 1877 book *Peru: Incidents of Travel and Exploration in the Land of the Incas* describes his experiences. On one level it is a superb travelogue, set in the same mold as his earlier volumes on Nicaragua (1852). On another level it continues the trend set even earlier in the 1848 treatise that he published with E. H. Davis on the Mississippi Valley mounds, a work that must be regarded as one of the earliest attempts systematically and objectively to present a corpus of ancient architectural remains. In his 1877 book Squier likewise described his excavations and surveys of Andean ruins. Significantly, this work included considerable effort spent in surveying Chan Chan, the Moche Valley capital of the Chimú polity. In his book he presented his maps and descriptions of the ancient city and also numerous drawings of pottery, much of it in the Moche style, which he called Chimú. Moreover, after leaving Trujillo he continued down the coast to the

*Figure 1.2 The Moche pyramid complex of Pañamarca, Nepeña
    Valley in the 1860s. (After E. G. Squier 1877, p. 201)*

Nepeña Valley where he explored and drew the large Moche
platform mound at Pañamarca, now believed to be an important Moche administrative center (figure 1.2). Accompanying
this material description was a summary of legends and beliefs
about the ancient peoples of the coastal region, much of it
drawn from earlier Spanish sources.

   In this first comprehensive treatment of a pre-European culture, Squier anticipated the methods deployed by investigators
for the next 75 years. In the 1890s, the German, Max Uhle,
heavily influenced in the use of stylistic analysis for establishing
ancient chronologies by the work of the great Egyptologist Sir
Flinders Petrie, initiated three decades of meticulous excavation
and pottery seriation throughout the Andes. With regard to the
North Coast Uhle is best known for his work at the Cerro
Blanco site where he excavated the extensive adjacent cemeteries and established the first culture history for the region (Uhle
1913, 1915; Menzel 1977). Uhle identified the Moche, or
Proto-Chimú, style for the first time in its correct historical

context and initiated a scholarly tradition in which his successors, including a long line of prominent Berkeley scholars such as A. L. Kroeber and John Rowe, expanded his chronological framework to its current level of refinement (Kroeber 1925, 1930; Rowe 1962b).

Interestingly, this period of exploration that predated systematic modern archaeological study has become immortalized at Chan Chan, the Chimú capital. Here each of the explorers who ranged the Moche Valley during the nineteenth century has his name identified with one of the huge compounds or *cuidadelas* that comprise the heart of the city. It is fitting that this be so. For it was these individuals who as a group first regarded the indigenous inhabitants of the North Coast region as people whose rich cultural achievements could teach much of value to their modern successors, rather than as anonymous ancients whose only merit was the creation of a priceless extractable source of wealth. It was at this stage that the modern epoch of Andean studies was born.

Archaeological time   The north coast region of Peru provides the best-known archaeological record for a major pre-European Andean cultural tradition. The work of Max Uhle in the Moche Valley at the end of the last century set the stage for several decades of pioneering research by such prominent anthropologists as his great Berkeley successor, Alfred Kroeber, and the Peruvians Rafael Larco Hoyle and Julio Tello. These individuals concentrated their efforts on the most accessible components of the material record, the great pyramid complexes that were once the centers of coastal civilization, and the splendidly crafted ceramic, precious metal, and textile objects that embellished the extensive cemeteries lining the valley bottoms.

Larco and Tello were instrumental in the formation of a prominent Peruvian archaeological tradition. Larco was a wealthy hacienda owner of the Chicama Valley in the coastal "core area" whose lands contained extensive cemeteries and great monuments that provided the research source for his definitive work on Moche pottery and its antecedents. Larco also regarded the fertile coastal valleys as the places of origin of Andean civilization in general (1941, 1946:149). By contrast, Tello came from a poor Indian family. Starting in the highlands and later extending his work to the coast, he conducted pioneering work on the early monumental architecture of the Andes, identifying the pervasive Chavín civilization, and proposing the highland origin of Andean civilization (Tello 1942). The work of these two Peruvian scholars, so different in their backgrounds, methods, and aims, constitutes a fundamental part of our understanding of the cultures of the North Coast region.

By the middle of this century scholars had documented a succession of major artistic expressions for the Peruvian north coast based largely on changes in pottery decoration and form. With the notable exception of material from Vicús in the Upper Piura river drainage in the far north of the region, this research was conducted chiefly on pottery recovered from burials in the Chicama and Moche valleys. This sequence represents the chronological framework whose component styles are still used to date associated settlements with their varied material contents. The chief stylistic phases are noted in figure 1.3, where we can see the Moche style succeeding the Salinar and Gallinazo, and preceding the Chimú style in the south and Sicán in the north. While this general temporal juxtaposition is sound, its precise correlation with Western calendrical time is still far from certain. Furthermore, there are significant problems when the scheme is utilized as a marker of socio-cultural change. Its sequential nature tends to depict change from one phase to another as abrupt, thus precluding the notion of gradual evolution or the possibility that different styles can co-exist in the same region. Recent confirmation of the contemporaneity of the Gallinazo and Moche styles for much of their existence highlights this problem.

Finally, in the Moche case stylistic seriation has been carried even further. Rafael Larco Hoyle identified five phases which, with their subdivisions, have long been accepted as chronological markers (Larco Hoyle 1948). In this book I shall follow common usage and refer to them as Moche I–V. However, in investigating broader historical development, where it is difficult to correlate stylistic units with social and political change, I combine the individual phases into three historical periods, Early, Middle, and Late Moche (figure 1.3).

Iconography   In addition to providing the basis for a relative cultural chronology the intensive study of Moche decorated

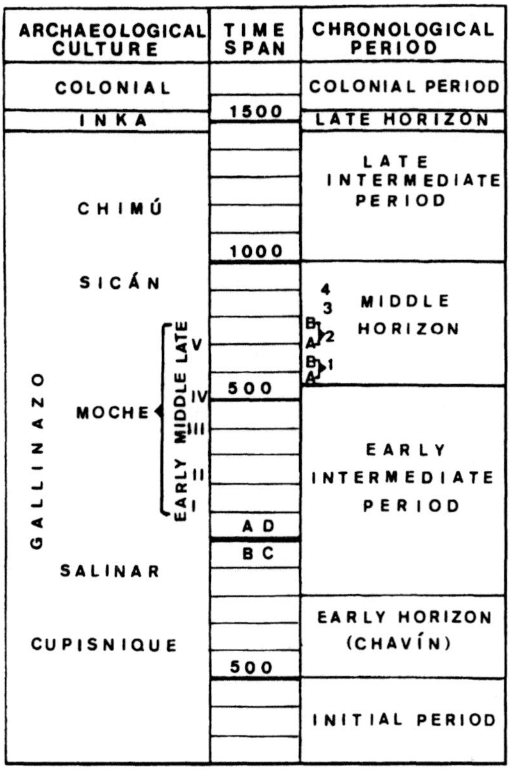

ARCHAEOLOGICAL CULTURE	TIME SPAN	CHRONOLOGICAL PERIOD
COLONIAL		COLONIAL PERIOD
INKA	1500	LATE HORIZON
CHIMÚ		LATE INTERMEDIATE PERIOD
	1000	
SICÁN		4 3 MIDDLE HORIZON B2 A B1 A
GALLINAZO · MOCHE {V IV III II I} (EARLY MIDDLE LATE)	500	
	A D	EARLY INTERMEDIATE PERIOD
	B C	
SALINAR		EARLY HORIZON (CHAVÍN)
CUPISNIQUE	500	
		INITIAL PERIOD

Figure 1.3 Cultural chronology of the north coast of Peru.

pottery has generated a very different category of information. Fine pottery embellishment of all phases, but especially of Moche III–V, incorporates a rich body of representational iconography executed in the characteristic fine-line painting style (figure 1.4). A variety of themes includes naturalistic portrayals of elite individuals, scenes from everyday life, and complex religious compositions portraying an array of supernatural beings as well as elaborately garbed humans. It is tempting to think of much of this art as the simple representation of familiar activities from daily life. Indeed for many decades it was largely accepted as such, although scholars recognized strong religious connotations in the obviously supernatural scenes.

Christopher Donnan of the University of California at Los

Figure 1.4 Middle Moche stirrup-spout vessel with scene of a deer hunt. (Peabody Museum, Harvard University; photo N27441, cat. 16-62-30/F726. Photo: Hillel Burger 1989)

Angeles undertook the most systematic research of Moche iconography as an important signifier of local social symbolism and belief (Donnan 1976, 1978). Building on the strong Berkeley tradition of stylistic studies, Donnan created a huge archive of Moche ceramic art drawn from private and museum collections from around the world and used this as the primary data base for his work. He is now increasingly focusing on the imagery of precious metal in his studies (Alva and Donnan 1993). Commencing in the 1970s he and his students have convincingly argued that Moche iconography is primarily religious in scope and communicates the tenets of prevailing religious belief as they were used in political ideology. While it appears at first glance to incorporate a wide range of subjects, Donnan demonstrated that Moche iconography actually communicates a surprisingly small number of themes that are repeated in different ways.

Donnan has used the analogy of Christian artistic symbolism to explain Moche religious iconography. In Christian art the fullest depictions of the Crucifixion scene contain not only the Cross of Jesus but its flanking counterparts, the mourning relatives and disciples and the Roman guard. However, these specific components are often used alone in religious art to symbolize aspects of Christian dogma, while the Cross itself is used without any human accompaniment as a universal symbol of Christ's sacrifice. All of these uses are easily recognized by Christian viewers, for whom they act as a kind of symbolic shorthand, triggering their wider meaning and enhancing faith through their imagery. The religious content of Moche art is similarly active on two levels. The first is inclusive and complex, depicting entire narrative compositions with their full casts of precisely identified participants. The second symbolic level involves portrayal of the participants either alone or in a very abbreviated portion of the larger composition. In this guise they act as symbolic referents to the content and meaning embodied in the major theme and were identified as such by North Coastal people of the Moche period.

Symbolic representation is also apparent in the burial accoutrements of important personages (Alva and Donnan 1993; Donnan and Castillo 1992). They often wear gold alloy masks and are accompanied by distinctive emblems of status and role (figures 4.2, 4.4). This paraphernalia duplicates the imagery contained in Moche painted ceramics and murals where it accompanies personages who are prominent performers in the activities being depicted (figure 4.3). Specific individuals can be related to the rituals in which they acted and the roles that they played in these rituals. In these ways iconography has become a valuable source of information regarding the belief structure of the Moche period. Numerous scholars are continuing to develop this arena of archaeological analysis by examining specific themes within the conceptual framework of Andean social

structure, promising even greater insight into the deeper motivations of this ancient people.

Settlement studies   While commencing much later than ceramic analysis and the exploration of architectural monuments,
study of the prominent settlement remains of the Peruvian north
coast has proven invaluable in adding social and historical
contexts to these rather restricted themes. The Virú Valley
Project of 1946, sponsored by the Institute of Andean Research,
was a pioneering multi-disciplinary examination of a small
coastal valley, undertaken to explore human occupation in the
region in its full historical and spatial dimensions. By recording
the residue of human settlement in the valley and using chronological data resulting from concurrent seriational (Ford 1949)
and stratigraphic (Strong and Evans 1952) research for his time-
frame, Gordon Willey, director of the survey component, was
able to document its changing occupation patterns and to construct the first comprehensive profile of economic, social, and
political development in a North Coast valley through several
millennia of the pre-European epoch (Willey 1953). This approach added an element of cultural process to previous stylistic
analysis, placing the well-known Moche phases for the first time
in broader historical context. The Virú Valley Project initiated
a tradition of North Coast settlement pattern studies that subsequently targeted numerous other valleys, mostly in the south
of the region, and continues to add valuable information regarding human occupation of the region (Donnan 1973;
Moseley and Deeds 1982; Proulx 1968, 1985; Wilson 1988).
   An important aspect of Willey's work was its description of
the changing patterns of land use and agricultural strategy in
the Virú Valley. While in itself rather tentative and largely
relying on associated human settlement distribution for its jus-
tification, this pioneering work initiated an interest in the field
investigation of coastal agricultural technology that still continues. However, later work regularly uses aerial photographic
interpretation in its methodology, something that did not feature in Willey's research. This method was initiated by Kosok
and Schaedel, working at the same time as the Virú Valley
Project, in an attempt to study multi-valley hydraulic and demographic patterns (Kosok 1965; Schaedel 1951a, 1966). In con-

junction these complementary micro- and macro-settlement strategies have formed the methodological base for all subsequent research into irrigation technology on the North Coast (Eling 1987; Farrington 1974; Kus 1972; Nolan 1980; Ortloff, Feldman, and Moseley 1985; Ortloff, Moseley, and Feldman 1983).

Together Willey's settlement study and Larco's pottery analysis suggested a scheme of historical development that has dominated Moche studies since the 1950s and has formed the basis for most subsequent interpretational research. Briefly, this scenario states that, having originated in the Moche and Chicama valleys, the Moche invaded the Virú Valley at the time represented archaeologically by the Moche III stylistic phase, where they conquered the existing Gallinazo society, establishing a territorial state. Lacking evidence to the contrary, this notion of a political state expanding symmetrically from its core was projected to the northern valleys. Thus, Moche supremacy was believed to have embraced the entire North Coast for several centuries until, in the Moche V phase, a combination of internal breakdown and foreign invasion brought it to an end. Versions of this unitary conquest scenario still persist (Makowski, Amaro Bullon, and Eléspuru 1995; Shimada 1994a, 1994b).

This scenario of origins and evolution, based on the integration of settlement pattern and stylistic analysis, has long provided a valuable conceptual framework for archaeological research. However, we now realize that the actual history of Moche society and its development was much more complex. The work that is reassessing our views centers on another aspect of settlement archaeology complementary to distributional analysis: the intensive examination of large settlements. Anticipated by the Virú Valley Project research of Wendell Bennett (1950) at the site of Gallinazo, this work commenced in earnest in 1968. The ambitious and multi-faceted study sponsored by the Peabody Museum was directed by Michael Moseley and Carol Mackey and focused on the urban Moche Valley site of Chan Chan, its supporting rural settlements, and agricultural systems (Moseley and Mackey 1974; Moseley and Day 1982). This vast city was capital of the Chimú polity that succeeded the Moche in the southern part of the region. The Chan Chan Project explicitly tried to reveal the strategies of social organization and hierarchy that ordered the population of Chan Chan. It accomplished this through a strategy that comprised a sort of town planning in reverse, whereby existing architectural patterns were first documented and mapped from aerial photographs, then examined by ground survey in order to establish their function in Chan Chan society. Their change through time was used to trace the evolution of Chimú kingship and governance.

The Chan Chan Project inspired a number of similar undertakings, mostly conducted in the Moche Valley at Moche period settlements. These included investigation of the Moche "capital" at the Cerro Blanco site (Topic 1982) and the Moche V town of Galindo (Bawden 1978, 1982a), founded after the abandonment of the capital and the collapse of the southern political sphere that it had controlled. Elsewhere, although important research at the great Moche V city of Pampa Grande in the Lambayeque Valley provided some early comparative information from the north (see summary in Shimada 1994a:32), little further intensive large-site investigation occurred until the 1980s. However, current work is drastically changing this picture. The dramatic splendor of the so-called Royal Burials of Sipán in the Lambayeque Valley is bringing new awareness of the creative capacity of local Moche rulers to harness intricate metallurgical technology on their own behalf and to use its abundant products as symbols of their personal might and status (Alva 1990; Alva and Donnan 1993). Continuing work at Sipán and at other comparable sites in the Jequetepeque and Chicama valleys is significantly adding to our understanding of the northern part of the Moche sphere and forcing a reassessment of its importance, while renewed examination of large sites in the "core" area is refining knowledge of this important zone. Taken together, this work points to a diverse and irregular scenario of social and political development in the Moche period.

Large-site archaeological investigation has provided two major contributions to Moche studies. First, it allows access to the direct expression of human social life – the villages and towns that are planned and shaped by the beliefs and customs of their makers. From these sources we now have good preliminary knowledge of Moche-period residential houses, their forms and contents, the ways in which they differ within the settlements and changed through time. This in turn illuminates the domestic life of the occupants, their patterns of social organization, and the role and development of class differences. In the domain of government, recognition of overall urban settlement plan and the nature of its component religious, administrative, craft production, and storage architecture, reflects the character of authority and provides a tangible way of tracing its change through time. Finally the burial architecture and contents associated with these settlements provide direct information on the group affiliation of the deceased and to some extent the status of specific individuals in Moche society.

The second contribution of large-site archaeology is that it provides information regarding the specific organizational and formal dimensions of human settlement. This in turn comprises the data base for accurate comparison of settlements and facilitates the task of discovering meaningful spatial and temporal variation. Without stringent application of this strategy, comparison is mostly intuitive and based on general and subjective criteria, leading to unwarranted conclusions of affinity or difference. For much of its course Moche settlement archaeology has relied on such an approach. On the one hand this has engendered erroneous ideas of architectural similarity in the dispersed Moche administrative and religious centers. On the other hand through quite vague similarities between Moche V urban forms and distant highland sites, it has encouraged the interpretation of invasion from outside in this final Moche phase, accompanied by the imposition of foreign settlement customs. Continuing work by Walter Alva at the great Moche complex of Sipán in the Lambayeque Valley (Alva and Donnan 1993), by Luis Jaime Castillo at San José de Moro in the Jequetepeque Valley (Castillo 1993; Castillo and Donnan 1994), and by archaeologists from the University of Trujillo and the Trujillo Division of the National Institute of Culture at Huaca El Brujo in the Chicama Valley (Franco, Gálvez, and Vásquez 1994) and the Huaca de la Luna in the Moche Valley (Uceda, Morales, Canziani, and Montoya 1994), is supplementing the evidence of earlier settlement investigation in showing significant diversity along the North Coast during the Moche period and indicating that late change was not directly imposed by invasion.

Documentary and ethnographic sources

While knowledge of the Peruvian northern coastal region, in common with all areas of the pre-European New World, is overwhelmingly drawn from archaeological research, this is by no means exclusively the situation. Valuable, if limited, information on the late periods was passed by Andean informants to early European observers and recorded by them. In addition, a considerable quantity of data concerning legal complaints by indigenous litigants, population censuses, individual and community property rights, and other official business of the incipient colonial system, represents a relatively objective corpus of information regarding indigenous social and economic life. This documentary information is complemented by ethnographic research on the modern descendants of the pre-European indigenous peoples, using the assumption of historical and wider pan-Andean cultural continuity to reconstruct aspects of the earlier society.

Documentary records must be used with care. The chronicles – texts written by Spanish observers which describe Andean peoples and their customs – were written at a time when Europeans in the Americas generally regarded Indians at best as benighted idolaters, at worst sub-humans. Their culture was seen as a potential obstacle to their transformation into servile Christian subjects of the Hapsburg Crown and thus something to be modified or destroyed in the interests of the new order. Of course, these preconceptions and objectives precluded any real understanding of indigenous social strategies or religious beliefs. However, the chronicles do provide valuable descriptions of the land and people as they appeared to the foreign intruders in the early post-contact period and are useful as long as their inherent bias is taken into account.

Also problematic are indigenous accounts of the pre-European past. First, many were written as media for political change. Such well-known works as Guaman Poma de Ayala's *Nueva corónica y buen gobierno* (1614) and Garcilaso de la Vega's *Comentarios Reales de los Incas* (1609) were written over a generation after the initial conquest, by elite natives who had been largely integrated into the ruling class. These works were largely revisionist accounts of the greatness of the lost Inka order and justifications for Colonial administrative reform. They cannot be considered as objective narratives. Even when referring to events that, on the surface, appear to reflect simple historical progression, these indigenous accounts cannot, as has often been the case, be accepted as fact. Some individuals continue to believe that embedded in the chronicles are actual events and personages that can be identified and used to reconstruct the general course of pre-European history. However, it is becoming more and more apparent that indigenous American conception of the passage of time was fundamentally different from that of Western peoples. Prominent among the scholars who are demonstrating this distinctively Andean conception is Tom Zuidema, who has probably done more than anyone to illuminate native Andean cosmology and social structure (1990), and Frank Salomon who has accurately stated: "Action over time was not conceived as changing the world, but as representing on the canvas of time the same supra-temporal structures that were also represented in space through the sacred geography of holy places, in plastic material through the use of imagery, and in social interaction through ritual" (1986:7).

Thus indigenous accounts of the past are inseparably linked to myth and metaphor, representing the structural categorization of social group identity and organization and the holistic integration of these with the wider physical and metaphysical universe. However, on the purely descriptive level they can provide very useful information about indigenous society.

For the North Coast region, probably the four most important historical sources are *Arte de la lengua yunga* (Carrera [1644] 1939), a source that provides interesting cultural details; a section of *Corónica moralizada* (Calancha [1638] 1976), a useful document for the culture and history of the Jequetepeque Valley in Chimú times; M. Cabello Balboa's *Miscelánea antártica* ([1586] 1951) which presents the history and legends of the Lambayeque Valley; and the *Anonymous history of Trujillo* ([1604] in Rowe 1948:28–30), which relates the founding myth of the Chimú dynasty and its subsequent history. In addition, other fragmentary accounts enhance information of the Chimú and more remote past in the region (Donnan 1978:86–101).

While most of the specific information in these historical accounts relates to the immediate pre-European period of the fifteenth and sixteenth centuries AD, the time closest to that of the writers, there is little doubt that many of the religious and wider cultural beliefs described in them had much earlier origins. They are also relevant for understanding the Moche period. In fact, an account by Bishop Bartolomé de las Casas ([1555] 1948) specifically describes the era that preceded the Chimú as preserved in later oral tradition and probably refers to the Moche period. Las Casas describes a time when the North Coast was divided among a number of independent "chieftaincies," none of them totally dominant over the others (Means 1931:65–6). The account also mentions that exchange and trade existed between these polities; moreover, that competition for the control of land and water sometimes led to warfare. Thus the central importance of irrigation agriculture to inhabitants of the North Coast through time has long historical continuity.

Of much more direct use is the impressive body of Spanish judicial and administrative documents relating to the subjected peoples. Compiled for purely practical administrative purposes by fieldworker-bureaucrats, these records represent the efforts of an emerging colonial administration to collect the demographic, economic, and organizational data necessary to impose order in the vast Peruvian territories and exploit them on behalf of the Spanish Crown. Absent from such records are both the biased criticisms of Andean civilization and the admiration of its political achievements that permeate the chronicles. As the pioneering work of John Murra first demonstrated in his account of a sixteenth-century Aymara Kingdom of the Lake Titicaca region (1968), it is possible to use these administrative data as a valid research inventory upon which to undertake cultural inquiry into the Andean past. For the North Coast an excellent example of this work has been provided by Patricia Netherly (1984, 1990) in her examination of water management systems and their social context. This work goes far to correct simplistic assumptions regarding the nature of indigenous social and economic organization and admirably asserts their distinctly Andean structural grounding in principles of kinship.

That strong continuities do exist has been convincingly shown through ethnographic research into modern and recent societies of the North Coast region. Various studies of local communities, modern shamanism, and specific cultural customs suggest a great deal of continuity through time. Even though the impact of European culture on indigenous societies has been strongest on the coast, it seems clear that views of the active supernatural presence within the physical world and holistic conceptions have transcended time and continue to be widely held. Moreover, Douglas Sharon's important study of a modern Moche Valley shaman-healer (1978) suggests the persistence of distinctive practices that were depicted many centuries ago in Moche art. In sum, this work identifies considerable evidence of material and ideological continuities between modern inhabitants of the region and their distant ancestors.

In addition to this relatively restricted inquiry into the North Coast region, a large body of ethnographic research attempts to demonstrate continuity of cultural beliefs between modern inhabitants of the Andean area in general and their ancestors. All such work assumes the existence of persistent cultural traditions and uses both historically documented societies and their modern descendants to detail the nature of shared conception and custom. In this view the social institutions and ideological beliefs of modern indigenous groups represent a pan-Andean pattern of shared physical, social, and ideational structure that transcends immediate historical and spatial boundaries. It is thus valid to interpret cultural traits of a chronologically or spatially remote Andean group by reference to a better-known counterpart. While modern studies are increasingly being used to identify such pan-Andean cultural patterns, historically the Inkas, as the best-documented contact period society, serve this purpose. Of particular significance to this book is the attempt by scholars of Moche iconography to interpret the cosmology of the Moche period within this theoretical context. By regarding the complex iconographic patterns of Moche art as symbols of wider structural concepts, they link this ancient culture with modern Andean society and interpret it accordingly.

Language

We have some indication of the language spoken by Moche people, knowledge that offers support for the idea of long-term continuity and represents a dramatic link between our own time and the distant past. The shortest chapter in E. G. Squier's superb 1877 description of Peru and its pre-European monuments recounts the then little-known history of the Chimú. At the end of this chapter, almost in passing, Squier also noted some information regarding the language of the local inhabitants. He wrote:

The inhabitants of the Indian village of Moche still speak, in confidential intercourse, the ancient language of the Chimús, which, from all I can learn, is identical with that spoken in the village of Eten or Eteng, about one hundred miles to the north, on the coast [author's note: Eten is located in the Lambayeque Valley]. Of this language I have a brief vocabulary. . . . The most that can be said of the language of Eteng is that it has no relationship with the Quichua, or with that of the Incas; and if it were that spoken by the people and princes of Chimú, it goes far to show that the latter were a distinct family. (Squier [1877] 1973:169)

In fact, much more can be said of this indigenous language of the North Coast, Yunga (Quechua for "hot land" or "valley"), as it is generally called. Writing over 60 years later in the second volume of his important treatise "Los Mochicas," Rafael Larco Hoyle presented an extended description of the vocabulary and grammar of Yunga, some words of which were still remembered by natives of the Lambayeque region (Larco Hoyle 1939:45–82). Larco drew heavily on primary sources for his information – a number of Spanish officials and writers of the early Colonial period. Most prominent among these early sources were the works of Fernando de la Carrera, Fr. Antonio de la Calancha, and the earliest informant of them all, Reginaldo de Lizárraga, who travelled through the region sometime in the late 1550s ([1560–1602] 1916).

Between them, these early and modern writers document some important implications of the Yunga language for unveiling the ancient people of the North Coast and their relations with other Andean peoples. First, as Squier recognized, the language of the Moche, Chimú, and their descendants bore little resemblance to Quechua, the native language of the Inka and the *lingua franca* of their vast Andean empire. This, of course, goes far toward establishing that they were a distinct people, possessing ethnic and cultural qualities that differed profoundly from their neighbors, even while sharing the wider Andean world-view. Second, these sources imply significant continuity between the pre-European inhabitants of the region and their modern successors. Larco and other scholars have compared Yunga words recorded in the early sixteenth century with those still remembered in the twentieth century and have pointed out the close similarity between them, a strong indication of linguistic and wider cultural connection through history. On this basis, then, it is reasonable to suppose that members of the small surviving Indian population of the northern coastal valleys are to a significant degree the descendants of the Chimú and their Moche ancestors, sharing the long cultural tradition of the region.

History and Change in Moche Society

Who, then, were the Moche? This introduction has summarized the significant body of knowledge that we can bring to bear on this question. No longer inhibited by the conventional methods and goals of archaeology, vital for establishing basic information, but too often mired in materialist interpretation and general evolutionary explanation, we can now go much further in our encounter with the Moche. By seeing the Moche elite, the peoples that they ruled, and the society from which they emerged as part of the totality of an Andean and greater American Indian cultural tradition, we can understand their brilliant achievements in their own conceptual terms rather than using those inspired by Western ideas. Their great monuments, agricultural systems, and religion need no longer be regarded merely as examples of dominant economic and political systems but as products of real people as they actively manipulated their living environment in their own distinctive and historically derived terms. We begin to humanize the material record, at the same time giving ourselves the opportunity to understand more closely the actual motivations and processes that governed society.

Through the use of archaeological, artistic, historical, and ethnographic information, I will place the people of the North Coast during the period of Moche preeminence in their historical context. Specifically, I set them solidly in the continuing lineage of their region, more generally in the wider sweep of Andean cultural tradition. Like all people they comprise various diverse interests and alliances. I will describe the nature and development of the individuals who created the Moche archeological record. As I noted, this record is actually the symbolism of an elite ideology of power, by definition the possession of an exclusive ruling group. But I will also examine as far as possible the lives and views of the general population of this period so as to reanimate the people whom Eric Wolf (1982) has called "The People Without History." After all, it is the interactions between individuals and groups within a society that create the dynamic tension that both shape its institutions of power and cause it to change.

In my endeavor I treat the material record as the window to human reality, not the substitution for that reality as has so often been the case, especially in archaeological writing. The Cupisnique, Salinar, Gallinazo, Moche, Chimú, Colonial, and Republican phases of the chronological table must be stripped of their independent lives as "archaeological cultures." By dissociating these purely stylistic constructions from their connotations of social change we can see them in their true light as arbitrary denominators of a single, distinctive cultural tradition that continues to this day; a cultural tradition created by the structural sub-stratum of Andean social conceptions and by a unique historical course. In removing this materialist curtain we can more easily focus our vision of the Moche on the people behind the art, using the stylistic categories as useful, if not very accurate, chronological ordering devices, or in their social context as ideological symbols.

We can thereby view Moche history as the temporal product of continuous tension and negotiation between the competing groups of people that constituted a particular society and their interaction with the external social forces with which they came into contact. Moreover, given the volatile natural environment of the area within which it unfolded, Moche history must also take into account the potential for environmental change and even for ecological catastrophe. Such history must necessarily be unique, made up as it is of the events and processes relating to a specific society. Moreover, to be truly history it must take into account the ambitions, achievements, and failures that motivated people and relate these to the deep structure that shaped all social activity and the cultural arenas within which they were acted out. For it is these human motivations and emotions, acted out in the daily social domain, that shaped distinctive Moche social, political, and economic systems, and that are symbolized in the ritual art of the period.

With this approach in mind, I will first describe the people in their various roles and alliances and the distinctive physical and metaphysical world within which they lived their lives. Only then shall I discuss the course of Moche history. In this way I hope to make the people of the Moche period familiar as the ancestors of many of the modern dwellers of northern Peru. Significantly, I shall try to de-objectify them and bring them into the realm of living history.

2

The Andean Natural World
as Culture

In this and the following chapter I introduce the people of the North Coast and the concepts that influenced their lives. It is appropriate in a book such as this to describe the natural environment within which people lived and which influenced such important factors of their existence as the procurement of food, the ease of long-distance travel, and vulnerability to outside attack. However, it is not possible to conduct this discussion of the physical world in isolation from that of the cultural experience of the people who lived in it. The people of the Moche period, in common with all Andean societies, experienced the natural world and human existence as integrated parts of a unified reality in which the spiritual forces of man and nature interacted in all aspects of their lives. This unity played and still plays a dominant role in determining Andean subsistence strategies and the rituals that are integrally related to them; in shaping religion in both its communal and political guises, and in determining the nature of social relations.

The Natural Environment of Northern
Coastal Peru

It is impossible to comprehend the course of Peruvian cultural development without an awareness of its physical setting. The

Andean natural environment, one of the most dramatic and diverse in the world, is one in which contrasting geographical and climatic zones, aligned on a north–south axis, abut one another. These longitudinal zones extend from the Pacific littoral eastward across one of the most arid deserts in the world, to the high Andes, where peaks soar well over 20,000 feet, and on to the boundless equatorial rainforests beyond. These diverse zones are all compressed within a distance of 300 miles. While I focus on the coastal zone in this book, the geographical relationship of this area to the other Andean environments is essential to understanding the wider connections of its inhabitants.

Sea and shore   The coastal environment consists of two ecological zones, the sum of whose characteristics is most evident in the north. These are the coastal waters of the Pacific Ocean with its adjacent shoreline, and the river valleys that wind through the coastal desert creating linear oases in this otherwise desolate area (see Moseley 1975a, Shimada et al. 1991 for summaries of the maritime ecology). Turning first to the maritime zone, the Pacific Ocean as it washes the coast of Peru creates a complex natural environment (figure 2.1). For human purposes, the most critical consequence of this situation is the generation of a constantly renewed marine food supply. The source of this abundance is the Peruvian Coastal Current, often called the Humboldt Current after the great nineteenth-century German natural historian and explorer of South America, Alexander von Humboldt. This current is the easternmost segment of the great counterclockwise circulation of the South Pacific Ocean which sweeps northward along the coasts of northern Chile and Peru before veering to the west. The juxtaposition of the Coastal Current above a deep offshore ocean trough creates an oceanic pattern that vitally affects the potentials for human occupation in the coastal zone.

The naturally warm tropical surface flow is constantly being replaced in the Coastal Current by the upwelling of cold water from the offshore ocean trough. This deep water is rich in the basic nutrients of minute sea vegetation. In turn, these microorganisms constitute the first link in an elaborate food chain which includes small marine herbivores, fish and crustaceans,

Firgure 2.1 A schematic cross-section of the Pacific Coast physiography and ocean current system. a: Clouds moving on-land are warmed by the land mass, causing a temperature inversion that prevents precipitation on the low coastal plain. b: Rainfall occurs in the high, cooler Andean slopes, feeding the Pacific coastal rivers. c, d, and e: The oceanic current and cool coastal current sweep north along the Peruvian coast while the deep counter-current pushes in the opposite direction. f: This configuration of currents causes the upwelling of cold ocean waters carrying abundant nutrients and stimulating a rich food chain for coastal dwellers. (After Moseley 1975a, figure 2.1)

sea mammals and fowl, and ultimately humans. Through the centuries the great abundance of these maritime resources has offered coastal dwellers a stable source of food that persists to this day. Thus, modern Peru ranks high among the world's leading commercial fishing countries and, prior to a recent decline resulting from a combination of adverse climatic conditions and overfishing, led the world in anchovy production: 12.3 million tons were caught in 1970. Because the Coastal Current sweeps back into the Pacific off the Santa Valley of Peru, its effects are most strongly felt along the central coast.

However, its benefits extend throughout the North Coast region.

Access to a plentiful natural food supply along the Peruvian coast, supplemented by inland plant–gathering and animal hunting, allowed its inhabitants to create one of the earliest expressions of civilization in the New World. Soon after 3000 BC the pattern of small villages that had characterized human coastal occupation for many centuries gave way to increasingly large and complex communities. The mud brick pyramidal mounds that dominated these settlements with their attached terraces and multi-room enclosures heralded a brilliant tradition of coastal architecture and its associated civilization that ultimately produced the Moche. Other elements that came to characterize later coastal Andean civilization also originated in this early maritime society. On the technological level, the invention of reed and balsa boats to fish the offshore waters anticipated a custom that persists thousands of years later in northern Peru (figures 2.2, 2.3). On the artistic level, the decorated textiles of the period originated an industry unmatched in the versatility and complexity of its intricate weaving techniques. Finally, many of the stylistic conventions that characterize later coastal art may be seen in their formative stages at this time.

There are two specific maritime considerations that fall somewhat beyond the confines of the North Coast but were important to its inhabitants, involving the formation and operation of long-distance coastal trade by boat and land. First, a useful by-product of the prolific maritime life is provided by sea-fowl that nest on the small barren offshore islands. The countless seabirds that made the coast their habitat for many thousands of years have deposited vast quantities of guano on the islands, a resource that has been mined as a valuable fertilizer since the pre-European period. The largest of these island groups, the Chincha Islands, lie off the southern Peruvian coast and were possibly visited by the Moche. The considerable distance of the guano islands from the mainland Moche hegemony makes this contact significant in terms of understanding wider interactions of the period.

Second we must mention the rather different resources of the

Figure 2.2 Northern Peruvian fishermen making tortora reed boats ca. 1930. (Peabody Museum, Harvard University; photo N8209, cat. 42–40. Photo: G. Holstein)

Ecuadorian marine environment to the north (see Stothert 1992 and Currie 1995 for summaries). Situated beyond the influence of the Peruvian Coastal Current, the Ecuadorian offshore waters are warmer and the coastal environment damper, especially in the north. In this setting a way of life emerged based on a mixed spectrum of hunting, gathering, and fishing, with easy access to the interior by means of large river systems. Agriculture emerged as an important complement to these activities. The societies of this region engaged in long-distance trading from early times. Of the significant resources traded from the Ecuadorian coastal region, a number of warm-water shells were of great religious importance to the inhabitants of ancient Peru. These were the *Spondylus princeps* (thorny oyster), *Strombus galeatus* (conch), and *Conus fergusoni* (cone), all of which have

Figure 2.3 Reed fishing boats beached near Chiclayo, North Peru.
(Photo: Garth Bawden 1995)

been found commonly in ceremonial and religious contexts along the North Coast region. It appears almost certain that Moche rulers engaged in this Ecuadorian trade in order to acquire these items of symbolic importance.

River and desert   The entire Peruvian Pacific coastline adjacent to this rich marine zone is bounded by a narrow desert plain, the northward extension of the great Atacama Desert of Chile (figure 2.4). The existence of desert in this tropical region immediately adjacent to the lush coastal jungles of Ecuador may at first seem surprising but is understandable as the product of a distinctive geoclimatic pattern. In combination, the cold Coastal Current, the prevailing eastern Pacific winds, and the tropical landmass of continental South America create a rare geoclimatic configuration that determines the potentials for human life along the coast (see summaries in Moseley 1975a; Shimada 1994a: chapter 3). The Pacific trade winds are cooled

Figure 2.4 Coastal desert near the Cupisnique Quebrada, north of the Chicama Valley. (Photo: Garth Bawden 1972)

as they blow over the Coastal Current, then warmed when they reach the tropical land mass. Consequently, the thick clouds formed over the cool ocean have their moisture-bearing capacity enhanced by onshore warming and they blow over the coastal plain leaving it arid and rainless, though constantly foggy (figure 2.1). Thus there is the multiple anomaly of a coastal desert only 5 degrees south of the equator adjacent to the tropical forests of Ecuador; one, moreover, in which the cold coastal currents and prevailing fog maintain an average annual temperature in the 60s Farenheit. While representing one of the most arid environments in the world and in most areas totally unsuitable for human settlement, the coastal plain is narrow, rarely exceeding 50 kilometers in breadth except in large northern valleys like the Lambayeque, and bounded to the east by the Cordillera Negra of the Andes mountains.

Precipitation occurs when the clouds come into contact with the great upthrusting wall of the western Andean mountain flanks. The rainfall flows back down to the coast in the form of small rivers that meander across the desert to the Pacific (figure 2.5). While over 50 of these rivers extend from the borders of present-day Ecuador down to northern Chile, the 12 that flow through the North Coast region are generally the largest in volume and are located nearer to each other than in the south, a configuration that permits relative ease of communication across the intervening desert. Canal systems, originating at the points where the rivers leave their mountain courses, spread like great fans across the desert floor, bringing water to all available agricultural land.

Andean coastal irrigation technology rivals that of the great early desert civilizations of the Old World in its capacity to produce the food needed to support a long tradition of complex society. Indeed it still provides most of the subsistence for the greatest population centers of present-day Peru. However, unlike the ancient civilizations of the Indus Valley, Egypt, and Mesopotamia, Andean coastal civilization was not naturally united by a drainage pattern whose canals or drainage basins were physically part of a single great system centered on dominant rivers like the Indus, Nile, Tigris, or Euphrates. By contrast, each of the coastal Andean rivers provides the water source for its own irrigation system that serves the fields flanking its lower course. The resulting pattern is one of a succession of numerous independent linear oases, separated by expanses of desert of varying width. Such a system depends on its own local society for maintenance, and administration thus tends to encourage self-sufficiency and autonomy rather than unity, a factor that is of significance in the story of the Moche.

These coastal hydraulic systems, which date back to the early second millennium BC and required considerable organization of labor for their construction and maintenance, reached the apogee of their development prior to the Spanish Conquest. Since then, in the face of changing agricultural regimes and geomorphological variation, they have declined in size, leaving vivid reminders of their earlier dimensions in the great areas of abandoned fields that extend along the flanks of many valleys. Agriculture practiced in these coastal valley systems of temperate tropical climate yielded a profusion of crops that included

Figure 2.5 Space shuttle view of the northern Peruvian coast showing (top to bottom): Moche, Virú, Chao, Santa, and Nepeña Valleys. (Courtesy Michael Moseley)

all of the staple subsistence foods of tropical South America. Thus maize, beans, squash, peppers, potatoes, and manioc were supplemented by a rich variety of tropical fruits and vegetables, while for protein, llama from the highlands, turkey, and guinea pig formed a varied and plentiful diet. These artificial valley systems, complemented by the harvest of the nearby ocean, represented essentially self-sustaining subsistence zones. Collectively, they constituted a chain of fertile oases which, if consolidated under any single authority, held the potential to create a major economic, demographic, and political entity.

The horizontal shape of coastal ecology   The 12 valleys between the Piura and Huarmey rivers that constitute the habitable areas of the North Coast region (figure 1.1) are similar in their general topographical forms and capacity for agricultural and maritime production. Nonetheless, they differ in particulars because of variations related to geographical and climatic diversity. The coastal valleys should not simply be regarded as a series of repetitive ecological units with equal and identical physical features and economic resources. Their variation raises the opportunity for occupants of one valley to better their condition by trading with their neighbors or more directly controlling them so as to appropriate their coveted resources. This coastal pattern which the Peruvian scholar Maria Rostworowski de Diez Canseco first described as an horizontal economy (1975, 1977) is a fundamental condition of the North Coast and operates both within the region and between it and more distant coastal zones, creating a dynamic for economic and political expansion that, as we shall see, is the exact opposite of highland patterns.

Because of the level coastal terrain, absence of the effects of the inshore Coastal Current, and greater rainfall nearer the equator, it is possible to irrigate considerably more land in the northern valleys of the region. Indeed, in several places the relatively level character of the coastal plain allows the merger of adjacent rivers by means of inter-valley canals. This linkage permitted the construction of great multi-valley hydraulic complexes capable of sustaining large cities, and provided the economic basis for major political development (Kosok 1965). In the far north the Motupe, Leche, Lambayeque, Zaña, and

Jequetepeque rivers were linked into such a unified entity, while late in the pre-European period the Moche and Chicama valleys were also connected by an extensive inter-valley canal intended to bring additional water to the great city of Chan Chan, though it may never have been fully operative. South of the Moche Valley it was not possible to create such extensive hydraulic agricultural systems. Here, even though the Santa possesses the largest drainage of all Peruvian coastal rivers, it runs though a deeply incised course, preventing its water from being distributed far into the surrounding desert. This characteristic, combined with a generally lower rainfall, reduces the agricultural capacity of the southern valleys. Moreover, their lack of a subsistence base sufficient to support large populations like the valleys further north, tended to lessen their ability to sustain lasting polities in pre-European times, laying them open to predation from outsiders.

Just as the productive capacity of the North Coast valleys varies, so their actual resource inventories differ. Thus the wide valleys of the Lambayeque complex and the Upper Piura Valley in the north of the region contain thick semi-tropical thorny forests (figure 2.6), a situation not found further south. These northern valleys are transitional between the more arid southern areas and the rainforest that characterizes parts of Ecuador. Like the latter area they provide the habitat for a large variety of exotic birds and animals often imagined to be restricted to the Amazon jungle, such as parrots, pumas, boa constrictors, and iguanas, creatures that were of special religious and social significance to peoples of the North Coast (figure 2.7). It is also possible that gold was mined in the north while the larger valleys throughout the region were used for breeding and herding llamas (Shimada and Shimada 1985). Thus, because of a differential distribution of agricultural potential, symbolic and economic resources, the possibility always existed for inhabitants of one valley system to increase their access to these valued commodities through exchange or outright conquest along the coast, a factor that becomes important to understanding Moche developments.

I have already mentioned the evidence of coastal interaction between the peoples of the North Coast, the offshore Pacific islands, distant northern mainland areas, and possibly locations

Figure 2.6 The Upper Piura Valley. (Courtesy James Richardson III.
Photo: James Richardson III)

Figure 2.7 Early Moche stirrup-spout vessel in the form of a parrot. (Maxwell Museum of Anthropology, University of New Mexico; cat. 57.5.8. Photo: Garth Bawden 1995)

to the south. Such far-flung interaction represents a logical projection of the "horizontal" tendencies within the region for valley communities to try to supplement their agricultural and other economic resources from better-endowed coastal locations. However, in both the case of the offshore islands and the far northern Ecuadorian coast, economic factors were closely linked with those of religion. It seems evident from historical sources that northern islands such as Lobo off Lambayeque, Macabí off Chicama, and Guañape off Virú were used by pre-European peoples as fishing and sea mammal hunting stations as well as for mining guano for agricultural fertilizers (Shimada 1987). This commerce presumes the use of craft possessing the capacity to travel quite long distances with substantial quantities of cargo. Moche painted depictions of large reed and balsa log boats, some with considerable superstructure, sometimes carrying bound prisoners, probably represent the means of transportation (figure 2.8; McClelland 1990). Wooden images of prisoners have also been found in excavations in the guano deposits of offshore islands together with other elaborate items of metal, pottery, and shell (Kubler 1948). Whatever the specific meaning of these materials, it appears most probable that they reflect the integration of religious and economic activity associated with the Moche use of the offshore islands.

While on one level "horizontal" coastal traffic with Ecuador may well have been an extension of this pattern of offshore economic interaction concerned with the acquisition of food commodities, the best available evidence concerns materials of religious significance, particularly the warm-water seashells from Ecuador that were long used by coastal communities as religious symbols. For instance, *Spondylus* shells were used both whole or ground into small fragments, in contexts of sacred importance as offerings and burial goods. Conch and conical shells also played important roles in religious rituals. Thus in addition to any rituals that may have accompanied the actual process of acquisition, the Ecuadorian commerce was to a large extent religious in motivation. Whether it be the

Figure 2.8 Fine-line drawing of reed boat carrying bound prisoners and cargo of large pottery vessels. Compare with modern boats in figure 2.3. (Redrawn from McClelland 1990, figure 2)

acquisition of guano, maritime comestibles, or materials of ideological significance, the more remote "horizontal" commercial enterprises of coastal peoples incorporated the innate conceptual structure of Andean peoples by uniting material and ideological aspects of human experience in their acquisition of natural resources.

Highlands and forest   No matter how separate an area may seem from its neighbors, they actually exist in a state of mutual interaction and influence. While the Moche, their ancestors, and their descendants were coastal dwellers, their horizons were not confined by the desert and ocean. The Andes ranges are omnipresent, always in plain view as they loom high over the coastal plains (figure 2.9). While in pre-European times the societies of the desert river valleys were usually politically isolated from the mountains and their inhabitants, in the realms of economics and religious belief the highlands were part of the northern coastal experience. Indeed, not only the mountains, but the tropical forests of distant Amazonia also played important roles in these aspects of coastal life. In order to understand the total Moche social sphere we must become at least superficially familiar with these other areas and the ways in which they were involved with the coastal regions.

The Andes mountain chain, actually a complex series of generally parallel ranges, runs the entire length of the South American continent, separating the narrow desert plain from the limitless tropical forests of Amazonia. The Peruvian Andes inland from the Peruvian north coast present a varied highland topography. Approaching from the west the traveller ascends the foothills of the Cordillera Negra, the western of the two chief Andean ranges. The rugged slopes are almost devoid of vegetation except near the banks of the rivers that plunge downward through deep and precipitous gorges to the coastal plains below. These breaks in the mountain wall have always formed the chief corridors between coast and highland and, throughout history, permitted the exchange of people and ideas. This transitional *yunga* area, in addition to being farmed where possible and used as a source for mineral ores such as copper, silver, and gold, also formed the border between coast and highlands. Moreover, in its lower elevations, the important highest eleva-

Figure 2.9 Neck of Moche Valley looking inland and showing high-level canals, 1969. (Chan Chan-Moche Valley Project)

tion irrigation canals, sources of all coastal irrigation networks, had their intakes in the descending rivers. Control of these points by coastal societies was of crucial importance for independent operation of their life-providing agricultural systems. Archaeological evidence of defensive works supports this indication that the *yunga* was at times actively contested between inhabitants of the two elevations (Topic and Topic 1987).

Between the permanently snow-capped peaks of the Cordillera Negra and its higher eastern counterparts, the highlands in the north are broken by irregular transverse ranges into fertile grassy basins and river valleys, almost all of which drain eastward into the tropical lowlands. The single major exception to this pattern is the Santa River which arises high in the Andes and flows northward through the great valley of the Callejón de Huaylas before breaking through the Cordillera Negra to the coast (figure 1.1). This river course offers the best communication route between the two zones, one that has been regularly used through time, in latter years accommodating road and rail traffic. Colder areas of rainy grassland overlook these islands of agricultural fertility. The highest of these, the *puna*, is the natural habitat of llama and alpaca, the large domestic animals of the Andes, the former serving as a pack animal as well as a source of meat, the latter chiefly used for its fine wool. Further east the Amazon-facing slopes of the Andes, unlike those of the west, fall within the Atlantic climatic pattern. They are hot and humid, subjected to heavy rainfall, and thickly forested. Moreover, their steep gradient carries them through a large variety of environmental zones in a relatively short distance.

The vertical stacking of highland subsistence zones, each with its own natural resources, has had great impact on economic strategy (see chapters in Masuda, Shimada, and Morris 1985 for a comprehensive treatment of this theme). In general, subsistence in the mountains depends on a narrower range of crops whose habitat is conditioned by altitude. Llama and alpaca are herded in the highest *puna* where very few food plants can survive. Above 8,000 feet the chief food crops are potatoes, other tubers, and quinoa. Below, in the valleys, maize thrives, while a wider range of crops including beans, squash, peppers, and coca grow on the lower mountain slopes. However, nowhere is it possible to produce in one place the broad assortment of subsistence crops that flourish together in the valley oases of the coastal plain.

Highland socio-economic structure has skillfully conformed to this "vertical" zonal pattern. Most land in indigenous societies is communally owned and scattered in a discontinuous chain through the various subsistence habitats. Thus, a single group can conduct llama herding in the high *puna*, potato cultivation on the high slopes, often utilizing elaborate terracing for this purpose, and maize farming in the river valleys below, all within a day's walk from its home village. Where distances are greater, highland villages maintain satellite colonies in the more remote zones so as to exploit resources inaccessible to them. The members of these colonies maintain their full rights in their home community, thus transforming holistic social principles of kinship into an effective economic strategy which perfectly accommodates the diverse requirements of the distinctive highland geography. One important consequence of this vertical configuration of natural resources has been that highland populations were predisposed to reach downward to the tropical forest and coastal lowlands to fulfill their economic needs. In pre-European times this tendency was occasionally accompanied by political expansion, with strong highland centers forcibly incorporating lower areas into a centrally controlled economic and administrative entity. Such direct impact was rarely felt on the North Coast before the Inka conquest. However, there is little doubt that the ever-present tendency for vertical interaction was expressed through more peaceful mechanisms of exchange and diffusion of ideas.

On their eastern slopes the Andes fall rapidly to the thick tropical forests of Amazonia, the *selva*, which blanket more than a third of the South American continent. This vast region produces the entire spectrum of Andean edibles including tropical fruits and manioc that were adopted in the areas to the west. While this region was rarely if ever in direct contact with the coast, it is clear that exchange included not only food commodities but items of social and ideological value. Thus brightly colored bird feathers from the tropical rainforest appear quite commonly on the coast, fashioned into the elaborate works of art that were the symbols of status and religious belief. While some of this material may well have come from the far north of the coastal region and the tropical areas of present-day Ecuador, it is probable that a significant quantity was obtained though long-distance exchange from the eastern forests. Moreover, there can be little doubt that important religious tenets that were adopted throughout the Andean region had their origins in the *selva*. For example, precise iconographic likenesses of cayman, monkeys, serpents, and condors first appear as central motifs in the religious art of the Chavín-related cults adopted by coastal peoples in the first millennium BC. This imagery represents the infusion of visual and symbolic elements inspired by the tropical forests into the wider Andean ideological systems.

These highland and forest regions, as well as more distant coastal areas, were influential in providing many of the economic and ideational foundations of coastal society. Coastal peoples like the Moche actively utilized material strategies and spiritual qualities of these distant areas for their own use, transforming them to fit their own particular needs, and at the same time modifying them.

Environmental instability on the coast　　So far I have discussed the North Coast region as a segment of a much larger maritime environment with consistent features and well-defined connections, both immediate and distant, each with its own potentials for interaction and influence. Although I have noted internal variation in topography, irrigation capacity, and natural resources on the North Coast, my depiction could well leave the impression of general stability based on a reliable environment and predictable marine-agricultural food sources.

Nothing could be further from reality. The Andes and their adjacent coastal regions are among the most physically volatile areas in the world. The mountains themselves are still evolving, and there are numerous active volcanoes and the regular occurrence of violent earthquakes. The impact of this tectonic dynamism is vividly described by Barbara Bode in her book *No Bells to Toll* (1989) in which she describes the physical and long-term cultural consequences of the 1970 earthquake whose catastrophic effects were most strongly felt in the Callejón de Huaylas. Here a combination of an earthquake of 7.7 force on the Richter Scale and an accompanying glacial slide from the highest slopes of Mt Huascarán completely obliterated the town of Yungay and almost totally destroyed its neighbor Huaraz, taking over 70,000 lives. Smaller quakes are regularly felt throughout the highland and coastal regions of the Andes, constituting an omnipresent facet of human experience (figure 2.10). A less dramatic but more lasting effect of this steady maturation of the earth's form is felt on the coastal plain. Here the land is constantly being lifted, albeit at different rates in different locales (Moseley 1983). This phenomenon has profound impact on the coastal drainage system, causing the rivers to cut down into their beds in compensation for the rising

Figure 2.10 Ruins of Spanish Colonial mansion Casa Madelengoitia, Trujillo, Moche Valley, following 1970 earthquake. (Chan Chan-Moche Valley Project)

land surface. The consequence is limitation of the water supply available for canal irrigation and restriction of agricultural capacity. Clearly such a process is of great detriment to the communities of the coastal valleys, limiting as it does their subsistence capacity.

The sea itself also undergoes dramatic fluctuations that can have catastrophic consequences for the peoples of the coastal regions. The most immediately destructive of these are the *tsunami*. These great tidal waves, while very infrequent, engulf broad stretches of the littoral when they hit, overwhelming the coastal areas for several kilometers inland and devastating local

communities. Of even greater long-term impact, the more frequent "El Niño" events, named after the Christ Child because
they often commence in the Christmas season, involve drastic
changes in the marine environment of the Andean coast (Arntz
1984; UNESCO 1980). While the causes of this phenomenon
are not well understood, the "El Niño" is known to be part of
a general disruption of the prevailing currents and associated
climatic conditions of the Pacific Ocean. The El Niño reverses
the usual environmental conditions. The cold Peruvian Coastal
Current is replaced by a huge mass of warm equatorial water
that can raise the normal 15 degrees centigrade temperature
of the coastal waters to well over 20 degrees. This elevation
of temperature devastates marine life. Suspension of cold
upwelling water from the ocean depths interrupts the flow of
nutrients and microorganisms that supports the prolific Peruvian coastal food chain. Cold-water fish either die or move
away from the land, together with the abundant sea-fowl that
prey on them. While sea life adapted to a warmer equatorial
ocean moves in to partially replace the natural species, these
cannot compensate for the immense loss of resources. The El
Niño of 1972, coming at a time when the coastal waters were
being overexploited, is regarded as one of the major factors in
the extended decline of the Peruvian fishing industry. This vital
enterprise has only recently recovered much of its previous
strength.

El Niño is not merely an oceanic phenomenon. It often rav-
ages the land. Although weak occurrences need not have any
direct terrestrial effect, the stronger ones bring with them heavy
precipitation caused by suspension of the drying effects of normal atmospheric conditions. The savage thunderstorms that
afflict the coastal plain bring flooding that may be very local or,
in periods of severe El Niños, may cause widespread destruction
of roads, bridges, and buildings. The storms can last with
varying intensity for several years. Most significant for human
subsistence, the irrigation systems are especially vulnerable to
flooding. Canal intakes, banks, and aqueducts are easily
breached, while channels and fields are buried in flood
sediments. One of the worst El Niños of modern times, that
of 1925, deposited 395 millimeters of rainfall during a single
month on Trujillo in the Moche Valley, an area that normally

averages less than 2 millimeters annually. While most El Niño events are not as severe as this, they nevertheless cause major damage to the areas most badly hit and result in widespread economic disruption due to destroyed communication routes and agricultural capacity. The combination of the marine and terrestrial consequences of the El Niño can bring long-term deprivation to the inhabitants of the coast, requiring massive mobilization of resources to alleviate it.

There is abundant evidence for the occurrence of these calamitous oceanic events in previous centuries. Beginning in the late sixteenth century, the Spanish Colonial records note a large succession of El Niños. For instance, in 1720 massive floods that afflicted the North Coast almost destroyed the village of Zaña in the valley of the same name. The surviving architecture still bears the legacy of this event in the heavy erosion of the lower walls that extends to a height of over 10 feet (Nials et al. 1979). There are also dramatic archaeological examples from the northern coastal region. On the basis of extensive flood damage to important architectural monuments, Bird (1987) argues that a massive tidal wave dating to the ninth century BC was partially responsible for major socio-political disruptions that signalled the end of Initial Period civilization on the Peruvian coast. Moreover, extensive recent work in the Moche Valley by Michael Moseley and his colleagues has demonstrated that a number of massive floods damaged important sites of the pre-European period. These include the important Cerro Blanco site, which, together with much of its nearby agricultural land, appears to have been severely damaged around AD 500 (Nials et al. 1979). Also bearing the marks of environmental devastation is the later Moche town of Galindo, whose center has been repeatedly destroyed by flood channels (Moseley, Feldman, and Ortloff 1981). Somewhat later, the flood of AD 1100, one of the largest ever to hit the north coast, laid waste Chimú towns and villages, destroyed the all-important irrigation system, and led the state to restructure its economic and political strategies completely (Moseley 1983). All of these events are believed to have resulted in major economic and political breakdown, underscoring the gravity of environmental stress in the lives of peoples of the North Coast through time.

While there are various accounts of such calamities, it is

probably Charles Darwin's eyewitness account of the major earthquake and accompanying tidal waves that affected a large part of the Chilean coast in 1835 that constitutes the most vivid earlier record (Darwin 1839). Several strong shocks, destroying many coastal towns, occurred while the famous "Beagle" was anchored off Valdivia. However, it was the accompanying terrestrial and oceanic cataclysms that vividly illustrate the broad scope of the phenomenon and underscore the instability of the Andean physical world. Concurrent with the earthquake, a number of volcanoes, extending from southern Chile well into Peru, erupted simultaneously. At the same time the sea temporarily receded from the port of Talcahuano, leaving the harbor totally dry and ships stranded on its bottom. This strange event was immediately followed by a succession of huge tidal waves that picked up the beached ships and flung some far into the devastated town. To Darwin the most momentous result of this paroxysm was the fact that the level of the land above sea level had risen several feet during these events in the vicinity of Talcahuano and its nearby inland neighbor Concepción. As we shall see, this experience deeply affected Darwin and brought him at least a brief awareness of the sense of transcendent power and supernatural awe felt by Andean peoples in their relationship with the physical world.

The Cultural Meaning of the Moche Natural World

The Andean relationship with nature is well expressed in these prayers by Aymara Elders of the Bolivian *altiplano* quoted by Joseph Bastien (1985:75-6):

Ayllu shrines, lords of the ayllu and seasons, Isqani Tuana, Makku Tuana, Mallku Ik'ituana, these Apachetans invite you to eat this llama and to drink its blood. Small and large valleys grant us abundant food. This we ask of you Mother Earth, and we give you blood with all our heart. Today the children break the earth for potato planting, and as fine children we will work and we will break the earth.

Lord of the qochu, lords of the season, receive this blood from the qochu. Give us an abundant harvest, grant increase to our flocks, and grant us good fortune in all. Mother Earth, drink of this blood.

In these prayers there is realization of the interdependency of nature and man, acceptance of the active spirituality that permeates the entire physical world and its inhabitants, and realization that all living things rely for their very existence on the munificence of the Earth itself.

This conception is, of course, very different from that of its counterpart – Western society – which has produced most of the individuals who have written of Indian culture. A brief summary of this more familiar Western experience helps to illuminate further the Andean vision of the natural world. The conceptual gap between the two traditions is easily apparent in the writings of the early Spanish chroniclers, who tended to regard Andean integration of nature, social life, and religion as idolatrous, or who completely misunderstood its significance and meaning. Western conceptions, of course, generally view the natural world as separate from the human being. While there is clear realization that the life course of people shares many qualities with those of other living forms, humans are set apart in their character as intellectual and cultural beings.

This partitioned Western view of nature also dominates perception of the landscape which is its physical context and the universal forces of nature that dominate all living things. Since Thoreau some Western thinkers have realized the significance of the broader natural world in terms of the physical and spiritual wellbeing of humanity; in large part, though, the earth itself and surrounding seas have been seen as a vast reservoir of natural food and mineral resources, to be exploited for human gain. Alternatively, the destructive impact of such natural phenomena as hurricanes and earthquakes is regarded by the Western scientific perspective as the impersonal force of a natural system whose processes can be understood if not yet controlled. The Judeo-Christian tradition, the religious pillar of Western civilization, not only promotes this separation of the natural world from humanity, but dictates it. In the following text from Genesis 1:26 this conception is very clear:

And God said, Let us make man in our image, after our likeness: and let them have dominion over the fish of the sea, and over the fowl of the air, and over the cattle, and over all the earth, and over every creeping thing that creepeth on the earth.

The great contrast in basic conception of the relationship between man and nature is easily apparent by comparing these texts with the Aymara prayers I quoted previously. Christian belief sets forth the separation of the natural from the human world and dictates its subjugation and domination by humans for their welfare. Few would see this relationship as mutual dependency and obligation dictated by an all-encompassing spiritual context which accepts the need to recognize and honor the forces of nature and its inhabitants in return for good fortune in the social world.

It is therefore no coincidence that Western anthropologists have taken the same direction in their efforts to understand cultural systems. For instance, in the "New Archaeology" of the 1960s the natural environment was seen as one among several distinct and compartmentalized cultural systems. It interacted primarily with the economic system in terms of setting the limitations and potentials for food acquisition and technological manipulation, the chief factors in social construction and change. While in this ecological view scholars accepted the importance of the environment, they did so on the material, systemic plane. Conversely, they avoided any notion of the natural world as a vital, living, and spiritual force, integrally involved in all aspects of human social and religious existence. But it is precisely this latter view that animates Indian holistic thought of the Andes and characterised that of the ancient inhabitants of the north coast of Peru during the period of Moche ascendancy.

Darwin's account of the 1835 Chilean earthquake (1839), although written by a leading proponent of empirical inquiry, provides us with important insight into the transcendental sense of awe that the powerful forces of nature arouse in human beings. On the descriptive level he forcefully affirms the purely physical magnitude of one of the larger of the physical convulsions that regularly strikes the Andes. He speaks of the broad scope and diverse nature of environmental volatility in the area.

This encompasses sea, coast, mountain, and weather in a network of related physical phenomena that causes the very shape of the earth to change as part of the endless course of evolution. However, Darwin also succumbs to very real feelings of helplessness and vulnerability in his brief confrontation with irresistible natural power. In his words, "A bad earthquake at once destroys the oldest associations; the world, the very emblem of all that is solid, had moved beneath our feet like a crust over fluid; one second of time has created in the mind the strange idea of insecurity, which hours of reflection would not have produced" (quoted in Moorehead 1969:135).

Can we, then, wonder that the inhabitants of such a dramatically diverse, beautiful, yet frightening world, are profoundly influenced by the ever-present potential of the earth and sea to unleash these momentous forces and their powerlessness to physically control them? The North Coast natural world with its imposing visual and topographic contrasts, its dual potential for bringing agricultural abundance and complete destruction, was an omnipresent feature of indigenous human life in pre-European times as well as the present. Understandably, natural features and forces played an influential role in the awareness and cultural expressions of its people, regularly appearing in their art and legends. However, this concern was not with a distant external force, always present, yet separate from human life. In reality the natural world was an integral component of the total human experience, sharing in the unity of human and physical spirituality that pervades and molds all physical and social existence.

While overwhelming on the physical plane, natural phenomena are innately understood as manifestations of supernatural force by the indigenous people of the Andean world who have from time immemorial lived out their lives close to them. Andean people integrate human, natural, and spiritual life into their total conceptual experience. In such cultures understanding occurs on the level of religious conviction. Myths explain the origins and meaning of the ever-present natural forces and order their relationship with human society. Rituals continually constitute these myths in daily life, reaffirming and enacting the cosmological system in which humans and natural world alike have their appointed places. Through the spiritual mediation and offering that is an integral part of ritual, the supernatural cores of natural forces are mobilized on human behalf. Ultimately this world-view infuses a sense of balance and mutual control between humanity and nature that can never happen on the purely physical plane.

Through historical references, chiefly of the Colonial Period, and the rich content of painted scenes on Moche pottery, we can recognize that northern coastal people of the Moche period conformed in general to what we know of broader Andean conceptions regarding the relationship between the human and physical realms. On the purely social plane I noted earlier Bishop Bartolomé de las Casas' description of the concern expressed by various local "chieftaincies," probably of the Moche period, with land and water rights (Means 1931:65–6). The economic importance of agricultural land and water in this desert environment is underscored by las Casas' indication that contention and strife between the various polities was chiefly due to competition for these scarce but vital resources.

The political implications of the environment are certainly understandable in terms of jurisdiction over scarce resources. However, the natural world also possessed great political significance on a much deeper and pervasive conceptual level. In the 1638 volume of Fr. Antonio de la Calancha, *Corónica moralizada* (see Means 1931), there is a description of numerous natural boulders which possessed supernatural significance and were associated with the ancestors of the living people of the Chimú period on the North Coast. These features, together with more formal shrines or *huacas* that stood in each district, probably reflect the North Coast variant of the common Andean assignment of sacredness to natural features which were of special importance to specific communities.

Calancha's boulders were probably the sacred boundary markers of community lands. Other natural features were also recognized as having special religious significance to specific communities as the homes of ancestral and nature spirits and, in the case of springs, as the sacred bringers of life to their fields. Netherly (1984), writing of the somewhat later Early Colonial Period, expands on the importance of natural features at all levels of social integration by illustrating the importance of water courses in delineating the jurisdiction of the local kinship-derived corporate groups who inhabited the valleys of the

North Coast. The pattern made by water on the landscape represented the physical manifestation of the social organization and political control which ordered peoples' lives, thus an integral constituent of their communal identities and wider social relationships.

Some of the most important religious practices in the lives of Andean peoples were centered in these places of social integration and in the food-producing fields with which they were closely related. These included rituals that secured the quiescence of the most dangerous physical forces, celebrations of the vital presence of ancestral spirits in their society, and the universal Andean rituals connected with the natural life cycle where special religious rituals accompanied the planting, growing, and harvesting phases of agriculture, ensuring the continuing nourishment of the community. These activities manifest both the interconnectedness of people and the natural world and the mutual dependency that affected human existence.

In these practices, centered on the distribution of land and its natural attributes, the Moche, Chimú, and their Colonial successors are linked with their ancestors and descendants in viewing the natural landscape as sacred geography. On the purely practical level the landscape serves as the precious resource that permits human occupation of the region. However, on a broader social level the distribution of land and water is the essential factor in asserting and reinforcing the kinship rights and connections that were central to Andean social structure on living and ancestral, physical and supernatural levels. The vital spiritual force that infuses all of nature manifests itself in the spirits of the rivers, canals, ocean, and sky, the great mountains that dominate all, and in the variety of discrete sacred places that carry specific supernatural meaning to each social group. These *huacas* are the physical foci for the rituals that mark the interface between the physical and metaphysical aspects of human experience, equally sanctifying the landscape and its inhabitants and linking them in an interdependent relationship, at once tenuous and fundamental. The natural world in this relationship *is* culture.

Particularly in the Moche period the Andean consciousness of the immediacy of nature and its vital participation in human culture was expressed through the symbolism of art. Realistic depiction of the terrestrial and marine landscapes and their

associated flora and fauna constitute the largest single iconographic focus of elite Moche pottery, the most abundant medium for artistic representation in the North Coast region.
Executed in the characteristic Moche fine-line painting style as
well as in molded vessels, the iconography includes numerous
animals and birds, either portrayed alone (figure 2.7) or participating in activities such as deer or sea lion hunts (figure 2.11;
see also figure 1.4), llama caravans (figure 4.12) and pumas
attacking or protecting human beings (figure 5.1; see discussion
in Benson 1974). In addition, the landscape itself plays a role
in this painting, with care often being taken to emphasize the
particular physical setting of the activity being portrayed. Thus
desert, sea, and mountain are each clearly designated by their
topography and flora (figure 2.12). A large class of iconography
depicts supernatural beings, usually exhibiting a combination of
human and animal characteristics and often engaged in complex
ritualistic events. Christopher Donnan (1978) has convincingly
shown that all of these thematic categories have religious meaning and were meant to convey specific information through their
symbolic connotations.

Donnan suggests that the subjects of Moche painting,
whether of naturalistic or composite human–animal form, represent specific participants in rituals that were very familiar to
coastal peoples of the time. These scenes are of two categories:
those that represent complex, formal ritual scenes and those
that show individual figures. The complex scenes regularly

*Figure 2.11 Fine-line drawing of sea lion hunt. (After G. Kutscher
1955:10)*

Figure 2.12 Fine-line drawing of Moche warrior escorting a prisoner across the desert. (After Disselhoff and Linné 1961)

show participants wearing distinctive garb and regalia that mark them as individual characters with distinctive identities. The same characters appear as discrete subjects on another category of molded vessels, their physical attributes and dress also communicating these same well-defined identities and ritual connotations. One segment of this category depicts individual shamans or curers with the tools of their occupation. It is clear from these examples that the flora and fauna of the natural world played vital roles in giving Moche *curanderos* the ability to conduct their healing functions. These include a variety of plants, both native to the North Coast and brought from adjacent regions. An important example of the former category is the San Pedro cactus, still used by local shamans as an hallucinogenic drug to initiate the magical journeys during which they commune with the spirit world on behalf of their patients (Joralemon and Sharon 1993). From further afield come examples like the espingo seed, native to the eastern Andean slopes, and still used today to effect cure.

Moreover, creatures such as puma, owl, hummingbird, and eagle which figure prominently in Moche iconography (figures 2.13, 5.1) probably possessed supernatural significance as the actual mediums through which human practitioners assumed

Figure 2.13 Middle Moche stirrup-spout vessel in the form of an owl. (Peabody Museum, Harvard University; photo 10144, cat. 979-14-30. Photo: Hillel Burger)

their supernatural abilities, while foxes and deer symbolize keenness in detecting dangerous spirits in the curing activities (Alva and Donnan 1993; Donnan 1978). While this association is clearer in the depictions of individual shamans, it is probable that a similar meaning applies to the more complex Moche ritual scenes where prominent participants bear attributes of the same birds and animals. We can reasonably assume that this iconography symbolically marks certain personages with qualities of supernatural ability to enter the spiritual world during the enactment of formal ritual. Such a religious belief conforms to the practice of many modern Andean and Amazonian peoples. Thus Moche religious conception shares the integration of social, natural, and spiritual qualities with its modern successors in a structural tradition that can be traced for many centuries. The significant point to be made here is that Moche religious belief identified the beings that symbolized their spiritual experience with creatures from the broad natural world, both human and animal, integrating them into the same active supernatural context.

However, the natural world that provides the setting for such rituals also plays an important role in Moche religious symbolism. While on a superficial level land, ocean, and sky could be construed as secondary to the events enacted in them, in the context of Andean conception this only begins to explain their significance. The natural world and its wider forces occupy dominant positions in Andean religious thought. Indeed, in Inka religion the supreme divinity, misconstrued by Europeans as Viracocha the Sun God – personalized as the senior deity in a state pantheon – was more probably conceptualized as the all-encompassing spiritual manifestation of the diverse force incorporating the ultimate power of creator of nature, ever-changing yet transcendentally supreme, (see Demarest 1981 for discussion). While its solar aspects were emphasized, the supreme Inka deity was a multi-faceted divine complex which embodied the national forces of sky, ocean, and land revealed through sun, celestial constellations, storm, thunder, and earthquake, not a discrete god with well-defined features.

It is probable that the Inka supreme deity, in addition to reflecting the customary Andean conception of the natural world, also assimilated pre-existing local conceptions, more representative of the various peoples that they subjugated. Such a process manifests a common practice in imperial expansion, of replicating political dominance in the religious domain through the construction of all-encompassing state ideologies that both subsume and transcend local belief systems. Thus, the Chimú people of the North Coast, descendants of the Moche, are believed to have held the Moon rather than the Sun in the greatest religious esteem (Rowe 1948). In addition the Sea, and various stars and constellations such as Orion's Belt and the Pleiades, were of great religious importance. We can assume that these sparse cosmological references signal a North Coast variant of the general Andean pattern whereby the predictable movements of celestial bodies were used to mark the natural cycles and to herald related rituals of seasonal change, rainfall, and agriculture (Reinhard 1991; Urton 1981). It follows that northern coastal religious belief shared with the Inka the general Andean recognition of the preeminence of the natural forces in the spiritual world while differing significantly from it in details of expression. Depictions on Moche pottery of the physical world, then, should be perceived not just as contexts for their related events, but also as religious symbols in their own right, with meaning deriving from the forces inherent in nature as these were experienced by North Coast people.

The many illustrations of activities occurring in the mountains or on the sea signify the great religious importance of these two natural contexts. Visually, of course, the Andes tower above the coastal valleys where Moche civilization was centered, linking earth and sky in their upthrusting peaks. They are also the direct sources of rains that provide lifegiving water to the coastal people and of the storms, believed to be the manifestations of powerful spirits, that at times threaten their existence through flooding. Indeed mountains are regarded as the homes of the powerful deities which control the distribution of water and the related fertility of livestock and fields (Reinhard 1991, 1993; Sallnow 1987). They are thus of vital importance to the existence of life on the coastal desert. It is therefore quite natural that people of the Moche period, in common with their descendants today, viewed the mountains with awe and regarded them as places of spiritual potency. Donnan (1978) notes the great importance of mountain peaks to modern coastal *curanderos*. They give direct access to the supernatural world. They are the places where herbs with magical properties are found. They are the residences of guardian spirits. It is thus not surprising that novice shamans are often initiated on mountain slopes. Moreover, in their supernatural flights shamans journey to the mountains to confront the spirits and either mobilize them on behalf of the sick or, in the case of malevolent spirits, to combat and subdue them (Joralemon and Sharon 1993). Various rituals that Donnan reasonably interprets as shamanistic in nature are situated among mountain peaks in Moche art (Donnan 1978: figures 222–7), suggesting that these beliefs have very ancient ancestry in the region.

The importance of mountains is also vividly manifested in the architecture of Moche social control and the sacred geography of which it formed a part. The very form of the pyramidal platforms carries symbolism that evokes the mountain peaks. They are in a real sense man-made mountains which bring the supernatural qualities of real mountains into the human social arena. The location of most Moche platform mounds further expresses this connection between the physical and spiritual aspects of human experience. These great edifices were usually situated between mountain slope and river, sometimes directly aligned with a prominent peak (figure 2.14; Conklin 1990). This location visually articulates valley bottom, mountain, and sky through the form and location of important architecture,

Figure 2.14 Oblique air photo of the Cerro Blanco site as it appeared in the 1930s. The summit of Cerro Blanco is seen in the left foreground with the Huaca de la Luna at its foot, the Huaca del Sol at center-left, and the rectangular burial platform excavated by the Chan Chan-Moche Valley Project in 1970 between them. The Moche Valley runs east–west in the distance. (Courtesy Department of Library Services, American Museum of Natural History (negative 334917).
Photo: Shippee-Johnson)

thereby manifesting the deep-seated Andean practice of integrating topography and cosmology in all aspects of life.

The location of architecture of religious and corporate authority on top of platforms both visually and symbolically
associated Moche authority with the spiritual forces that ensured cosmological balance and the human social order that
was dependent on it. Specifically, the visual location of the
platforms at the intersection of the terrestrial and celestial
spheres and their mountain-derived character as entrances to
the supernatural world provided Moche leaders with a powerful context for their claim to penetrate the spiritual world as
shamanistic mediators on behalf of their people. Moreover, the
identification of platforms with mountains would have carried
for the Moche populace the implication that they possessed a
similar spiritual capacity to provide water and fertility to the
human community. Again, this quality would have identified
the leaders of rituals conducted on their summits with the life-
giving powers of mountain deities. Thus platforms, by repro-
ducing the form and function of the mountain at the center of
social control, generated omnipresent awareness of the essential
forces of the nature and, as we shall see, permitted Moche
leaders to harness these forces in the interests of political
control.

Finally, the sea, the other pervasive natural presence in the
lives of the peoples of the North Coast, was also a vital part of
their cultural experience. On the most fundamental religious
level the sea is regarded by many Andean peoples as the source
of all waters. Understandably, then, the sea, its various disposi-
tions, and its inhabitants figure large in the religious obser-
vances of inhabitants of the desert plains with their dependence
on the unpredictable flow of the coastal rivers (Reinhard 1993).
Such well-documented Andean practices as covering the floors
of shrines with beach sand (Reinhard 1991:45; Sherbondy
1982), employing *Spondylus* shells in religious rituals and offerings, and the pervasive use of maritime imagery in religious art
are all explicable in this context. Also significant is the fact that
Spondylus workshops and offerings, and maritime imagery in
general, are often associated with coastal mountains (Menzel
1977:40) and platform summits (Shimada 1994a:213–16). By
these means the actual and symbolic terrestrial features whose

related spirits control water in Andean cosmological belief are linked to the ultimate source of these waters – the Sea. This pattern strikingly illustrates the efforts of coastal people to conduct the rituals that maintain harmonious balance between the spirituality of human beings, the earth, and the ocean in order to ensure the provision of the vital substance that provides them with their very existence.

The fruits of the sea were, and still are, a vital part of the regional economy. For the Moche, the nearby sea and its coastal margins provided rich and varied food supplies, while more distant northern regions of Ecuador provided items of religious use such as *Strombus* and *Spondylus* shells through maritime trade; offshore islands provided fertilizer for the agricultural fields. So critical was this age-old concern with the sea that it shaped a distinctive component of the regional cultural tradition. In Chimú times we know of specialized fishing communities which constituted an exclusive social and economic caste with its own religious and administrative structure and distinctive dialect (Rabinowitz 1983; Rostworowski 1975, 1977). It is probable that the same situation existed in the Moche period. No wonder, then, that the sea, its creatures and the involvement of human beings in the affairs of the sea, are conspicuous subjects of Moche art. Naturalistic fine-line paintings and molded examples of fish, crustaceans, birds, and sea mammals are common in all media. Moreover, one-man fishing boats with upturned prows made from bundles of reeds, of a type still used in the region, appear in Moche art together with larger double-decked forms of balsa construction, no longer seen, which were apparently used to carry cargo and passengers from distant regions (figure 2.8).

The supernatural connotations of the sea and its denizens can also be discerned in several categories of Moche imagery. On the most basic religious level, that of the shamanistic healers, sea lions are almost always shown with round objects, actually beach pebbles commonly swallowed by these animals, in or by their mouths (figure 2.12; Donnan 1978:136). Modern folk healers of the North Coast region regard such stones as having strong healing properties and use them in their practices. Moche depictions of such stones in all probability express a similar belief. On a much broader level individuals, naked and bound, are portrayed as being conveyed over the sea in large double-decked Moche boats propelled by supernatural beings (figure 2.8). Because ceramic and wooden figurines of the same form have been found in the offshore islands, it has been supposed that this iconography depicts a sacrificial ritual concerned with ensuring the abundance of sea and islands and perhaps propitiating the spiritual forces of the ocean.

That such beings existed in the Moche belief system is affirmed by the frequent portrayal of numerous supernaturals with the characteristics of sea creatures as well as humans (figure 2.15). These beings are repeatedly depicted in combat with human warriors or with each other, suggesting that they represent on the mythic plane the struggle of Moche society to

Figure 2.15 Middle Moche stirrup-spout vessel with scene of two marine beings in combat. The figure on the left holds the characteristic Moche sacrificial knife. (Maxwell Museum of Anthropology, University of New Mexico; cat. 57.5.4. Photo: Garth Bawden 1995)

prosper in the real world against the manifold forces that oppose human success. Indeed, Hocquenghem (1979, 1987:124–31) suggests that such maritime scenes may well illustrate actual rituals in which religious dignitaries act out the myths of Moche society in order to reaffirm social foundations and continuity. The natural marine environment thus played a potent role in maintaining the religious foundations of Moche society as well as symbolizing the various supernatural forces that people encountered daily. Finally, the importance of this part of the natural world as symbol and the reality that it reveals is underscored in late Moche art and that of its successors on the North Coast by the stylized use of the ocean wave as a persistent component of narrative and abstract ceramic and architectural art (McClelland 1990). Here in its broadest form the marine environment and its multi-faceted spiritual forces are manifest as an integral part of cultural symbolism and belief.

We have seen that the dramatic natural world of the North Coast played a vital role in every aspect of the life of the people of the Moche period. On the purely economic level it determined the nature of subsistence techniques, provided abundant food resources, and offered marine and terrestrial routes to more distant regions. On the supernatural plane the always-volatile Andean environment represented tangible spiritual forces at once beneficial to human society and possessing the potential to destroy it. This awareness operated on the structural level of cultural conception to direct the relationship of man and nature. The result was total articulation of the natural and supernatural and their active manifestations in the social realm. Thus subsistence practices possessed indispensable ritual components that drew on natural features and forces for their motivation and symbolism. In the social domain the symbols of group organization and corporate authority derived much of their symbolic power from their natural form, alignment, and relations, while religious ritual incorporated the supporting essence of supernatural power inherent in its physical setting and associations. At all levels the natural world was part of the cultural fabric of people of the Moche period.

3

Life and Work in Moche Society

As is the situation at all times and places in human history, Moche society was a mixture of the sacred and the mundane, of the notable and the inconsequential, the uncommon and the familiar. Moche people experienced the wide range of hopes, goals, accomplishments, and disappointments faced by all people, and conducted the wide variety of occupations and roles characteristic of all human social life. In this chapter I introduce the actual people of the North Coast during the Moche period and the various social settings in which they lived their everyday lives.

At the basic level of Moche society were the ordinary men and women who, with their families, represent the indispensable center of all social existence. Their homes were the focus of daily activity. These people included farmers, fishermen, craftsmen, builders, and transporters, whose labor was the foundation supporting the edifice of Moche society. Further up the social hierarchy were priests, curers, soldiers, administrators, and ultimately rulers who ensured that the necessary economic, political, and religious underpinnings of society remained secure and that the interests of the elite were safeguarded. Collectively this diverse human community comprised Moche society and built its brilliant civilization. In this chapter, I use archaeological information, together with available historical records and the evidence of linguistic affinity to describe that segment of the population who were primarily concerned with producing the food commodities, raw resources, and finished items required to support the economic and social needs of Moche society.

Language, Specialization, and Social Organization

One of the most useful bodies of information on the nature of Moche production comes not from archaeology but from early European accounts of the languages spoken by North Coast people. We shall see that this information carries important implications for understanding occupational specialization. At this distance in time it is, of course, difficult to determine whether the variability described by the early Spanish visitors was due to dialectal difference or distinctive language structure (see Rabinowitz 1983; Rostworowski 1977; Torero 1987). I noted in the first chapter of this book that one early writer, Calancha, asserted that a common language, Yunga, was spoken along the coast from the Sechura Desert in the north to at least as far south as the Virú Valley. Calancha also tells us that within the language there were three variants:

Fr. Francisco de Monroy ... was sent ... to affect the conversion of the communities of San Pedro de Yoco and Xequetepeque, which at that time had large populations ... the tongue they speak is the Muchic and the Quingan, rough sounding and of harsh pronunciation. The Pescadora is in general the same, but it uses more guttural sounds; few have known it fluently, and of these the men of our religious order have learned it outstandingly well. (Calancha [1638] 1976:606, translation in Rabinowitz 1983:249)

While this passage might suggest that Pescadora was linguistically distinct from its fellows, most modern scholars suggest that the three tongues mentioned by Calancha differed in terms of dialect rather than in basic structure. Two of these, Muchic and Quingan, appear to have been geographically delineated. The former was used by dwellers of the valleys extending from Jequetepeque north, the latter in the southern valleys. This linguistic difference corresponds to similar cultural differences, thus revealing real diversity between northerners and southerners in the North Coast region. By contrast, Pescadora, first identified by Lizárraga ([1560–1602] 1916:66–7) soon after the Conquest when little demographic disruption had yet occurred, accompanied the other dialects in the Virú, Moche, and Chicama valleys and possibly the entire region. Consequently, it cannot be explained as a local geographical variant like Muchic and Quingan. In fact it appears to reflect an outgrowth of basic Andean principles of occupational specialization and social organization.

Deeply ingrained in native Andean social conception is a correspondence between occupational activity and community organization. In the highlands this belief has its most striking expression in the "vertical archipelago," a pattern that has been traced back to the pre-European period through ethnohistory and archaeology and still exists today, especially along the eastern slopes of the Andes (Masuda, Shimada, and Morris 1985). In this socio-economic pattern, highland societies maintain separate communities in several environmental zones located at different altitudes so as to utilize their specific climatic, agricultural, and natural resources. Moreover the various communities often specialize in particular crafts. By these means the society as a whole commands a wide range of resources and economic productivity. Fundamental to this "archipelago" pattern is the fact that even though geographically separated, the members of the various communities remain integral parts of the same wider social unit, together with its accompanying kinship affiliations and obligations.

The coastal variant of this pattern of economic and residential segmentation in the context of wider social unity has been well documented by archaeologists and, more prominently, ethnohistorians. The Peruvian scholar Maria Rostworowski de Diez Canseco has been instrumental in showing that pre-European coastal societies were organized by principles in which groups of people conducting various important tasks such as fishing, farming, and craft production were separated into their own communities (Rostworowski 1977, 1981; also see Netherly 1984, 1990). Some of these communities appear to have been internally self-governing, with their own local administrators. However, it is also clear that such autonomy was exercised within the wider prevailing political structure, whether this encompassed a particular valley or a broader hegemony, as in the cases of the Chimú and presumably the Moche.

Although there are many instances around the world of

smaller groups within a society holding specific occupations, it is not often that they practice this to the exclusion of other tasks. It is even rarer that such social segregation is so rigidly formalized that it leads to cultural separation within society. Nevertheless, this is what occurred on the north coast of Peru in the case of fishermen and their families. Fishing communities dwelt in their own villages near the shore under their own governors, or "lords" as they are usually termed. Even though they lived at the mouths of river valleys that produced abundant agricultural commodities, they did not conduct any farming activity. Instead, they obtained agricultural products through exchange with farming specialists located elsewhere in the valleys. Moreover, it seems that the fishing groups adhered to their own variants of prevailing local religion with their own divinities and associated rituals. Most significantly, they married within the fishing communities, thus ensuring continual reproduction of their sub-culture.

It is not surprising, then, that the fishing communities of the North Coast developed their own distinct dialect of the prevailing Yunga language – one that has been appropriately termed Pescadora since the time of Lizárraga's visit to the North Coast in the 1550s immediately preceding the *reducción* policy of Viceroy Francisco de Toledo which permanently disrupted this indigenous demographic pattern. *La lengua pescadora*, with its equally distinctive occupational, residential, and cultural associations, illustrates the basic social framework that regulated the daily life of the population during the Moche and succeeding periods. We can assume that beyond the great pyramid centers from which Moche rulers governed their domains the bulk of the people lived in small villages like those described for the fishing groups. The great majority of the inland communities would have contained specialist farmers, speaking either the Muchic or Quingan dialects of Yunga, depending on where on the coast they lived. It is likely that skilled craft specialists – potters, metalworkers, and weavers – resided in their own communities near the centers of Moche government, where they produced the high-status items that enhanced the importance of the rulers and constituted the symbols of their ideology of power.

Domestic Life

Our current knowledge of Moche domestic life derives from a relatively few examples of archaeological research which have focused on the residential areas of settlements. These were conducted in the 1970s. Teresa Topic investigated the great Cerro Blanco site (1977, 1982) which was occupied throughout the Moche epoch, but reached the peak of its importance in the Middle Moche Period (Moche III–IV), roughly AD 350–600 (figure 1.3). In addition the Moche V towns of Galindo and Pampa Grande (ca. AD 600–750) were the foci of research by the author (Bawden 1977, 1982a, 1982b, 1990) and Izumi Shimada and his colleagues (for synthesis of the Pampa Grande research see Shimada 1994a). These focused site investigations are complemented by the results of settlement distribution studies in various valleys (Donnan 1973; Moseley and Deeds 1982; Proulx 1968, 1985; Willey 1953; Wilson 1988). The entire corpus gives us a good preliminary view of Moche residential patterns through time and within their specific occupational settings. I shall regularly refer to this site information in this chapter to illustrate my discussion of domestic life and the nature of production in Moche society.

This settlement research suggests that for much of the Moche history most people lived in relatively small villages scattered along the peripheries of the valleys. Exceptions were the great centers dominated by flat-topped pyramids like the Huaca del Sol which represented the symbols of paramount social authority and were the places from which Moche rulers wielded their power. Residential access to these centers was probably strictly controlled and limited chiefly to administrators and the artisans who created the brilliant inventory of elite items that we regard as Moche art. In this sense they can be regarded as specialized symbolic centers of ceremony and power.

In the final Moche period this pattern changed. Large urban settlements were constructed at Galindo and Pampa Grande (figures 1.1, 9.7, 9.10) and were occupied by large variegated populations clustered around the most prominent structures. This urban pattern contrasts markedly with the earlier Moche rural settlement configuration and denotes profound internal social conflict and change between the Moche IV and V phases, whose implications I will explore later in this book. Most of the specific information regarding the domestic context of daily life comes from this late period of increased urban development. It is likely that internal tensions accompanying the Moche V changes had some impact at most levels of social behavior and organization. My portrayal of Moche domestic life must be taken as applying chiefly to the latest period although many of its basic features undoubtedly apply to earlier times.

It is always easier to interpret the archaeological record of domestic life in terms of the tasks represented than of the families that performed them. We too easily regard the domestic sphere solely as the place where people lived and were nourished. Because we regard these functions as universal to humanity, their importance is accepted as given and their specific cultural implications ignored. Human actors remain anonymous, hidden by the generalizing shield of their "domestic activity" while domestic life is seen as the constant backcloth to the stage of history on which vital social dramas are played. While recognizing the difficulties of the endeavor, I believe that it is possible at least to glimpse the faces of the people who lived in Moche houses and to begin to identify some of the specific ways in which they influenced Moche social organization and its structures.

The Moche residential house was probably quite similar in construction technique, if not appearance, to those still built in the rural areas of coastal Peru (figure 3.1). Low stone walls and wooden corner posts supported superstructure and roofs of cane which also shaded small outside patios. The basic house plan consisted of three separate functional spaces (figure 3.2). A large room lined with plastered stone benches, with an open central space, served as the general living and probably sleeping space. In the Late Moche Period some people, adults and children, were buried in these benches. Abundant remains of copper sewing needles, spindle weights used for spinning yarn, and remains of weaving implements reveal that the production of domestic cloth took place in this room, while remains of food and eating utensils suggest that meals were consumed here. This center of domestic activity was not directly accessible from the

Figure 3.1 Rural house in the Upper Moche Valley, ca. 1970. (Chan Chan-Moche Valley project)

exterior. An adjacent food preparation area served this purpose and contained hearths for cooking, grinding stones and work surfaces for food preparation, the remains of *cuy* (guinea pig) pens where these Andean domestic animals could scavenge the food scraps while fattening for eating, a great deal of plant and animal residue, and a variety of domestic storage containers. Finally, a small space, usually entered from the living room, contained large storage vessels for domestic storage.

In some cases block-like groups of these houses surrounded a large central patio in which domestic activities were pursued in a more communal manner. In these more public areas the remains of stone and wooden implements used in agriculture, and uncooked remains of plants are frequently found. These patios also sometimes contain rough hearths although these are not normally as well-constructed as the indoor examples, suggesting that they were not the chief loci of family cooking. We can assume that here the occupants of the houses, possibly related families from the house blocks, met to relax after their

Figure 3.2 Foundations of Late Moche residential house at the site of Galindo, Moche Valley, dating to ca. AD 700. The food preparation and cooking space is on the left and gave access to the house. The benched room with rectangular patio was the general living area. Adjoining this area are two small domestic storage rooms on the right. (Photo: Garth Bawden 1971)

daily work, much as modern Andean villagers do today. Here also men fashioned new agricultural tools, repaired broken ones, and shared with women the preparation of fruits and vegetables for cooking. Here women spun the yarn from which rope and string were made and wove on their back-strap looms in the shelter of overhanging ramadas. Here children played. Finally, it is interesting to note that it is only in these patios that we find evidence for tasks clearly associated with men, a fact that has implications for understanding domestic organization.

However, it is also clear that the domestic life of common Moche people was not totally taken up with attending to basic physical needs. Small ceramic figurines, some hollow, many solid, were an integral component of the domestic setting in all status categories. Depicting a wide range of subjects including humans, animals, and a range of non-human figures, these items probably reveal the importance of artistic, decorative, and religious needs in the context of ordinary family life (figure 3.3). Some of the more complex figures of fanged and anthropomorphic beings may well signify the existence of domestic religious belief much like that associated with the icon and crucifix in the Christian home. However, it would probably be a mistake to interpret them all in this way. More naturalistic representations of mothers with babies, monkeys, lizards, and simply-dressed men playing flutes and pipes are equally validly seen as domestic ornaments and playthings. The presence of such items underlines the fact that Moche families, like their counterparts everywhere, not only aspired to be free from hunger and abuse, but also created a domestic sphere enhanced by relaxation, aesthetic pleasure, and play.

We have seen that the evidence for specifically male activity was primarily confined to the outdoor patios adjacent to the buildings. By contrast it is clear that women played important roles within the houses. Most artifacts found in the benched

Figure 3.3 Figurines from Late Moche houses at Galindo, Moche Valley. (Photo: Garth Bawden 1973)

rooms that served as the centers of domestic life were associated with women. Sewing, cooking, and weaving implements are commonly found in this room. At the domestic level weaving, a primarily female activity, carried, and still carries, great social importance in Andean society. In the area of social reproduction, weaving incorporates family history, the myths of the community, and the maker's status. However, textiles possess broader importance as ritual gifts that cement inter-family relations and accompany the dead into the supernatural. Because of this latter role it is probable that women were principal actors in funerary rituals that accompanied the interment of family members in these same rooms. They may also have participated in the domestic economic distribution network whose presence is marked by the storage rooms attached to all Moche residences. This prominence in the relations of domestic production and related ritual is reflected in broader political structure where, although men were the principal participants, women to a lesser extent figured in the myths and ceremonies of Moche social integration.

Although Moche dwellings quite closely approximate modern rural coastal homes and the domestic life that they shelter, when examined in their settlement context, patterns of variation emerge that disclose wider social and economic traits peculiar to their time and place. First, though most obvious at Galindo, it is clear at each of the three settlements mentioned above that the residential population was internally organized according to social status (Bawden 1982b; Shimada 1994a:168–80; Topic 1982:266–70). Houses differ in size, elaboration, and content, in terms of the quality of their decorated pottery, metal items, and access to meat, especially llama. Moreover, some of the houses of higher status were associated with facilities used for bulk storage, and corrals where llamas, the means of transportation, were kept. The elite occupants of such homes probably controlled a portion of the economic resources of the community and were responsible for the acquisition, storage, and distribution of valued commodities. It is also clear, especially at Galindo, that the various categories of dwellings were strictly segregated into different residential zones. Passage between the zones was controlled by a high wall, suggesting the presence of social differentiation and, its logical accompaniment, internal tension. In all sites the most elaborate residential structures, presumably the homes of the rulers, were located on or adjacent to the great platforms and compounds that symbolized supreme corporate authority.

As a final note on Moche domestic life it is significant that the later Moche pattern of functionally compartmentalized homes and socially segregated population groups was not always present. While the situation in the Early Moche Period (Phases I–II) is not known, the prevalent Gallinazo and later Chimú residential pattern, with the exception of the highest social strata, does not exhibit the rigid differentiation of the later Moche phases (Bawden 1990). This more generalized pattern spatially conforms more closely to the pattern of Andean holistic society where principles of kinship rather than class are the basis for social order. The late Moche pattern, as seen most vividly at Galindo, indicates a progressive trend toward social differentiation. We will see more fully in chapter 9 that this trend was ensured by an extreme form of physical coercion imposed by the rulers. Such separation strongly suggests social tension, a situation that is of vital importance in understanding the evolution of Moche political history.

The Contexts of Daily Life

Food producers

Fishermen Knowledge of the occupational and residential separation practiced by the Moche and their descendants and its relationship to deeper Andean cultural conception helps us to understand coastal social organization. This historical and linguistic information does not provide us with specific details on how the fishing communities or other groups carried out their work, the implements they used, or the houses and villages that they occupied. These details derive from other sources. I have noted that most of the representational scenes in Moche art depict events of political and religious significance. Very little in this specialized elite art concerns the daily life of the great majority of the population. However, contained in the subject themes are many elements that were used in various social contexts, commonplace as well as exclusive. Accordingly, we can use this otherwise restricted imagery to learn a great deal about the artisanship, architecture, and dress of the wider society and the settings in which they functioned.

From the exquisite ceramic representation of fishing craft and marine scenes we see that Moche fishermen used craft that in most respects were the same as those still used on the North Coast. These boats consist essentially of bundles of local reeds tied together to form a rounded raft with upturned prows on which the fisherman sits astride or kneels, propelling the craft with a split cane paddle (figures 2.2, 2.3). The *totora* reed used in boat construction is still grown by the boat builders along the shore in sunken gardens adjacent to their villages, together with cotton for their lines and nets and gourds which serve as their net floats (figure 3.4). We may assume that then, as now, entire families shared the diverse tasks involved in making this marine fishing gear. Moche ceramic illustration depicts line and net fishing, crab traps almost identical in form to those used today, and sea lion hunts by club-wielding hunters (figure 2.12). All of these implements have been found through excavation of coastal sites, together with abundant remains of the fish, mollusks, and sea mammals that they procured. This complex archaeological record clearly reflects a highly self-sufficient way of life that in many ways continues today.

Farmers   The other chief source of coastal subsistence is intensive agriculture in the river valleys. Because of the arid environment, agriculture is only possible where water can be drawn from the river channels onto the plain to irrigate the fields. Irrigation agriculture of this kind requires at least local collaboration of farming communities in the construction of canals and ditches and their regular clearing of silt. In fact during the Moche period the canal systems of the coastal valleys incorporated much more than local initiatives, for the large trunk canals extended many miles from their intake points down toward the sea (figure 2.9). This rather complex technology encouraged the development of the other vital economic specialty in coastal society – agriculture.

Figure 3.4 North Coast family in a coastal fishing village, ca. 1930. Note the reed house, unused reed bundles for boat construction, split cane boat paddles, and fish nets. (Peabody Museum, Harvard University; photo N8037, cat. 42–40. Photo: G. Holstein)

Agricultural adaptation along the coast developed much later than did marine-oriented life, only becoming widespread in the centuries following 2,000 BC. This long deferral relative to marine adaptation may have been caused by the greater need for coordinated labor and the relatively difficult technology involved in coastal farming. However, once established, agriculture rapidly became the central economic component of coastal economy, surpassing fishing in its potential for providing a surplus of food resources.

As was the case with the fishing communities, farmers were specialists, engaging exclusively in agricultural endeavors. In the smaller valleys with their limited productive potential, farming villages were located in the desert on the edge of the irrigated zone so as to maximize the area of cultivation. In the larger valleys like the Chicama and Lambayeque such conservation was not as necessary, a fact that, together with the greater distances involved between home and field, encouraged the location of villages within the field systems. Judging from information available from the later Chimú period, an important part of the Moche farmers' working life was conducted in fields held in common by their home villages, in wider Andean terms the heritage of a corporate kinship group (Netherly 1984). Local field systems, with their relatively small feeder canals and ditches, were probably maintained and operated by the members of local communities. Such work would have been organized at the local level according to a farming schedule sanctioned by traditional knowledge and accepted by Moche society as a whole.

However, construction and maintenance of the principal irrigation canals which, with their extensive courses and stone aqueducts, provided the essential water supply that drove the entire agricultural system of each valley, demanded more intensive labor organization than could be mobilized at the local community level. Archaeological evidence suggests that Moche farmers contributed their labor to such construction and also worked fields controlled by the elites. Michael Moseley, who has studied the development of pre-European agricultural systems in the Moche Valley, believes that small adobe platforms located in some agricultural areas are the bases of small structures that originally served as the field stations used by field supervisors (Moseley 1992a:178). He suggests plausibly that this type of government-managed work was an early counterpart of the well-documented Andean system in which workers owed a portion of their labor to the state in return for their subsistence while on official duty and the provision of ritual feasts that were closely associated with all agricultural activity. This pattern is an extension to the broadest corporate level of basic Andean structure with its emphasis on communal cooperation and reciprocal responsibilities among all members of the social unit. State agricultural labor in the Moche period, then, would have involved the actual planting and harvesting of crops, chiefly the staple maize, and construction and maintenance of the larger canals.

Archaeologically, a variety of implements used by farmers for community and corporate work have been found in and around the remains of residential houses of the Moche period. These include tools used for preparing and tilling the fields – wooden digging sticks and shovels, stone blades that may originally have come from the Moche equivalent of the Inka footplough, and the round "doughnut-shaped" stone heads that were originally affixed to wooden handles and were probably used to break clods of soil during field preparation. While quite simple in form and construction, these tools were adequate for fulfilling the requirements of a labor-intensive agricultural system. Indeed modern Andean farmers still use these tools, the chief exception being that blades are now made of metal rather than stone or wood.

In the tropical climate of the coast the Moche farmer produced almost the entire spectrum of Andean food crops. Among these were maize, several varieties of beans and squashes, peppers, sweet potato, manioc, avocado, and a large range of tropical fruits, while the vital accompaniment of Andean labor – coca – grew in the inland valley slopes. The leaf form of this basic Andean commodity was, and is, used universally in the higher elevations to relieve altitude fatigue. It is chewed and lime is added as a catalyst to help extract the medicinal alkaloids from the leaf. In Moche ceramic art coca leaf is usually depicted in ritual contexts (figure 3.5). In the Moche lands where altitude was not a problem coca may have played a sacred role as religious offering and ritual drug. The ritual associations of both coca and maize in Moche society added special significance to their production and consumption, involving farmers in deeper aspects of Moche social integration.

It is probable that, as in later periods in the Andean world, farming activity was carried out by able-bodied men and women according to a sacred calendrical cycle. Vital accompanying rituals united humans and the natural world in a mutual endeavor to ensure the health and fertility of Mother Earth (see Urton 1981 for full description of a modern example). Such rituals celebrated and spiritually assisted the agricultural stages of ground preparation, planting, weeding, and harvesting. Important roles in this process were held by women of the farming communities who prepared the alcoholic corn-based beverage, *chicha*, used in rituals, a function which is still conducted by

*Figure 3.5 Fine-line drawing of Moche personages using coca.
(Redrawn from Kutscher 1955:9)*

their descendants today. A basic quality of Andean agricultural
religious practice involves the offering of items of sacred significance to the spirits of nature. Maize and coca, both plants that
were cultivated widely by the Moche, were prominent in this
regard as offerings. Moreover, maize, in its alcoholic form as
chicha, was not only offered to the spirits of the earth and to
those of communal ancestors at these religious gatherings but
also consumed in large quantities during the feasting that accompanied them. These events, whether conducted at the specific community level or as more formal ceremonies organized
by the central Moche governing authorities as their obligation
to state workers, incorporated the entire social community in
actions of solidarity, cooperation, and religious unity, regularly
reinforcing the foundations of social existence. Of course, at
the official level they also permitted the ruling body to display

their own prestige and power, thus infusing a deeper political purpose to basic religious belief. Farmers, in their apparently mundane occupation, were involved in functions vital to wider social cohesion, as were their fishing counterparts.

Artisans

Another chief category of Moche producers – artisans – differed in important respects from the food-producing groups. Fishers and farmers constituted their own communities and, especially in the case of the fishing peoples, these appear to have extended through generations. Moreover, fishing communities were essentially autonomous in terms of their local administration. Artisans lived and worked in very different social circumstances. Their special skills directly served the interests of the ruling Moche elite by fashioning the material symbols of formal political ideology. The brilliant Moche creations that grace the shelves of museums and private collections the world over were the active symbols of authority. Formal iconographic themes painted on the surfaces of ceramic vessels, woven into textiles, or formed in gold and silver, proclaimed the principal tenets of an ideology that supported Moche leadership and the political system through which it exercised power. While there were also specialists in wood carving, basketry, featherwork, and mural painting, here I shall concentrate on the textile, precious metal, and pottery media which have contributed most of our knowledge of Moche craft production.

The expert metallurgists, weavers, and potters who made these prestigious items were producers in a very special sense. Fishermen and farmers devoted most of their efforts to obtaining the food that satisfied the subsistence needs of the entire population. By contrast craftsmen worked in the restricted arena of social integration producing a commodity that had value principally in the political domain. Moreover, their products – symbols of prestige and power – were not the assets of society as a whole. Instead they were appropriated by a restricted segment of society, the ruling stratum, to maintain their political position at the apex of society and to strengthen their prestige. Craft specialists were dependants of the food producers who sustained them as they exercised their skills. At the same time they were dependants of the ruling elite, their skills part of the continuous effort to perpetuate the political order that gave this exclusive social group its power.

Weavers Because of the important social arena within which artisans performed we have numerous representations of their work in elite Moche pottery, a medium that largely depicted ideological themes and their related activities. Thus the famous weaving scene on an elaborate flaring bowl (figure 3.6) reveals the importance of this occupation to Moche society. It also demonstrates that weaving occurred as an formally organized enterprise as well as a domestic activity and that women were the producers in both cases. In this depiction, a number of women sit under shady cane ramadas weaving on the traditional back-strap loom in a setting still to be seen in the Andes (figure 3.7). They fashion cotton or wool thread, spun from raw material provided by the Moche administration, into intricate patterns that adorn the unfinished cloth shown on their looms. Several officials are seated at intervals among the weavers while lesser attendants move between them. These individu-

Figure 3.6 Fine-line drawing of weaving scene with female weavers using back-strap looms and supervised by officials. (Redrawn from Donnan 1978, figure 103)

Figure 3.7 North Coast weaver seated under ramada, using back-strap loom, ca. 1925. (Peabody Museum, Harvard University; photo N33550, cat. 30–1)

als are overseeing the weavers and presumably monitoring production.

This scene illustrates the Moche version of an activity that played a major role in wider Andean society where cloth was (and is) employed in contexts of central importance to social integration. In the better-known Inka setting women were selected from local communities and brought to live and work in special centers where they wove as part of the labor tax that they owed to the state. The high status that this conferred on them is suggested by the fact that they were also officiants in official religious ceremonies and that they often became the wives of important members of the Inka hierarchy. In both Inka and Moche societies cloth served to designate the position and status of its owner, the highest-ranked personages wearing garments of the greatest elaboration in design, color, and embellishment with other valuable material such as feathers, gold and silver thread. Rich cloth served as a ritual gift, circulated among high-ranking persons to confirm political and kinship alliances. It was also used as a sacrificial offering in religious ceremonies, and as an elaborate symbolic ingredient of funerary ritual, denoting the position and rank of the deceased. Thus, the high degree of organization and supervision conveyed by the painted Moche weaving scene is quite understandable in the light of prevailing beliefs concerning the vital social significance of cloth. The great importance of weaving persists in many areas of the Andes today where the identity and social histories of the makers and their groups are woven into the intricate decorative symbols of textiles.

Metalworkers Metallurgy in the ancient societies of the North Coast region played a role that was similar to weaving. Again, the products of metalworkers were actively used to display rank, status, and the symbolism of political ideology. In Moche society, the rather complex activities involved in metallurgy were similarly organized by the government and conducted in special facilities devoted to this purpose. Moche metalworking incorporated a wide variety of techniques. In addition to producing many smaller molded and sheet metal items, metallurgists joined together intricately decorated metal sheets by means of sweat welding and soldering techniques to create elaborate three-dimensional objects such as masks and animal figures (Jones 1979).

Moche metallurgy was part of a brilliant regional tradition that extended back to the Chavín period a thousand years before and continued through the succeeding Chimú phase

(Lechtman 1979, 1980; Shimada and Merkel 1991). The tradition was characterized by alloys of gold with copper and silver, mixtures that emphasized the golden color, although not necessarily the purity of the metal that formed the finished product. The reasons for this emphasis on color rather than content can be found in Andean structural values: its non-corrosive nature made it an ideal symbol for the permanence of divinely ordered power (Lechtman 1979; see also Sallnow 1989).

Both Moche ceramic art and the actual excavation of metalworking sites help us to reconstruct the activities of Moche metalworkers. Several stages of work were involved. First, miners obtained the necessary ores from deposits located in the Pacific Andean foothills inland from the coastal plains. Whether these miners constituted another group of specialists or whether they were prisoners taken in inter-group conflict we do not know. However, recent surveys in the upper reaches of the Lambayeque and Zaña Valleys tell us that they worked numerous shallow deposits with triangular, stone-headed picks. The raw ores were then taken to smelting sites that were probably located nearby. None of these have yet been located. Following the smelting process the resulting metal ingots were transported down to the coastal centers where the actual production stage took place in closely supervised shops, two of which have been studied at the Late Moche towns of Galindo and Pampa Grande (Bawden 1977:202–7; Shimada 1994a:200–6).

The evidence from remains of these sites reveals that metalworking activities were centered around large, sturdy hearths where metal ingots were melted in kilns prior to being shaped into finished items. Workers blew continuously into these kilns through ceramic tubes inserted in holes set into their sides in order to maintain a temperature high enough to work the metal. Elsewhere in the work areas the presence of molds for molten metal, stone beating and shaping tools, and plentiful remains of fragments of cut sheet metal are evidence of the other tasks involved in metal production. At Galindo the presence in the work area of both finished and unfinished ceremonial items such as copper bells, small axes, and perforated discs demonstrate the specific types of commodities manufactured in the workshops and their association with elite social functions. Significantly, both of the excavated workshops were located in exclusive parts of their towns near administrative architecture and in settings where access was restricted. Such concern with supervision and control clearly indicates the great value placed on metalworking by Moche rulers and underscores the importance of items of precious metal as symbols of authority.

Potters The third major group of specialist craft producers of whom we have considerable knowledge are potters. Pottery was used in most social contexts and thus is abundant in the archaeological record. A large array of vessel shapes, techniques and levels of decoration are represented in the Moche ceramic inventory. Thus, the finest molded and painted vessels are regularly found in elite burials, and the centers of administration and religious activity. Some distinctive shapes appeared to have been used exclusively in one or another of these contexts. Pottery of this same type, though less carefully crafted and decorated, also occurs in residential settings. Field research at the large town of Galindo in the Moche Valley has shown that the degree of elaboration of fine-painted residential pottery correlates with the status of the occupants and the location of their homes (Bawden 1982a), a pattern that indicates the use of ceramics as a general symbol of Moche social status. Finally, a wide variety of undecorated pottery vessels were used in the domestic domain for such mundane functions as food preparation, cooking, serving, and storage.

We now know a fair amount about the work of Moche potters. It appears that fine pottery used to define high status and for ceremonial purposes was made at manufacturing sites disinct from those that produced utilitarian forms. A large Middle Moche period ceramic workshop has recently been found at Cerro Mayal adjacent to the major Moche ceremonial center of Mocollope in the Chicama Valley (Russell, Leonard, and Briceño 1994). Cerro Mayal consists of the production site itself and a nearby residential area where the specialist potters lived. Here archaeological research has defined an extensive depression filled with dense deposits of ash and wood fuel, covered by a cap of smaller vegetal materials as the primary firing site. This firing area also contained numerous fragments of pottery vessels and molds which revealed that the principal output of the workshop was in fine forms such as stirrup-spout jars (figure 3.8) floreros (large, flaring-rim bowls), faceneck jars, figurines, and ceramic trumpets. Vessels made at workshops like Cerro Mayal were most commonly formed in ceramic molds, many of which still exist. Following the application of surface embellishment through shaping, smoothing, and painting, vessels were fired in the pits or kilns. Interestingly this technique is still used today by some North Coast potters like the well-known curer Eduardo Calderón, who maintains the tradition in the modern village of Moche.

Elsewhere on the coast the residue of ceramic production, including deformed or broken vessels, molds, and ash, is quite common, but little is known of its associated workshops. The positive evidence that we do have strongly suggests that the vast quantity of plain utilitarian wares needed for domestic use and wider storage and transportation functions were made in shops located at the periphery of the settlements. A workshop of this type at Galindo was located near the main road leading from the site down toward the coast (Bawden 1977:187–202). This location away from substantial housing would have facilitated access to llama caravans bringing in fuel and clay and taking away the finished pottery pieces. Indeed, a llama corral adjoined the workshop, confirming the integration of transportation and production at the site.

The Galindo workshop was merely a crude stone-walled compound in which a large open pit functioned as the firing kiln. The pit was filled with ash, fragments of burnt wood, and a large quantity of llama dung, the residue of fuel used in the firing process. Many pieces of broken and deformed pottery, all from large plain cooking vessels and storage jars, indicated the

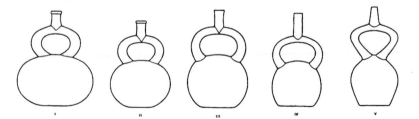

Figure 3.8 Moche stirrup-spout sequence based on Larco's five-phase seriation.

product of the facility. Numerous whole and fragmentary stamps were used to decorate the necks of jars. Significantly, the presence of several small molds used to make figurines of human and supernatural form (figure 3.9) of the type found commonly in residential structures (figure 3.3) suggest that these rough symbols of domestic religion were made in the workshop and indicates their low status compared with the fineware. These small figures may well have played a role similar to that of the domestic icons and medals of today which carry religious meaning without the sanctity reserved for the paraphernalia devoted to formal religious settings.

It appears that the large class of pottery which carried no special value in terms of prestige was produced in rather informal settings remote from the centers of government. By comparison, we can reasonably assume that the elaborately painted Moche fineware would have been made in exclusive, supervised workshops, much in the manner of fine textile and metal production. This is certainly the pattern at Cerro Mayal, whose

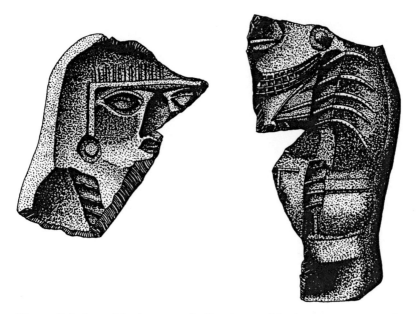

Figure 3.9 Late Moche ceramic figurine molds from pottery workshop, Galindo, Moche Valley.

location adjacent to the elite center of Mocollope would have permitted close supervision of its production. In addition, at Pampa Grande in the Lambayeque Valley a small production site where potters apparently manufactured somewhat more ornate forms was located in the center of the town (Shimada 1994a:191–200). Here, approached by narrow streets, access and production could have been easily controlled, lending support to the notion of corporate supervision over the potters who crafted vessels that conferred symbolic importance to the ruling body.

Finally, a few random discoveries allow us to glimpse the individual persons who created the profusion of Moche ceramic vessels. Numerous plainware jars, often with faces stamped on their necks, contain rough marks that were scratched or pressed into the wet clay before firing. Such marked vessels, although a

Figure 3.10 Rim fragment of a pottery vessel from Galindo, Moche Valley with "graffito" probably drawn by the maker before firing. (Photo: Garth Bawden 1995)

small percentage of the total volume of plain jars, have been found throughout the North Coast region. The Galindo excavations discovered several instances of identical patterns being used on numerous jars at the site. It is probable that potters made these crude designs on the vessels to mark them as their own work, imposing a personal quality to their work that is not commonly visible in Moche craftsmanship. A final example of this intrusion of the individual personality into ceramic craft is unique in the record. A rim fragment from a plain jar from Galindo bears a graffito of a stylized human face, etched into its surface (figure 3.10) before firing, presumably by the maker. Such a deed poignantly exposes the humanity of its executor, reflecting universal attitudes and sentiments that transcend the passage of centuries and the cultural gulf between ourselves and the Moche, bringing us face-to-face with the individual potter who helped to create Moche society.

Transporters and traders

A final group of specialists is important not because of its capacity to produce food or craft items, but because its members ensured that commodities perceived as valuable to the functioning of Moche society were distributed efficiently. This group comprised the merchants and transporters without whom elite items could not have been procured from distant regions, raw materials acquired for the production of utilitarian and symbolic articles, or finished products circulated throughout the Moche region and beyond. Transporters of goods worked on the sea and on land, ensuring the maintenance of economic links with Ecuador in the north, southerly areas of the Peruvian coast, the offshore Pacific islands, and the adjacent highlands to the east.

In addition to their primary occupation of gathering the harvests of the coast and sea, it is probable that Moche fishing groups participated in wider domains of social and economic importance. Given their great familiarity with the sea, it is likely that they also provided crews for the large, sometimes double-decked boats that engaged in long-distance travel. Boats of this type were recorded by European sailors of the sixteenth century off the coast of Ecuador (Heyerdahl 1995) but have not been built since the early Colonial period. The Moche and their successors used boats of this type to convey cargo and passengers to and from the offshore *guano* islands and to transport commodities of high social value such as the *Spondylus* shell from the Gulf of Guayaquil in Ecuador (figures 2.8, 9.6; Cordy-Collins 1990). Ethnohistorical records tell us that this trading activity was conducted by a distinct group of merchants, who worked exclusively for the rulers (Netherly 1977; Rostworowski 1975). Most probably these merchants were a special group of seafarers drawn from the fishing population. This group played an extremely important role in specialized economic functions of great significance to the established political order. Their important contribution to wider society goes far toward explaining the status of the seafaring community as a locally autonomous administrative body within the Moche political system.

There is no similar evidence for a discrete group of merchants on land with special status in Moche society. However, it is clear from the archaeological record that a considerable amount of overland transportation took place and that this activity played a vital role in maintaining the flow of prestige and raw materials required by the Moche socio-political system. Effective land traffic of bulk commodities depended on llamas which, in addition to providing meat and wool, were used intensively throughout the Andes as draft animals. Historical accounts assert that by Inka times state caravans sometimes contained several thousand of these animals, each bearing its burden of food or prestige items (figure 4.12). Similarly the archaeological record indicates that llamas were bred on the coast by the Moche (Shimada and Shimada 1985) and intensively used by them for transportation purposes. Large llama caravans required the services of a large number of drivers who, with their families, constituted a semi-nomadic group of specialists devoted to the movement of goods along the coast.

Llama caravans acted as the terrestrial counterparts to the ships used in offshore traffic between Ecuador, the *guano* islands, and the Moche settlements of the Peruvian north coast, using roads whose remains have been identified to traverse the coastal desert from valley to valley. They probably also exchanged local subsistence and finished products for resources from the Central Coast and highlands such as alpaca wool and obsidian, and, indirectly, prestige items such as exotic feathers from the tropical forests. At the local level, caravaners ensured that raw resources were brought to the manufacturing sites. In this respect I have already noted the transportation of metal ores from the slopes of the northern Andes, and possibly the highlands above, to the nearby smelters and ultimately down to the towns of the plain for final production. Similarly we have seen that llama corrals accompanied the ceramic workshop at Galindo, indicating the means by which clays were brought to the site and finished vessels distributed. Thus in all aspects of local and interregional transportation, llama caravans and their drivers complemented their marine counterparts in supporting a widespread economic network that connected the Moche to their neighbors and ensured the supply of necessary materials of production, prestige, and subsistence.

Builders, laborers, and servants

So far in this chapter I have described the activities of those groups who performed specialized occupations concerned with production and transportation of food and items significant to the position of Moche rulers. Of course, not everyone fell within one of these exclusive categories. A large number of people must have been engaged in other activities concerned with production, such as building the immense Moche platform mounds and trunk canals, assisting the specialist craftsmen, and acting as the personal retainers of the ruling elite.

Although most of these other domains of production were probably occupied by non-specialist retainers and laborers, it is almost certain that Moche society supported surveyors and architects who provided the designs upon which the great agricultural systems, roads, and corporate construction depended. Unfortunately, we have no information regarding these persons, so their existence, together with their status in society, can only be inferred by the impressive products of their creativity. While direct information about the workers who actually implemented these plans is similarly lacking, archaeological research

and knowledge of wider principles of Andean labor mobilization does give us a fairly good idea of the strategies employed by
Moche rulers to create their elaborate corporate projects.

During the Inka period most members of the population were
required to devote a certain part of their time to working for the
government. This type of labor tax is well documented and was
an extension of the basic Andean principle whereby mutual
obligations were shared by community members (Rowe 1946;
Murra 1980). At the village level people were bound to help
each other with such important tasks as agriculture, house
construction, and ritual. In the period of Inka domination these
obligations were expropriated by the government with each
subject community being responsible for its allocated share of
labor and production on behalf of the wider polity. Archaeological research suggests that Moche corporate agriculture used
the same basic labor pattern. I have already mentioned the
presence of small, regularly shaped building foundations in the
fields of the Moche Valley. These structures, the precursors of
even more elaborate Chimú examples, were probably the stations used by government officials to supervise agricultural
laborers employed by the Moche rulers to work their fields as
part of their labor obligations.

Michael Moseley has examined the great Huaca del Sol in the
Moche Valley to explore strategies used in Moche large-scale
construction and believes that a similar system operated there
(Moseley 1975b). The body of the great edifice consists of a
number of contiguous vertical sections (figure 3.11), erected
over an extensive period of time. Construction bricks, though
homogenous in form within each section, differ between sections in size and proportion. Moreover, from 20 to 50 percent
of the bricks of each section are marked with distinct "maker's
marks" – simple impressions that appear to distinguish the
construction material of each segment. This pattern suggests
that bricks incorporated into each discrete construction segment were made in the same molds by the same specific work
crew.

Moseley reasonably concludes from this evidence that the
Moche utilized a system of labor organization that was similar
in its fundamental structure to that of the Inka a thousand years
later. The Inka empire demanded a regular *mit'a* labor tax from

Figure 3.11 North face of the Huaca del Sol, Cerro Blanco site, Moche Valley, showing the segmentary construction technique. (Chan Chan-Moche Valley Project)

its subject peoples, with each local community contributing a required work quota toward state-sponsored projects. Within this conceptual framework Moseley sees each vertical adobe segment of the Huaca del Sol being erected by a work crew drawn from a specific community on the coast. It thus represented the work of a distinct social unit contributing its taxation obligations to the Moche polity.

This segmentary labor system has been identified elsewhere in the Moche sphere. Most of the important structures that I discuss in this book, including the Huaca de la Luna at the Cerro Blanco site, the Castillo platform at Huancaco in the Virú Valley, the Huaca El Brujo in Chicama, and the Sipán burial platform, conform to the construction style of the Huaca del Sol, while the enormous Huaca Fortaleza at Pampa Grande in the Lambayeque Valley presents a modification caused by the needs for more rapid construction in a time of changing social and political conditions at the end of the Moche period

(Shimada 1994a:162–6). Indeed it appears that the system had a long history on the North Coast. The Gallinazo culture used it prior to the Moche period while the impressive walls of Chan Chan, the Chimú capital, were also constructed in segmentary technique long after the Moche demise.

In summary, we can confidently assume that other occupations important to the smooth operation of Moche production, though not visible in the available record, were conducted along the same lines as those discussed here. Certainly, we have seen in this chapter that wherever there is sufficient information to allow us to glimpse the workers who provided the subsistence for society and the craftsmen whose products helped to maintain a stable social system, well-defined canons of occupational organization consistently prevailed. These canons of production were deeply grounded in Andean structural principles of occupational specialization and reciprocal obligation of community members to each other. On one level specialization permitted skilled artisans to develop a brilliant array of artistic techniques and devote them to the elite in return for their physical and religious sustenance. On a much broader level specialization distinguished entire communities of farmers from fishermen as distinct social groups.

All these various producing groups complemented each other by providing the full range of commodities required to sustain the Moche social system. The basic Andean concept of interdependence between community members was broadened in scope by the Moche to become political strategy. Each group within society owed its distinct form of productivity to the wider body, politically represented by the ruling elite. The Moche elite, in return for the labor of the many, maintained the subsistence and ritual requirements of social order with the material and psychological rewards that accrued to the producers. Moreover, they assured their ideological authority by enforcing exclusive command over its material symbols. Concurrently, they secured their economic power base by controlling production of subsistence commodities and its related labor organization. As is the case in all complex societies, these mechanisms ensured preservation of the existing political order. Within the parameters of Andean social conception, Moche rulers manipulated basic beliefs to their own ends, achieving not only long-lasting success but a structural conflict of interests within society that demanded constant negotiation and adjustment of the ideology of rule. It is to these other specialists – the Moche elite – and their strategies of power, that I now turn.

4

Symbols of Power

Political ideology as religious practice

Most of the artifacts traditionally regarded as distinctive of Moche "culture" are manifestations of a restricted and exclusive social domain – one of the most successful and persistent political ideologies of precolumbian Andean history. Magnificent Moche pyramids still dominate the landscape of Peru's north coast. Many of the world's most distinguished museums possess examples of exquisite Moche art. They are the products of craftsmen and artists whose imagination and skill created a treasure of aesthetic and technical splendor whose quality has rarely been equalled. Their aesthetic qualities alone place them among the great testimonials to the artistic achievement of indigenous New World peoples. However, to the Moche these formal attributes were of secondary importance to their specific social meaning. They were the active material symbols of an ideology of power, produced at the behest of an exclusive body of rulers, calculated to assert and sustain its authority.

Numerous overlapping meanings are ascribed to ideology in the social sciences (see Eagleton 1991 for a comprehensive summary). When applied to the establishment and reproduction of social groups, ideology encompasses a variety of roles. It can be regarded as the set of beliefs that gives psychological identity to individuals in a social situation, the shared ideas that symbolize the experiences and aspirations of a particular group within society, those that identify and promote the interests of different groups in conflict with one another, and, most relevant for this book, the ideas that legitimize and sustain the position of a dominant group over all others. In the Moche instance this was largely accomplished through minimizing the effect of social opposition by creating the illusion that social asymmetry was inevitable, supernaturally sanctioned, and that it served the interests of the general population. By helping to sustain inequality in this way, ideology entered the domain of political relations where the Moche elite manipulated beliefs grounded in the cultural experience of the society as a dynamic mechanism of power.

It is important to realize that society is always in a state of transition. Internal tension, whether between the forces and relations of production, competing views of social order, or individual interest relative to that of wider institutions, impels negotiation and change. Ideology as both cause and product of social imbalance cannot ultimately possess greater inherent stability than the conditions it seeks to mask. Thus, it is constantly adjusting to changing situations, whether to maintain the position of the privileged, to confront opposing ideologies, or to mediate challenge by those whom it seeks to subordinate. When it can no longer resolve the contradiction presented by such situational challenges there is breakdown in the social process.

In the Andean political domain it appears clear that elites used ideology as a vital mechanism for the construction of power. Ethnohistory reveals that Inka rulers consciously translated traditional concepts into ideologies of authority to surmount the constraining effects of local belief systems (Collier, Rosaldo, and Wirth 1982; Conrad and Demarest 1984; Zuidema 1990). Similarly, archaeological research reveals the importance of ideological manipulation of concepts of descent and kinship by Chimú rulers (Conrad 1981, 1990). These ideologies employed ritual enactment of mythic events and processes – the supernatural structure that underlay group integration – to maintain social order. By conducting these rituals, rulers and their political order were identified with the transcendental quality of myth and the social permanence that it fostered.

Material symbols played active roles in this political process. Symbols are potent forces in ordering, interpreting, even reconstituting reality. They help resolve social contradictions by connecting humans to the shared cultural experience from which they derive group identity. Such diverse symbols as dress, regalia, religious and funerary paraphernalia, ritual iconography, monumental public art, and the architectural contexts of power, all act to connect human leadership with the structural foundations of society. By so doing, material symbolism confers both secular and supernatural status on elite leaders, closely identifies them with the foundations of social order, and legitimizes their exercise of power. In the next two chapters I discuss the Moche ruling elite and their use of ideology and its material expression. First I examine the symbols of elite position and the social contexts of their use; in the next chapter I address the dramatic ritual events that were the central agencies through which Moche rulers constructed their ideological power and demonstrated it to the wider community.

While the various symbolic expressions of Moche power all served a single social *raison d'etre*, for purposes of discussion they can be separated into various material categories. These comprise complex iconography painted on fine pottery and the walls of pyramids, exquisite crafted items of precious metal and stone used both in ritual contexts and for personal adornment, and the huge architectural forms that were the omnipresent manifestations of power. As is generally the case, these physical symbols functioned through a combination of passive display and action. As visual referents they proclaimed a specific canon of social order to their viewers. They were also active agents in the ritual recreation of mythic social order in Moche daily life. In public rituals they evoked widely shared social principles to link all members of the community in affirmation of the prevailing order and the rulers who maintained it.

A century of archaeology and art history has familiarized us with the outward expressions of Moche ideology. However, two recent discoveries in the northern river valleys have greatly added to our understanding of their meaning. Moreover, these findings, to an unprecedented degree, proclaim the exclusive status of Moche rulers by bringing us face-to-face with the individuals for whose benefit Moche symbolic art and architecture was created. First, in 1987, at the Lambayeque Valley site of Sipán, several previously undisturbed burials – the Moche

"Royal Tombs" – were found in a large architectural complex, long the target of looting. They are currently being excavated by Peruvian archaeologists under the direction of Walter Alva (Alva 1990; Alva and Donnan 1993). The burial chambers, dating to around AD 200–300, were located within an adobe platform which stood near the main pyramid complex, clearly a site of great importance, in the midst of the fertile fields of the coastal plain (figure 4.1). Information to date suggests that the platform contained the remains of some of the paramount rulers of the Moche polity centered at Sipán. Elsewhere, in the Jequetepeque Valley, another elaborate ceremonial center, San José de Moro, has yielded further knowledge about the individuals who wielded authority in Moche society. Here, in 1991, several rich tombs, dating to around AD 500, were discovered and excavated by Luis Jaime Castillo and Christopher Donnan (Castillo 1993; Castillo and Donnan 1994; Donnan and Castillo 1992). The project is continuing under Castillo's direc-

Figure 4.1 View of the burial platform at Sipán where the "Royal Tombs" were discovered. Photo taken from the adjacent huaca. *(Photo: Garth Bawden 1995)*

tion. At both sites lavish inventories of burial goods contain the objects used by persons who stood at the apex of Moche society in the elaborate rituals that vitalized Moche power as a political force. Moreover, these items and their contexts allow us to identify the specific roles played in these rituals by the individuals who occupy these tombs.

At Sipán all of the deceased possessed exquisite gilded copper, gold, and silver ornaments whose profusion, composition, and form symbolically proclaim their elevated status (figure 4.2). Some were attended by sacrificed retainers, a certain mark of extraordinary, if not divine, status. One was buried in full armor and with the weaponry that affirmed his warrior status. The San José de Moro tombs also contained the remains of elite persons accompanied by sacrificed humans, and elaborate, ceramic and precious metal objects. Significantly, a minority of individuals at both sites wore the headdresses, garb, and ceremonial objects that identify them as officiants in the so-called "Sacrifice Ceremony," possibly the most important Moche religious ceremony.

Christopher Donnan has described the Sacrifice Ceremony in detail (Donnan 1978; Alva and Donnan 1993). The complex theme and its components appear frequently on elite fine-line painted pottery vessels and their molded counterparts, objects of precious metal, and monumental architectural murals from throughout the North Coast region (figure 4.3). I shall discuss the meaning and social significance of elite Moche ritual more fully in the next chapter. For the moment it is sufficient to note that the Sacrifice Ceremony was conducted in a pyramid pre-

---

→

Figure 4.2 Reconstruction of principal Sipán burial, showing the "Lord of Sipán" buried with the full acccoutrements of the principal officiant of the Sacrifice Ceremony. From top to bottom – A: Gold face mask; B: Six earspools bearing the forms of deer, Muscovy duck, and Moche warrior; C: Necklace composed of gold and silver peanuts; D: Large metal crescent-shaped headdress components; E: Sceptre bearing the depiction of sacrifice near the right arm; F: Two bells depicting the Decapitator holding a sacrificial knife in the right hand and a human head in the left; and G: Backflaps with the same image near the feet. (Photo: Garth Bawden 1995)

Figure 4.3 Fine-line drawing of the Sacrifice Ceremony. (Redrawn from Kutscher 1955: 24–5)

cinct where bound prisoners, presumably taken in warfare, were sacrificed and their blood ceremonially presented to distinctively dressed and masked officiants. The sacrificial scene invariably includes the same participants, with a central figure who wears a rayed headdress with large crescent appendage and warrior's metal backflap and holds a ceremonial rattle. The supporting figures include a warrior wearing a beaked bird mask and accoutrements and a woman who carries a ceremonial goblet of sacrificial blood and wears a distinctive tasselled headdress and gown. The material symbolism of garb, ritual accoutrement, and physical location, clearly plays a vital role in the meaning of this important event.

Three of the occupants of the Sipán burial platform appear to have owed much of their status to their assumption of specific roles in the Sacrifice Ceremony. The so-called Lord of Sipán wore the distinctive crescent-shaped headdress, copper backflap, large earplugs, and ceremonial accoutrements of the central being in the ritual (figure 4.2). He was also accompanied by the tools and symbolism of blood-letting and decapitation, large *tumi* knives and various depictions of the "Decapitator," a figure holding a knife in one hand and a human head in the other (figure 4.2; compare with figures 5.4, 5.8). Significantly, several items of regalia, most prominently a necklace composed of large peanut-shaped segments, were constructed half of gold, half of silver, a coupling that Donnan sees as symbolic reflection of the duality basic to the Andean conception of the social world. A second, older burial contained an individual who is commonly termed the "Old Lord of Sipán." He was also interred with the implements and symbols of sacrifice, suggesting that he too performed the central role in the Sacrifice Ceremony. A third personage, probably of slightly lower status, wore the owl headdress emblem that may well designate the bird warrior who often attends the principal figure of the ceremony (figure 4.3).

From the Jequetepeque Valley comes the well-documented instance of another of the ritual officiants in the Sacrifice Ceremony. The most elaborate of the burials at San José de Moro was of a high-status female, dramatically revealing that women played roles of importance in the Moche hierarchy. Her rich array of accoutrements, in addition to confirming her high social position, also signified her precise status as the female principal of the Sacrifice Ceremony. Her body was covered with large hammered metal sheets, one of which was a silver-copper alloy mask, while others replicated human limbs (figure 4.4). She wore the large headdress with gilded silver tassels of her ritual identity and was buried with the goblet and blackware dishes that she would have used during the ceremony.

The Sipán and San José tombs, located in the precincts of the great architectural monuments that symbolized central authority and conferred it on their occupants, thus represent a dramatic advance in our understanding of Moche power and its vital dependence on material symbolism. The paraphernalia of authority and status interred with these persons provides crucial information about their roles when alive and their ongoing social importance when dead. We now know that the themes identified in Donnan's studies of Moche narrative art illustrate actual events rather than being solely supernatural representations, and introduce us to the actual persons who participated in them. They show that the elevated rank of the members of the Moche ruling elite to a large degree depended on their ritual positions which, significantly, were actively proclaimed and given meaning by distinctive physical symbols. In the remainder of this chapter I shall elaborate more precisely on this integral relationship between the material and the conceptual in the social contexts of Moche leadership.

Figure 4.4 Burial of the Priestess, San José de Moro. Large metal headdress with the characteristic tassels of the female officiant of the Sacrifice Ceremony can be seen at her head and accompanying attendants at her feet. (Courtesy Luis Jaime Castillo)

The Language of Power

Moche art as text   While, long after their deaths, we are meeting some of the actual rulers of the Moche world, their funerary monuments are only the final and most abiding signifiers of their social importance and exercise of power. Throughout their active lives these persons and their counterparts at the top of the Moche social hierarchy maintained authority by combining the same mixture of lavish display subsumed in ideological symbolism and ritual practice. It is largely through the rich Moche narrative art style, especially as preserved on fine ceramic vessels, that we see these rulers in action, wielding the items whose actual counterparts we see in the Sipán tombs. In addition, the great architectural symbols of corporate authority allow us access to the actual centers where power was consolidated through public ceremony and ritual. The information provided by these combined sources tells us that symbolism enhanced the official Moche political order by visually associating rulers with their contexts of power. Symbols communicated the high status of the rulers and the narrowly prescribed group of which they were part, at once clearly defining their place in the ruling hierarchy and separating them from the rest of the populace. Moreover, symbols proclaimed the roles that endowed these powerful persons with social importance and ritually mobilized the powerful forces of supernatural belief on behalf of the established order which gave them power. In combination, these functions formed an essential element of an ideology of power whose composition and evolution allows us access to Moche political society.

We are now in a position to define more precisely the means by which symbolism visually achieved its effects as a key element of political ideology. In the Royal Tombs of Sipán and their San José counterparts, symbols are clearly defined and easily recognizable, each being endowed with meaning that is specific to its social role. However, it is in their cumulative association in ordered sets that these distinctive symbols acquired social meaning. Ritual roles were each identified by a tightly defined group of objects which included distinguishing apparel and ceremonial accoutrements. While different officiants may sometimes use the same object or item of clothing, the total inventory associated with each role forms a discrete symbolic set that cannot be confused with that used by any other actor. These individual sets and the roles that they identify symbolically represent the specific ritual context in which they acted and gave it meaning that could be easily recognized by participants and viewers alike. Recent work has identified this pattern as it refers to one central ritual, the Sacrifice Ceremony – however, it is certain that the same function was shared by other ritual events and contexts (see Castillo 1989 for an analysis of mythical personages in Moche iconography using this approach).

Moche art functioned to communicate the text and context of elite power to the public. Like all text this information was composed of a set of codified signs, the words of the language. In Moche art visual symbols constituted these basic components of the language, each carrying meaning, some precise, some more general. These symbols, like words, acquired narrative meaning by being organized into regular groupings, in this case a set of thematic conventions, the grammar of the language. Again, conforming on the visual plane to the quality of a grammar, strict representational canons directed composition and content. Variation was minor, minimizing chances of misunderstanding. Moche iconographic themes were consistently repeated through the visual media of fine pottery, architectural embellishment, and precious metal, and displayed in strictly defined settings. Themes include simple scenes of elite individuals involved in hunting, procession, and combat. More complex scenes, like the Sacrifice Ceremony, possess more overtly supernatural connotations, involving fantastic beings or human figures wearing the masks of animals. While obscure in meaning to researchers, all of these themes were undoubtedly familiar to their Moche predecessors, acquiring meaning from their unique cultural context.

While the Moche iconography of power corresponds to a text in possessing an organizational structure in which formally ordered components and sets of meaning serve to proclaim its message, the fundamental way in which a text differs from iconography also helps us understand its use. Words in a written text have a linear order and are read in succession to convey information in a discursive manner that conforms to the rules of logic as they apply to social practice. Moreover, they can be read, stored, and evaluated according to analytic rules. However, the visual media, even though their internal structure may be as ordered and consistent as the text, eschew the syntactical rules that govern language. Instead of revealing its components successively as in a text, the constituent themes and ideas articulated in the visual form are received simultaneously. Inevitably, the impact of the visual image is directed to the emotional and subconscious levels of experience rather than to the referential, informational, and logical. Moche ideological art combines these dual features. In its consistent articulation of elements it asserted an unmistakable message of power and social order. At the same time it did this in a mode that guaranteed a great impact not only on the level of conscious intellect but also on the vital level of individual and group psychology. Iconography in this sense became the language of ideological discourse.

The structure of Moche symbolic text   Like written language, the Moche visual text acquired its ability to communicate precise meaning through its basic components. In much of Moche iconography the elements that provide a unifying thread and establish the identity of the human subjects are size, dress, personal adornment, and accompanying regalia. Elite individuals often tower over their attendants (figure 4.3). This means of signifying a person's place in society is, of course, not unusual. The Egyptian pharaohs, rulers of the Sumerian states, their Assyrian and Persian successors, and the rulers of the Mayan states were commonly depicted in official iconography as of much larger size than their subjects and attired in their full regalia of rank. Modern counterparts are the uniformed monarchs of Western Europe and their dictator successors who are commonly honored by huge statues of superhuman size which proclaim their dignity and accomplishments and proclaim their political power.

Disproportionate size of elite representation in art was, of course, only an iconographic signifier of rank. The characteristic elements of personal ornament, regalia, and dress were more than artistic conventions. They were not only used in artistic depictions of Moche elite, but also appear conspicuously in the physical record, most prominently accompanying deceased rulers in such elaborate burials as Sipán and San José. This combined evidence indicates that they participated prominently in the context of day-to-day social control as well as that of iconographic symbolism. It follows that recognition of the ways in which these classes of physical objects denoted position and rank and the social contexts in which they were displayed assists us greatly in our exploration of the domain of power.

Moche elite personal adornment actively symbolizes authority on two levels. A variety of elaborately shaped and embellished articles functioned both to indicate the high status and to designate more precise attributes of the wearer. Prominent among these items are large, ornate earspools, fashioned from silver and gold alloys, semi-precious stone and shell (figure 4.2, 4.7). Such visible articles were universal signs of special importance in pre-European South America and were undoubtedly analogous to those worn by Inka nobles, the *orejones* ("Big ears") referred to by the Spanish chroniclers. Another type of high-status marker of similar character was the nose ornament, a flat, metal ornament that clipped against the nasal septum and hung below the nose (figure 4.5).

Earspools and nasal ornaments well demonstrate the two levels of symbolic meaning embodied in personal adornment. In many instances they are unembellished, in this form probably acting in a general manner to identify the wearer as a person of high social importance. In some cases they bear exquisitely crafted and very intricate images of humans and animals whose identity may well have marked exact characteristics of the wearer. Thus the highest-status occupants of the Sipán tombs, individuals identified as the principal officiants in the Sacrifice Ceremony, wore earspools and nose ornaments which bore the images of fully armed warriors. The images and articles of weaponry also interred with these personages associated them with that aspect of their wider ritual roles which involved the subjugation of sacrificial prisoners (figure 4.2). The images of animals such as deer that also appear on earspools and else-

Figure 4.5 Middle Moche stirrup-spout vessel in the form of a Moche warrior. (University Museum, University of Pennsylvania; cat. 39–20–9)

where serve the same purpose – the hunting and killing of these animals symbolically representing the events centered on the Sacrifice Ceremony.

Other articles of personal adornment were similarly used as social symbols. Elite Moche individuals commonly wear necklaces, pectorals, belts, and wrist bands made of precious metals and stones (figures 4.2, 4.5). These clearly marked the wearers as persons of importance. However, the Sipán burials again tell us that such items could also be used to denote specific position. Like the conspicuous items described above, the beads that formed some necklaces were fashioned into the specific images of ritual significance: the symbols of power. Thus, the spider beads contained in the gold necklace worn by the Old Lord of Sipán vividly symbolize the essential qualities of the ritual over which he presided: the taking and consumption of blood.

Another class of material symbols just as powerfully proclaimed the identity and status of their users. These are the
ornate objects that were wielded by the ruling individuals as
ceremonial signifiers of rank and position. In Moche fine-line
painting, elite individuals of specific rank are usually associated
with certain items of regalia, a pattern that is repeated in the few
cases where their actual remains have been identified. Thus, the
large *tumi* knives, crescent-shaped backflaps, and war club and
shield images found with the Lord of Sipán almost always
appear in iconographic depictions of the central officiant in the
Sacrifice Ceremony (figures 4.2, 4.3). Similarly the high-status
female personage from San José who has been identified as the
priestess of the Sacrifice Ceremony was buried with the decorated goblet that she presents in this ritual event. Somewhat
more enigmatic are the elaborately carved scepters found in the
highest-status Sipán burials (figure 4.2). At least two of the
scepters are embellished with images of individuals engaged in
the sacrificial act, again relating the deceased with the context of
his social action. The contextual association of these objects
with the same individuals indicates that they were also ceremonial emblems of role and position. It seems apparent from their
burial contexts that other so-far unique items served similar
functions.

While relatively few well-preserved examples of Moche apparel have been recovered, it is clear from the pieces that have
been found, and more especially from their representation in
art, that the wearing of richly decorated woven tunics, kilts, and
headdresses designated high status in Moche society. However,
these items, like other items of personal adornment and regalia
that I described earlier, also carried more precise meaning. The
dual social functions of dress – as a symbol of high social rank
and as an indicator of position – united to create a visual
language which effectively communicated and reinforced the
hierarchical and structural order that dominated Moche society.
In the light of current research, this function of dress is most
clearly seen through headdresses which appear to be consistent
markers of role and social context. The standard elite head
covering appears to have been a decorated turban, probably a
mark of distinction (figure 4.6). The designs of the turbans
may well have depicted information about the social position

Figure 4.6 Middle Moche stirrup-spout portrait vessel. (Peabody Museum, Harvard University; photo N30119, cat. 30/5050. Photo: Hillel Burger)

of the wearer. Further elaborate appendages affixed to many such turbans probably identify the wearer's specific role in society.

Headdresses can be grouped into two general classes. Most frequent are forms that are basically elaborations of the regular turban. Common additions to the turban are a large frontal disc or metal crescent, the former sometimes embellished with an emblem representing the three-dimensional head of an animal or bird (figures 1.4, 4.7). Alternatively, the emblem may appear alone. Both frontal elements appear in conjunction with a fan-shaped plume attached to the back of the headdress (figure 4.8). These types are accompanied by rich attire and ceremonial regalia and appear to distinguish personages participating in important religious ceremonies (figure 4.8, 4.3) supervising weaving (figure 3.6), hunting (figure 1.4), and undertaking long-distance sea and land travel (figure 4.12). This general

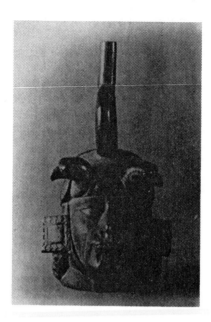

Figure 4.7 Middle Moche stirrup-spout portrait vessel. (Peabody Museum, Harvard University; photo N8243. Photo: G. Holstein)

category incorporates great variety and complexity of form. In all probability the specific type of headdress signified the particular social and functional status of the wearer. At this point, however, insufficient analysis has been conducted to significantly develop this line of reasoning other than to suggest the general contexts within which headdresses of this type appear and to contrast these with those of the second, more specific type of headdress.

The second category comprises a conical cap, sometimes surmounted by a large crescent-shaped crest. The wearer also usually carries weapons and a shield (figures 4.8, 4.9, 4.10). From the large number of scenes depicting personages wearing this headdress, it appears that the conical form is the headgear of warriors, a suggestion supported by Sipán personages, several of whom possessed the crescent-shaped headdress crest and were accompanied by weaponry and other accoutrements of

Figure 4.8 Fine-line drawing of the arraignment of prisoners. (After Kutscher 1954:23)

Figure 4.9 Moche warriors in combat. Relief mural from the facade of Huaca Cao Viejo, Huaca El Brujo complex, Chicama Valley. (Photo: Garth Bawden 1995)

combat. Most depictions of individuals wearing the conical cap in Moche art clearly and specifically represent combat, its immediate antecedents or aftermath, thus precisely identifying the chief social referent of the item. However, in a few important

Figure 4.10 Fine-line drawing of combat between Moche and non-Moche warriors, possibly Recuay. (After Kutscher 1954:21)

instances individuals wearing the warrior garb participate in non-combat activities. Again, the best described of these is the Sacrifice Ceremony which, although associated with the results of warfare, is not in itself combat (figure 4.3). In this event, the important participants each wear their distinguishing costume. Some of these, including the chief officiant, wear the conical cap with crescent crest; others wear the disc-emblem type indicating articulation of symbolism of chiefly martial meaning with that of usually non-military significance in a single complex social ritual.

The religious meaning of Moche symbolic text While symbolism as text described the prevailing system of social order, in a broader context it also proclaimed the source of the authority that supported this order. We have seen that the specific items of Moche elite symbolism, whether manifested as artistic motif or as physical object, acted as the codified units of a readable text, each having its own meaning. Combined into regular sets, these symbols served to identify the roles and status of the persons who headed the social hierarchy. We can now go further and examine the precise social contexts in which codified sets were used. These contexts, most commonly communicated to the observer through the medium of narrative artistic composition, tender the full meaning of the text, transforming it into a potent iconography of power which mobilized the Moche cultural and historical experience on behalf of established leadership.

Specifically, the visual language of iconography used familiar concepts to infuse the existing socio-political order with religious reality. While wearers of the two general types of headdress usually appear in separate combat and non-combat contexts, there are instances such as the important Sacrifice

Ceremony where they appear in the same ritual context. This functional and formal combination signifies, in the most explicit visual manner, a fundamental feature of Moche social conception and political authority. The unity of military and elite functions in a context charged with supernatural import characterizes a symbolic system that integrates the sacred and profane qualities of social existence. While I shall further discuss the actual themes portrayed in narrative art later in this chapter, at this point it is sufficient to note the linkage between occupations usually seen in Western society as distinctively religious on one hand and secular on the other.

The occupants of the Sipán Royal Tombs eloquently inform us that attire, personal adornment, and regalia were more than relatively passive media for artistic symbolism. They also demarcated status and role in active social practice. Thus, in the world of daily action they participated in dramatic ceremonies that stood at the center of social integration. In all probability these ceremonies were enactments of well-known Moche myths. Such events manipulated shared group concepts to regularly reconstitute and strengthen the social order through ritual practice. Moreover, they served to endow the high social rank of their principal officiants with a religious aura that greatly enhanced their authority. The Sipán and San José burial evidence, then, brings syncretism of the sacred and profane into the real world and supports my reading of Moche iconography, one that conforms to Donnan's much earlier proposition (1978). It is abundantly clear that the dominant status of the gold-bedecked occupants of the great Moche funerary monuments derived from both religious and secular authority – indeed, that these were fully integrated aspects of power.

It is understandable that individuals at the apex of government should participate in the rituals of power and that these ceremonial occasions should be celebrated in art. After all, this happens to some extent in all societies, ancient and modern. However, most elite art also portrays wider, more secular aspects of life, a feature that was long ascribed to many Moche scenes in which elaborately garbed persons engage in a variety of activities carrying no obvious religious significance. Yet the combined funerary and iconographic evidence demonstrates that the attire of these personages corresponds to that appearing in acts of obvious religious importance. Consequently, we must question this assumption. The evidence contextually supports Christopher Donnan's suggestion that most Moche elite art, whatever its content, carries religious import. This helps us to understand the social significance of those themes that we would otherwise simply interpret as depictions of daily life and reveals that they articulate social status, position, and religious affiliation, to legitimize the contexts of leadership and the individuals who filled them.

While there are many scenes that could illustrate this point, I shall confine my discussion here to a selective sample of broadly narrative compositions that represents the range of Moche power contexts as they are symbolized in art. In the next chapter I will discuss the religious significance of scenes of combat as they relate to the central ritual ceremony of Moche society. Where available I build on the research of other scholars who have studied this topic.

An obvious candidate for inclusion in the category of non-religious art is the common hunting scene which appears to represent economic or sporting activity. Scenes of hunts in progress are confined to sea lion (figure 2.11), deer (figure 1.4), and sometimes fox. This is a significant point given the archaeologically demonstrated reliance of the Moche population on a wide variety of fish and fowl which rarely if ever appear in art. If we look further at the two forms of hunting and the manner of their representation, the meaning of these scenes becomes clearer. I mentioned previously the widespread faith of modern shamans on the north coast of Peru in the healing qualities of stones that have been swallowed by sea lions, and their use in curing rituals. In Moche hunt scenes sea lions are always depicted with stones near their mouths, an artistic convention that strongly suggests the same supernatural quality of the animal. Moreover, such scenes sometimes include an offering to an individual seated on a covered and elevated dais, indicating that the hunt had connotations of ceremonial presentation.

In the case of deer hunts, the chief participants are men dressed in the full regalia of high rank. The hunters wear the elaborate headdress that we have seen worn by participants in explicitly ritual contexts. The great elaboration of dress is more indicative of a ritual than a sporting event, a conclusion that is further supported by the religious associations of the headdress. While it is difficult to generalize from the sparse data available on the cultural meaning of hunting, the histories mention that in Andean societies of the later, contact period deer hunting was largely the monopoly of the rulers. Most significantly, it appears that the yield of the hunt was used in religious feasts and sacrificial ceremonial (Paz Maldonado [1582] 1965, quoted in Salomon 1986:83). In other words it appears that deer hunting was an activity associated exclusively with the Moche elite and endowed with religious status. I shall elaborate on its meaning as a metaphor for the series of ritual activities that culminated in the Sacrifice Ceremony in the next chapter. However, at this stage it is sufficient to assert that in Moche elite ideology hunting is transformed into a context of power in which leaders participate in ritual that proclaimed and enhanced their social position.

Transportation scenes, while clearly containing economic elements, also were closely related to elite status and religious ritual. Long-distance maritime trade with Ecuador was conducted in order to obtain the warm-water shells that were used in Moche religious rituals. Participants in such events are shown blowing conch shell horns; these ceremonial objects have been excavated from places of exclusive religious association. Extensive iconographic analysis of other scenes indicate that the transport and transfer of conch shell was a very important component of rituals (Donnan and McClelland 1979). Likewise *Spondylus* was accorded supernatural qualities and used as a ritual substance. In the archaeological record, ground *Spondylus* endures as a physical marker of the sites of offering and sacrifice. An essential purpose of sea travel was to further Moche religious practice and, by association, the interests of the group that conducted and controlled this very important context of social integration. Previously we noted that scenes of ocean transport often displayed supernatural beings and bound prisoners (figures 2.8, 9.6). Moreover, figurines of such prisoners have been found in the offshore islands on which *guano* was mined for fertilizer (Kubler 1948). These figures also appear in sacrificial contexts on some of the most complex of Moche ritual scenes. These activities were far from being simple pictures of trade and economic production. Rather, they were associated with central aspects of Moche elite ceremonial, thus enveloping these superficially mundane activities in an aura of religious authority and political power.

Numerous fine-line painted themes show a variety of people being presented to personages seated on stepped daises. The appearance and context of the seated figures immediately indicate their high status. They are finely dressed, usually wearing the disc-emblem headdress (figure 4.11, 4.12). The daises stand inside small structures with ornate roof-combs that are sometimes placed atop platforms. The specific themes include presentation of naked prisoners, of other elaborately-garbed individuals whose smaller size shows them to be of lesser status, and of food commodities presented either on platters or gourds (figure 4.13), or being transported by llama train (figure 4.12). These scenes have been variously interpreted as victory parades, the delivery of tribute, or simple representations of important economic activity without any overt religious meaning. However, their symbolic and contextual qualities indicate otherwise.

The transportation scenes often represent llama caravans laden with such goods as marine shell, food items, and commodities contained in ceramic vessels (figure 4.12). These scenes may be related to another group of vessels which portray anthropomorphized packages of food tied into gourd containers (figure 4.13). While it is tempting to interpret these scenes solely as representing the conveyance of tribute items to the centers of Moche government or the acquisition of economic resources

Figure 4.11 Fine-line drawing of the presentation of prisoners. (Redrawn from Donnan 1978, figure 59)

Figure 4.12 Detail of fine-line drawing of the Late Moche Burial Ceremony. A llama caravan brings conch shells to a dignitary seated on a dais at the summit of a platform mound. (Redrawn from Donnan and McClelland 1979, figure 16)

Figure 4.13 Fine-line drawing of anthropomorphic offerings of food and ceramic container vessels presented to dignitary seated on an elevated dais. (After Larco Hoyle 1939, plate 31)

from afar, aspects of content and context indicate an additional meaning. First, the caravan escorts are dressed in the elaborate garb of the Moche elite while their disc-emblem headdresses convey an aspect of ritual, just as did those of the seafarers of the marine transportation themes. Second, a prominent commodity being transported is the conch shell which, as we have noted, was an item used primarily in religious activity (figure 4.12). Third, the anthropomorphic nature of some food items and the inclusion of what seem to be supernatural attendants strongly suggest that these scenes are not simple depictions of trade but of ritual or religious events. Fourth, and most significant for understanding this general composition, the caravans approach daises or stylized platform mounds where persons of highest status await, a composition which suggests a formal presentation theme rather than mere transportation.

Another scene in which the dais figures prominently is the Burial Theme (figure 4.12; Donnan and McClelland 1979) whose implications I will explore more fully later in this book. One important element of this theme is the approach of elite individuals up steep steps to the central figure of the composition who sits atop a platform. All wear distinctive forms of the disc-emblem headdress, their particular features probably identifying their specific role and status. In this theme the presenters bring conch shells. The incorporation of this scene into a broader composition that also includes burial and sacrifice again emphasizes the religious connotations of the conch shell in Moche society and that of the platform which forms the locus for ritual events.

Finally, a frequently described example shows the approach of nude prisoners toward the elevated dais (figure 4.11). This scene is convincingly interpreted as the aftermath of warfare and the arrival of the defeated warriors (Donnan 1978:34–5; Wilson 1988:339–41); however, its religious significance has not always been noted. The composition is clearly not just a victory parade. Elsewhere in the composition dead bodies and a severed head represent the ultimate fate of the prisoners, while a scene of human sacrifice performed by elaborately accoutred personages suggest the means by which they were killed. Other fine-line painted scenes which portray the transport of prisoners through the desert (figure 2.12), sacrificial events, and the dismembered bodies of the sacrificed illustrate the same sequence. Thus the presentation to the prominent occupant of the throne-like dais is more than a celebration of victory. It is the culmination of a longer ritual series that also involves capture and sacrifice. Clearly the small "throne room" with its elaborate roof embellishment and the platform on which it stands was the central physical location for events of great religious importance. The depiction of this place in other scenes – such as the sea lion hunt (figure 2.11) and food presentation scene mentioned above – imbues the scene with a quality of the religious and so was used in the Moche iconographic language.

From these examples we can see that many aspects of life were used by the Moche political order to assert its power through the visual medium of iconography. The economic, political, and social realms all figure prominently in the themes that I have discussed. Their common link is that they provide a setting for the ruling group to display its social status and the religious sanction for the authority that it wielded. A variety of other subjects are understandable in this system of meaning. The well-known Moche genre of explicit sexual art depicts an activity that also occurred in broader ritual narrative (Donnan 1978:177). Scenes of weaving and metallurgy represent the production of items for the Moche elite of materials endowed with deep social and supernatural importance. Scenes of *chicha* and coca production and use display actions replete with religious significance in the wider Andean social tradition in which the Moche can be located.

Together, the iconographic and archaeological evidence again stresses the impossibility of separating the religious and non-religious in either the configuration or practice of Moche power. This should not surprise us, for the people of the Andean North Coast, like American Indians generally, did not distinguish between these qualities in defining the domains of power. Rather, their world-view merged supernatural and secular aspects of human experience, making the imposition of such categories for describing Moche political structure largely meaningless. It is fully understandable that the body of information that survives about Moche rulers and their physical and social contexts of power should underscore the pervasive use of supernatural beliefs for political ends.

The Places of Power

At various times in this book I have had occasion to allude to the architectural monuments that dominated the Moche physical world as the most visible symbols of central authority. The

basic Moche platform mound was a massive mud brick structure incorporating ascending terraces connected by ramps.
Huge terraces, connected to the platform by means of ramps
and flights of steps, often abutted the central architectural element, visually emphasizing it and expanding the space available
for the ceremonial that formed a vital part of its function (figure
2.14). Archaeological studies indicate that these structures supported summit rooms whose roofs were often elaborately embellished by warclubs, decorative combs, or animal adornos
(figures 4.11, 4.12). Open to the front, these rooms were approached by steps and contained daises or "thrones." From
painted depictions it is clear that they were the focus of the
important ritual dramas that were conducted on the platforms.

While platforms as a class were built throughout the North
Coast, they varied considerably in details of size, form, and
construction method. Moreover, the major destruction that
time and vandalism have afflicted on many platforms make it
impossible to determine at this stage how far they conformed to
a precise architectural canon. However, general correspondence
of form and locational context strongly indicates that they
manifest a common concept regarding the use of architecture as
the focus of central political authority and its accompanying
symbolism of power.

It was on the broad terraces and summits of these symbolic
mountains with their aura of spiritual power and fertilizing
force that the rituals of power took place. It was here that
crowds from the surrounding valleys congregated at times of
religious festival and political ceremony to participate in the
events that strengthened their sense of communal identity and
to celebrate the prevailing social order. It was here, overawed by
their surroundings, that they transcended the constraints of
daily life to enter sacred space and time and commune with their
ancestral heritage. It was here, high above, that their leaders
conducted the rituals by whose means they penetrated the world
of the spirits to assure the fecundity of their arid land. It was
here that, in the drama of ritual sacrifice, the blood of humans
created the vital connection between physical and supernatural
dimensions of Moche experience and allowed shaman-rulers to
sustain the cosmological balance upon which rested the fortunes
of their society.

However, there was another means by which platforms served as the places where the physical and metaphysical domains of the Moche universe converged. While most served as the places where rituals of power were enacted and the rulers who conducted them most conspicuously manifested their positions of authority in society, some also represented the most elaborate Moche burial monuments (Alva and Donnan 1993). In this role they again identified rulers with the supernatural bases of their authority. By interring the dead members of the ruling elite in the greatest symbols of social domination, complete with the tokens of their social and political position, these great structures ensured their continuing active role in society as sacred presences whose influence transcended time and physical existence.

Platforms also possessed deep symbolic meaning. Politically, this meaning was calculated to ensure that the reins of power remained in the hands of the rulers of Moche society. Platforms were visual embodiments of the power inherent in the spiritual forces of the natural world and of the myths of Moche group identity and history, all of which were revealed in daily life through ritual enactment. By associating this powerful ritual system with a dominant architectural form, Moche rulers transformed physical context itself into the central component of the symbolic system that manifested and asserted Moche political ideology. As centers of ritual and the eternal abodes of its officiants, the massive adobe platforms articulated deep Andean structural belief pertaining to myth, cosmological balance, spirituality, and time, to proclaim the centrality and immutability of the social order that sustained the ruling group. These great symbolic edifices were the primary centers of social integration. They were the places where power was manifested most potently in the social domain. It is not by chance that the popular name for these platforms is the Quechua word for sacred place – *Huaca* – a meaning that projects the awe and religious aura that surrounded these places from Moche times to the present.

While there may well be other, as yet undefined, patterns of variation among the Moche platforms, the most obvious differences distinguish platforms located in the valleys north of the Chicama Valley from their southern counterparts. Northern platforms are higher in proportion to their base area than those further south and mounted by long zig-zag ramps, quite unlike their straight southern counterparts (compare figure 2.14 with figures 9.11 and 9.12; see also Kroeber 1930:163). Moreover the adobe bricks – the basic construction components for Moche platforms – differ in shape, in the north possessing rounded tops, a feature not present in the south (Kroeber 1930:58). In addition, in the later periods of Moche history, while the outer levels of the edifices of northern platforms are of mud brick, the interiors display a "chamber and fill" technique in which rectangular walled chambers are constructed from solid slabs, the resulting large spaces being filled with unconsolidated rubble (Shimada and Cavallaro 1986). Finally, they are mostly free-standing, unlike the majority of southern platforms which are built on the tops of hills or against their sides. Thus the Moche platforms can be organized into two broad categories that differentiate the south and north of the region. We shall see later that this stylistic difference in all probability was just one expression of deeper cultural variation.

For much of Moche history, the platform was the dominant architectural component of relatively specialized settlements. It appears that, with the possible exception of the Cerro Blanco site in the Moche Valley, the major platforms were not immediately surrounded by dense residential settlement. The traditional term "ceremonial site," while implying a generic quality that tends to deflect understanding of the precise activities conducted at these sites, generally conveys the configuration of the platform center as we glimpse it through archaeology (Isbell 1986:194).

Architectural accompaniments of the platforms in some instances include walled enclosures and terraces (Bawden 1982a; Willey 1953; Wilson 1988). At the principal Moche Valley center, the Cerro Blanco site, the Huaca de la Luna represents a distinctive architectural complex of platform, enclosures, and plazas that contrasts in form, and probably function, with its great counterpart the Huaca del Sol at the same site (figure 2.14). The Huaca de la Luna has been interpreted as a temple or royal dwelling with the Huaca del Sol as the locus of religious and administrative activities at the settlement (Topic 1982). In combination with exceptional residential areas and large associated cemeteries, these structures clearly denote a site of great importance and represent the nearest approximation to a fully urban settlement that has been identified in the Moche I–IV chronological phases.

Elsewhere, the occurrence of pottery workshops in the environs of platforms at Pampa de los Incas, the principal Moche site in the Santa Valley (Wilson 1988:211) and Mocollope, a Chicama Valley counterpart (Russell, Leonard, and Briceño 1994), suggests that specialized craft industries were located at these centers of corporate authority. As we have observed, fine ceramic and metal objects constituted the principal symbols of Moche ideology; thus the appearance of sites associated with their production at the centers of power is entirely predictable.

On the other hand, buildings that could have housed formal military units, exclusive administrative centers, and corporate storage facilities, were usually absent, at least in the first four Moche phases (Isbell 1986:194; Schaedel 1985:159–60). The general absence of these attributes of managerial complexity suggests that during this extensive period of time local leaders did not command clearly differentiated mechanisms of administrative authority, and that organized bodies of soldiers, the requisites for effective coercive power, did not exist. Central management was probably chiefly concerned with controlling the production of those individuals whose skills or labor enhanced the status of the elite – the specialist craftsmen who worked at the ceremonial centers and the farmers who fed them. However, we will see that in the Middle Period a somewhat different situation may well have emerged in the southern zone controlled from the Cerro Blanco site. Thus, a formal storage component, though of relatively small size, is associated with the Moche center of Huancaco in the Virú Valley while other indicators of centralized multi-valley control of agriculture are apparent. Moreover, it is clear that in the Moche Late Period substantial changes occurred in the structures of authority leading to more centralized control throughout the region.

In the Moche V Phase (ca. AD 600–750) the form and physical setting of these great places of power changed dramatically. The southern platforms become mere vestiges of their previous size and were replaced by very different structures that seem to have little basis in previous architectural tradition (figures 9.7, 9.8; Bawden 1982a, 1982b). However, the tradition of massive platform construction continued further north, with the central unit now placed within a formal complex of compounds accompanied by craft workshops and formal storage areas (figures 9.10, 9.11; Haas 1985; Shimada 1994a). In both areas the Moche V platforms stand within agglutinated urban settlements, a major departure from earlier periods that reveals a considerably different social context and function. I will discuss in detail the implications of these changes in chapter 9.

In conclusion, the Moche platforms and their associated specialized centers were the locations where political authority was exercised by the rulers. This is where they conducted the administrative duties of their office, where they exerted control over the production of prestige commodities and received exotic goods from afar, where they accepted prisoners for sacrifice, and where they led rituals of social continuance. These platforms were the cardinal symbols of the prevailing social order, communicating the aura and stability of power through their size and visually proclaiming the beliefs that sustained the social hierarchy through the murals painted on their facades. Most potently, as permanent homes of deceased rulers who had also acted these central roles of leadership, burial platforms linked past and present in a unitary temporal framework deeply grounded in holistic principles of Andean belief in the integration of the physical and spiritual experience. These two forms of experience were continually articulated through the enactment of religious rituals to constitute a Moche political ideology that transcended time and space and placed the rulers solidly at the center of the axis where spiritual authority and political reality converged. Thus the deceased rulers of the Sipán platforms were not merely honored dead; they were potent embodiments of metaphysical tenets that lay at the core of Moche political strength and ensured its persistence as the natural order of their society.

5

The Rituals of Power

In the last chapter I defined those items of material culture that archaeologists have traditionally regarded as being symbols of social rank and ritual role. In describing their forms, categories, and contexts of use, I proposed that they acted as symbolic language to communicate an ideology of power, both through codified iconography and as real objects used in the vital events of social control. I suggested that this ideology subsumed a wide variety of elite activities into a religious context which mobilized the force of sacred authority on behalf of Moche leaders. Essential for the sustenance of Moche power and the key to understanding its evolution were the ability to monopolize the material symbols that communicated central ideological precepts to the wider community and to assert them through the medium of dramatic ceremonies. The most important rituals were conducted in the precincts and on top of great platforms by political leaders who were ultimately buried in these sacred locations, thus elevating their identification with the centrality of power to a level that transcended time and event. In the daily world, the same effect was achieved by the narrative representation of ritual themes in iconography affixed to architecture, precious pottery, and metal items. In this chapter I examine the wider content, context, and meaning of these rituals as central components of the Moche ideology of power, specifically exploring their grounding in myth and shamanistic belief.

The power of myth

Almost by definition rituals of religious significance receive much of their potency from their association with deeply and broadly held beliefs. We are all familiar with the sacred stories enacted in the rituals of the great religions. In Jewish tradition, the annual festival of Passover recreates the events that immediately preceded the Exodus from Egypt. Similarly, the heart of regular Christian liturgy is the celebration of Holy Communion in which the officiant enacts the Last Supper of Christ and his disciples. These ceremonies, and many others like them, repeat through formal, prescribed performance, events that are believed to have happened centuries ago, but whose effects transcend time to sustain beliefs that are central to their respective groups. Essential to the persisting influence of such ritual is the mutually sustaining interaction between exact repetition of their elements and the constant meaning that they signify. Repetition in this context connotes continuity and stability, even in the face of wider social disruption.

Just as Judeo-Christian ceremonies ritually enact ancient events which have been permanently recorded as sacred narratives, so Andean rituals enact accounts, or myths, that have been passed through time as oral history concerning the deeds of human and supernatural beings. In the Andean world, ritual, and by definition its attendant myth, carries much more direct social significance than does modern religion in the Western world. Myths are stories which, through symbol and metaphor, provide explanations of how human life came to be as it is. They describe the opposing forces innate to the cosmos and stress that these forces remain in symmetrical balance. They express sacred beliefs held by the members of a human group as to its origins and structure, its relation to the wider natural and supernatural universe. These myths vividly portray the dangers resulting from disorder and chaos associated with alternative structures. As such, myths are of crucial importance in sustaining the ordered internal relations of the group and perpetuating these through established social roles and responsibilities.

Myth serves various social ends that help us understand the political use to which it was put by the Moche ruling group. At the basic level it has meaning only to its immediate group, providing a formalized statement of group values and attitudes and thereby promoting social solidarity. Through ritual enactment, myth helps mask individual and wider social insecurity by repetitive, anticipated activity that renders the future predictable by its conformity with the past. Myth makes permanent the organizational structures by which society is integrated and sanctions this order by involving supernatural agents in the affairs of the living.

While these qualities of myth influence society by promoting stability and continuity, like all social constructions it is susceptible to manipulation. The effect of myth in societies that do not record collective memory is to anchor basic structural principles in time through endless verbal repetition and ritual drama. Such a system gives the prevailing order the authority of long-term tradition and makes it resistant to change relative to that of groups whose rules and practices of social integration are written and thus readily accessible to scrutiny and assessment. Even so, myths and their associated social meanings are not immutable. For instance, modern myths of Andean highlanders sometimes include obvious European references in order to explain the profound impact of colonization (chapters in Hill 1988; Rappaport 1990, 1994). Similarly Hawaiian myths incorporated English practices and characteristics into their own mythic structures following the confrontations with Captain Cook and his followers (Obeyesekere 1992). Thus, in order to fulfill their role of explaining the circumstances and relations of a particular group through time and space, myths can and must adjust to address profound changes in the social condition.

Myth and ritual serve to cloak the rules and strictures of society in the authority of timeless social tradition. But within this context of structural continuity, they possess the flexibility to accommodate major historical events. This adjustment must, of course, occur through the intentional action of the group members who, after all, are the agents who construct and perpetuate myths. It is possible, then, for such human agents to redirect myths and their ritual dramatization to serve their own interests, especially at times of major social flux. By so doing, they assert their own interests within the powerful context of long-term cultural tradition and supernaturally ordained sanction. Here, myth and ritual can become potent political agents for normalizing unequal power relationships while continuing to perpetuate the embedded structures of social life. In this way Moche leaders, by manipulating the associations of basic North Coast myths and officiating as the central figures in their ritual enactment, were able to widen the scope of traditional belief and practice as the core of their formal political ideology.

Shamanism and religious ritual

Ritual varies broadly in its social context, the details of its enactment, and its purpose. Its social significance can be addressed on two levels. On the most general level, all rituals, whether religious or secular, share the suspension of normal time and its substitution by a special time–space setting in which the pragmatic rules and procedures of daily life have little place. In the religious sphere this suspension of "profane" time, as it has sometimes been termed, allows the transcendental quality of sacred time to pervade the ritual event and the space in which it takes place. Even in Western life with its separation of the sacred from most other domains of daily life and its experience of a distant, omnipotent divinity, we are familiar with this in the context of the rituals of Christian religion where the timeless presence of the Holy Spirit, the all-pervasive aspect of God, is evoked as an integral component of worship. It should be understandable that, in societies like those of the Andes, where secular and sacred aspects of life are far less clearly segregated than in the Christian West, the impact of rituals of sacred separation possess an even stronger social impact. Here, people live their daily lives in a relation of correspondence with the spiritual life of natural phenomena, objects, and the ancestors. With their daily experience of the supernatural as direct and immediate, the transformative potentials of sacred time add a greatly intensified potency to the ritual life of Andean communities.

Andean rituals are generally comparable in form and function to their Jewish and Christian counterparts. Through the medium of sacred performance they too evoke deep-seated beliefs concerning the spiritual basis of social order and thereby tangibly re-affirm the shared foundations of the community. However, Andean ritual, especially as it relates to the pre-European period, has additional significance associated with its distinctive cultural setting. Three factors are important here. One which I have noted above derives from the holistic Andean integration of everyday life with past and present time and the wider natural and supernatural aspects of human existence. In this context, ritual has much broader social significance than in the Judeo-Christian tradition which compartmentalizes the various aspects of social existence, thus tending to circumscribe the impact of religious practice.

A second important property of Andean ritual, also concerned with its encompassing world-view, concerns the concept of cosmic order. In Andean conception, the human universe is suffused with opposing beneficent and dangerous forces. Whereas Western religious belief seeks to resolve similar confrontation through total defeat of the forces of evil, the dualistic Andean state of cosmic order involves mediation of the opposing forces to create a condition of harmonious balance. In this context ritual becomes the sacred setting in which an officiant, such as a shamanistic curer endowed with special powers, enters the supernatural world in order to mediate the dualistic forces and to direct the power resulting from their confrontation to benefit the patient or the wider community (Bastien 1989; Joralemon and Sharon 1993). Here Andean practice reflects a universal social quality whereby dichotomous cultural perceptions are mediated in differentiated ritual space (see Bell 1992 for extended disussion of this subject).

The third factor that shapes the role of ritual in Andean life is that throughout the pre-European period, and to a large extent since, these societies did not have a system of writing. All past events, rules and regulations of a particular society – indeed the collective experience of the society through time and space – are perpetuated through human memory, verbal communication, and symbolic representation. The repeated ritual re-enactment of beliefs that carry deep social and spiritual meaning and their representation through imagery not only serves a religious purpose, it is a means of sustaining concepts that lie at the very core of social consolidation and cultural identity, ensuring their circulation to the entire group.

In the context of Moche political ideology the ritual enactment of myth was suffused by shamanistic principles. I believe
that high-ranking individuals, such as the occupants of the
Royal Tombs of Sipán and San José de Moro, who conducted
the rituals through which the ideology was continually reinforced and asserted in the social arena, acted as shamanistic
practitioners in their intervention with the supernatural. The
role of the shaman in Andean societies is diverse. In general the
shaman is the custodian of the unseen forces of good and evil in
society and an individual who, through direct communion with
the supernatural world, possesses the ability to direct these
forces on behalf of the community. The shaman cajoles or
coerces ancestral and nature spirits distinctive to the particular
group in order to effect healing, to cast spells or counterspells in
the interests of an individual or group, and to forecast coming
events. Of special relevance to my discussion of the Moche are
the abilities of the shaman to enter the spirit world and to cure
illness.

The means by which shamanistic practitioners achieve their
goals, while differing greatly in specific details from group to
group, include several widely shared practices. Of central importance is the use of a combination of supernatural journey
and specified ritual to achieve their goals with the expectation
of immediate positive response. The supernatural journey, in
which the shaman confronts the spirits, occurs during self-
induced trances caused by a combination of hallucinogens and
the hypnotic effects of drums and other musical instruments. A
common element of Andean and wider South American shamanism is the use by practitioners of personal mediums, usually
from the animal world, who assist them in their journeys and
interaction with the spirit world. Creatures such as foxes, felines, eagles, and serpents are known to play the role of medium; significantly, these are all frequently depicted in Moche
art (figure 5.1; see discussions in Benson 1974, Furst 1968,
and Roe 1982, especially 273–305). This belief finds its North
American equivalent in the intervention of animal mediums in
the spirit quest of the Plains Indians.

Joralemon and Sharon (1993) have recently described the
practices of a large group of modern North Coast shamans.

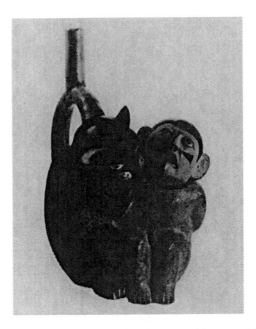

Figure 5.1 Middle Moche stirrup-spout with feline and bound pris-oner, probably from Chicama Valley. (Peabody Museum, Harvard University; photo 30324, cat. 16-62-30/F727. Photo: Hillel Burger)

Specific rituals are followed for each shamanistic objective, their rigidly prescribed elements usually including some combination of repetitive chanting and music and, in the case of curing ceremonies, the use of herbs and objects possessing supernatural power. An element common to many curing rituals is the suck-ing of stones bearing the illness-inducing force from the patient. With the subsequent discard of the stones, the patient is freed from their sickness. Significantly, shamanistic ritual involves activation of principles of opposition and balance lying at the heart of Andean cosmology. Thus the ritual table – the para-phernalia laid out to use in shamanistic curing ritual – includes items from both the precolumbian past and from the Catholic present arranged in two discrete sets that represent the domains of danger and good respectively (figure 5.2, 11.1). The active

Figure 5.2 Diorama from the Site Museum at Túcume, Lambayeque Valley, of a Curandero and his mesa. (Photo: Garth Bawden 1995)

mediation in the sacred sphere of these opposed and comple-mentary parts is the dialectic that creates dynamic unity and generates beneficial curing force.

Donnan (1978) notes that many components of modern heal-ing ritual and items of its associated paraphernalia appear in ancient Moche artistic depictions, indicating that these particular shamanistic practices possess long-term continuity on the north coast of Peru. The art of the Moche period includes ceramic representations of actual curers with their full inventory of ritual paraphernalia (figure 5.3) together with depictions of their shamanistic drums and rattles, animal and bird mediums, and the plants used for healing and inducing trances. Also prominent in art are the pebbles swallowed by sea lions, probably used by healers to absorb the sickness-causing spirits after they were sucked from the patient's body, battles between shamans and spirits, and the mountain peaks that are still believed to be the homes of powerful spirits.

Shamanism contrasts markedly in several important aspects with the tenets that motivate formal religious establishments and the procedures associated with them. First, at the institutional level, the shaman is an individual practitioner whose unusual powers are personal in nature. He usually owes no

Figure 5.3 Middle Moche stirrup-spout vessel of Moche shamaness and her mesa, probably from Chicama Valley. (Peabody Museum, Harvard University; photo N30230A, cat. 16-62-301/F728. Photo: Hillel Burger)

formal obligation to any faction within the community itself for his position. This status differs sharply from the priest who derives authority from his constituted office in an established religious organization which is usually sanctioned by the government. Second, the shaman's experience of the supernatural is personal and immediate. He directly confronts spirits whose significance is often exclusive to his society in the expectation of receiving prompt response to urgent group or individual needs. By contrast, the priest of a formal religion is usually concerned with the conduct of group events in which, through ritual practice, he brings a participating public into contact with sacred forces that are believed to possess universal authority. Moreover, it is far less common for the officiant of organized religious ceremonies to encounter supernatural beings directly or to expect immediate results from them. Instead he acts as mediator and intercessor for the participating group with a more remote divinity whose sacred power transcends the exclusive interest of local communities.

It is clear from religious studies that in practice shamanism and organized religion are not mutually exclusive. Scholars have thoroughly documented the shamanistic qualities of the complex religious rites that lay at the core of the ancient religions of the Maya region and early imperial China (Chang 1983; Schele and Miller 1986). In each of these cases, supreme rulers discharged the functions of a shaman within the wider context of formal and public religious practice. Thus, the Shang dynasty king consulted the spirits of his ancestors by manipulating oracle bones for divination and prognostication during a ritual that may have included music and alcohol-induced trances. Similarly, the Mayan ruler confronted the gods of his people through vision quest, hallucinogenically provoked by personal blood-letting using sacred stingray spines. Significantly, both practices were integrally associated with kin-based myths of origin and order and in each instance the principal officiant used a variety of ritual objects and procedures to attain his supernatural goal. These examples clearly indicate that the formally organized public rituals of highly complex societies could use shamanistic elements. Political leaders used shamanistic power to encounter the spiritual world directly, thereby reaffirming their supernatural authority.

Moche leaders adopted a generally similar strategy in their cultural domain. They also incorporated myths and rituals peculiar to North Coast peoples into the established religious ceremonies of their society. Given that a basic effect of myth is perpetuation of traditional social order through its continual ritual re-enactment, the highly charged sacred context of Andean ritual served the purposes of Moche leaders in two important ways. It created a setting in which the precepts of social order were infused with greatly heightened psychological impact and with more specific supernatural sanction. By taking the shaman's role in these sacred settings, Moche rulers gained the distinction of mediating directly with the supernatural world, thereby separating themselves in social and ritual status from their subjects. Moreover, by achieving this in the context of formal, public ritual they also brought members of the wider society into the sacred drama as participants in the enactment and assertion of the myths that explained social order. The elite associated themselves with the foundations and perpetuation of social order and this association conferred great status and power upon their positions.

The Myths and Rituals of Moche Power

In chapter 4, I described Moche symbolism and its artistic depiction in terms of a language, one that combined the strengths of logical structure and the emotional impact of a visual dialogue. In this sense the discrete objects that were the basic units of meaning communicated a particular message that was easily understood by the viewers. In this chapter I have described this setting as the ritual enactment of a sacred story, or myth, peculiar to North Coast peoples. We can now go further in examining the nature and social significance of Moche myth and ritual. In the absence of direct verbal or written information, the specific meaning of Moche myths is, of course, hidden from us. However, their frequent depiction in art allows us unusually good access to their formal and thematic content. From the examination of many hundreds of such depictions scholars have isolated a relatively small number of mythic themes centered on the acts of supernatural beings, and the important ritual performances in which human beings enacted them in the social domain.

At the outset we can identify several fundamental features of Moche myth and its ritual enactment. First, a persisting focus is apparent through the several centuries of Moche history even though accompanied for shorter intervals by other components and symbolic associations in response to historical circumstance. At the core of this focus lay the act of sacrifice. From what are tentatively known as the earliest phases, from the important Vicús metallurgical complex from the Upper Piura drainage (see chapter 6), through the roughly three centuries represented by the Sipán royal burials, to the latest Moche V period, the symbolism of sacrifice holds a dominant place in elite art and narrative ritual depiction. A second and closely related theme which persists through the course of Moche myth and ritual is combat. Whether portraying struggles between supernatural beings or between Moche warriors, combat held a prominent place in the social belief system of North Coast peoples during this period. The third part of the same ritual complex is the hunt, whose metaphorical and symbolic meaning centers around the sacrificial theme.

The relationship between these general thematic categories gives us the third basic feature characteristic of Moche ritual. It is clear from their consistent iconographic association that sacrifice and combat, and most probably the hunt as well, were parts of a wider mythic-ritual sequence. In most cases it appears that combat between humans preceded the sacrifice of prisoners, a relationship that can also be assumed in the mythic stories that underlay these actions. Thus Moche rituals did not stand alone but combined to form larger cycles.

The Sacrifice Ceremony

In the earliest Moche period sacrifice symbolism chiefly consisted of an individual holding a ceremonial knife in one hand and a human head by its hair in the other – the so-called "Decapitator" (figure 5.4). Significantly, this theme was used

Figure 5.4 Early Moche style figure of precious metal and inlaid stone from Loma Negra, Upper Piura Valley, in the form of the Decapitator, holding knife in one hand and human head in the other. (Drawing by Rebecca Bawden)

much earlier in the religious symbolism of the North Coast, during the Chavín period of around 400 BC (Cordy-Collins 1992). In later Moche periods sacrificial ceremonial centered around ritual taking of blood and killing of captives by a group of elite persons whose members included the individuals identified in the Royal Burials of Sipán. The articles of personal adornment and other regalia associated with these burials prominently display symbols and representations of sacrifice. In addition to explicit depictions of decapitation and bloodletting, these accoutrements transmitted symbolic meaning through such metaphors as the spider with its connotations of blood-taking, the deer with its links to the sacrificial hunt (figure 1.4), and the knives and goblets that release and receive the sacrificial blood (figure 4.3).

Christopher Donnan's excellent analyses of the Sacrifice Theme (Donnan 1978; Alva and Donnan 1993) provide the grounds for a detailed interpretation of this central element of Moche ideology. Figure 4.3 depicts the conventional Moche representation of the ceremony. The principal officiants appear in the top register. Most important in Donnan's terminology is the Warrior Priest, wearing the headdress and regalia that identify his martial status. Dignitaries who filled this central role were buried in the Sipán tombs. Almost invariably the Warrior Priest is accompanied by a dog who stands at his feet and was clearly an important player in the drama. Significantly dogs were also buried with the occupants of the Sipán Royal Tombs, indicating that the ritual relationship documented in narrative art continued beyond death.

The Warrior Priest is approached by the Bird Priest, in this case wearing the trappings of a warrior. In other representations the Bird Priest wears the disc-emblem headdress with an owl adorno commonly depicted in religious contexts other than combat. Accompanying these principal characters are the Priestess – known particularly from the San José de Moro tomb – and another priest wearing the disc-emblem headdress of religious status. The lower register depicts elaborately garbed and masked figures using ceremonial knives to take the blood of bound males whose bodies were subsequently dismembered. The ceremonial litter of the Warrior Priest shown adjacent to the sacrificial scene is adorned with human heads, while other depictions include the severed arms and legs of the dead. Often portrayed in these scenes and repeated on the actual regalia of the participants are fruits that have been identified as *ulluchus*, a member of the papaya family that possesses strong anticoagulant properties. Donnan suggests that this plant was used to prevent the sacrificial blood from coagulating during the ceremony.

The mythic aspect of the Sacrifice Ceremony is intensified by repeated visual references to supernatural beings. In figure 4.3 this is reflected by a variety of human and anthropomorphic figures who together participate in the ritual. These latter include the Bird Priest, whose human counterpart we have seen in the Sipán burials, together with a feline executioner and several other supporting players. Clearly this ritual possessed two important qualities. First, its location in the precincts of the central architectural symbols of Moche society imbued it with great importance to the people of the region. Second, the identity and roles of its participants evoked the deeply rooted power of the traditional myth with which it was inextricably connected.

Although complex narrative representations in fine-line paintings and architectural murals present the most complete depictions of the Sacrifice Ceremony, its component elements comprise the themes of much Moche portable art. Thus, all of the principal participants appear on modelled ceramic jars (figure 5.5; see also figure 2.13). In sum, the ceremony and its significance formed a central and pervasive presence in many domains of Moche social life.

The Sacrifice Ceremony and other important rituals provided the forum for rulers to participate in events that placed them firmly at the point in time and space where tradition and event, structure and practice, converged. The highly visible and super-

Figure 5.5 Pottery vessel in the form of seated captive with rope around the neck and hands bound behind the back. (Maxwell Museum of Anthropology, University of New Mexico; cat. 37.9.10. Photo: Garth Bawden 1995)

naturally charged context of Moche ritual replaced the haphaz-
ard vitality of daily life with the transcendental continuity of the
mythic world. Through the ritual manifestation of the precepts
of group cohesion and the dangers of uncontrolled chaos, subsumed in myth, these events continually justified and recon-
structed social order and reinforced the institutions that it
sustained. Clearly, the officiants at these powerful events, by
identifying themselves with the maintenance of established communal order gained great prestige and authority relative to their
wider group.

Sacrifice and society   The location of human sacrifice at the
center of Moche ritual cycles imparted added significance to the
already powerful ritual setting. In many distinctive ways blood
continues to have significance as offering and spiritual medium
in most Andean cultural traditions. Blood, as the life principle,
is vulnerable to attack by harmful spirits and is consequently
the focus of many healing rituals. Moreover, blood's vitality is
seen as the necessary symbol of individual and kin-group claim
to land. By pouring it on the ground during agricultural rituals
humans ensure that the land is energized by the sacrificed animal's life essence. The sprinkling of blood into streams and
lakes similarly sustains the life-giving force of water. Through
all of these practices runs the theme of the direct relationship
between human and natural life and the capacity of blood to
ratify the kinship relationship between them by acting as the
agent through which their dual spiritualities can meet for mutual benefit. Sacrifice in this respect is the vital element in a
reciprocal relationship between humans and supernatural beings, instigated by the shamanistic officiant while in a state of
trance. The use of human blood clearly brings a most potent
substance into the ritual, embodying as it does the life essence of
the active ritual partner.
  There is abundant evidence of the practice of both llama and
human sacrifice by the Inka during their important festivals (e.g.
Salomon and Urioste 1991:112,120) On the North Coast the
Chimú commonly buried sacrificed llamas in important ceremonial and religious places (see references in Moseley and Day
1982). Moreover, at their capital, Chan Chan, they also ritually
killed young women as part of the funerary rites of the para-

mount ruler, before interring them in his burial platform
(Conrad 1982). In the Moche domain the recently excavated
tombs at Sipán and San José de Moro furnish important information regarding the centrality of human sacrifice. Each of the
officiants of the Sacrifice Ceremony represented in these burials
was accompanied by some combination of mostly young male
or female retainers, dogs, and llamas (figure 4.4), all presumably
killed intentionally to enhance the transition of the principal
between the corporeal and supernatural world. Moche ritual
violence must be seen in the context of a wide complex of
generally similar beliefs regarding the relationship between humans and their broader physical and metaphysical universe.
Within this structural connection, each group evolved its own
distinctive cultural expression of the custom as an important
vehicle for communication with the spirit world.

I regard the Sacrifice Ceremony as the specific cultural arena
of the Moche in which human blood formed the principal
vehicle for the meeting of a shaman-priest and the supernatural.
In this ritual the Warrior Priest, in his dual role as shaman and
political leader, aided by his close adherents, performed the
society-renewing ceremony on behalf of his people. During this
ceremony he entered the supernatural world, facilitated, I believe, by a shaman medium, possibly the dog companion who
was always present at the sacrificial ritual and later accompanied the Warrior Priest to his transcendent spiritual state after
death. Further, even though the depictions do not confirm this,
I would suggest that the supernatural confrontation was undertaken during trance, as is usual in shamanistic practice. Certainly, other scenes show elite individuals in the trance state or,
alternatively, depict the hallucinogenic San Pedro cactus and
the musical drums, rattles, and other instruments that typically
accompany shamanistic ritual.

Thus, the act of ritual violence that is sacrifice allowed Moche
officiants to confront the spiritual by means of the blood of the
victim during the transformative ritual setting of sacred time.
Such spiritual confrontation was, and is, initiated by local village shamans in order to bring help to their patients or to
encourage continuing fecundity of the natural world on behalf
of their small communities. The formal priestly officiants of
Moche, Chimú, and Inka undertook the same journey to ensure

the health and continuity of the wider social order. In the Sacrifice Ceremony, the shamanistic element of Andean religions permitted the principal officiant, by means of the sacrificial act, to cross the barrier separating the mundane world from the sacred. In this journey he directly and immediately approached the supernatural, using the life principle of blood to draw the power of supernatural beings into the daily lives of the Moche. Again, artistic depictions of prominent Moche personages confronting supernatural beings through violent struggle vividly illustrate the sacred confrontation of shaman and spirit. In this confrontation the Warrior Priest mobilized the supernatural on behalf of society, thereby solidifying the social order.

However, we can validly venture further in this exploration of the meaning of the Sacrifice Ceremony and seek the specific benefits that it brought to Moche societies. By examining this sacred drama in its complete historical and cultural contexts its full significance becomes clearer. I noted above that there persists to the present time a pervasive Andean belief in the vital force of blood in its role as the essence of life. This belief is eloquently expressed in the words of the Aymara shaman which I quoted in chapter 2. He presents the blood of the sacrificed llama to Mother Earth in a ritual setting that represents the necessary and proper traditional procedure for communicating with the spirits of nature. Moreover, the ritual pouring of sacrificial blood onto the ground is intended to reinforce the balanced interdependency of man and nature, to assure the physical world of continuing nurture from its human partners, and to secure the reciprocal blessings of the earth in the form of abundant harvests and flocks. Blood is here the vital connection between the spirituality of people and nature, between the human and wider physical world.

Another essential quality of the Sacrifice Ceremony and its counterparts resulted from their performance on platform summits. As I discussed in the previous chapter, Moche platforms were far more than monuments of power: they were symbolic manifestations of mountains on the coastal plain. The soaring mountain peaks of the Andean world carry great religious significance. They are the homes of benign and malevolent spirits. Mountain deities control water and thus the fertility of the land and the health of livestock. Furthermore, mountains are access routes to the supernatural world. Such realities underlie the widespread association of mountains with shamanistic initiation, spiritual journey, and encounter with the supernatural. The Moche platform, through its shape, its common location on the desert plain between fertile valley and flanking hills, and its frequent alignment with prominent peaks, actualized these fundamental concepts in the social sphere. The platform visually signified the linkage of earth, sky, and humanity, the control of life-giving water, and the connection between the natural and supernatural duality of Andean experience. It thus became a supremely potent setting for rituals and the individuals who conducted them.

Through their symbolic and shamanistic association with the mountain the officiants of the Sacrifice Ceremony acquired aspects of its supernatural quality. As human representatives of the mountain deities they were responsible for conducting rituals that ensured the rainfall to sustain the life-giving coastal rivers. In these rituals, as community shamans they entered the spirit world by way of its mountain entrance represented by the platform. Through the ritual drama of the Sacrifice Ceremony, grounded in traditional myth and belief in the ability of blood to vitalize the relationship between man and nature, they effected balance between these complementary forces to benefit their societies. However, it must be noted that while these functions brought supreme importance to Moche rulers, they also raised the possibility that disruption in the natural world would be ascribed directly to their failure. We shall see that this danger became all too real in the later Moche period.

Ritual combat and supernatural confrontation

The second mythic-ritual theme that persists through Moche history is combat. Scenes depicting this contain human warriors, mythical or supernatural beings, anthropomorphic birds and animals, and even objects as combatants (figure 5.6; see also figures 2.15, 4.9, 4.10; Castillo 1989, 1991). This theme encompasses two types of action, one that pertains to the physical world, one to the metaphysical. Luis Jaime Castillo has effectively identified and analysed one specific expression of

Figure 5.6 Panels from the "Revolt of the Objects" mural originally discovered in 1925 by Alfred Kroeber at the Huaca de la Luna, Moche Valley, and now destroyed. (Redrawn from Kroeber 1930, plate 15)

Figure 5.7 Fine-line drawing of Confrontation Theme. (After Kauffman Doig 1973, figure 429)

supernatural combat and traced its origins to the earliest phase of Moche history. In this Confrontation Theme (Castillo 1991), a mythic hero, a figure with a deeply lined face and attired in the elaborate dress of the Moche elite, battles a non-human "demon." Both are armed with *tumi* knives with which they strive to vanquish and decapitate their opponent (figure 5.7). Castillo has traced this struggle through various sequential phases in which the supernatural being beheads a human victim before, in turn, suffering the same fate at the hands of the Moche hero. The final scene shows the hero holding his knife in one hand and the head of his antagonist in the other in a pose that closely resembles the many depictions of the "Decapitator."

It seems clear from other scenes involving the same protagonist that the struggle with the "demon" was only the most frequently depicted of a number of confrontations that the Moche hero experienced. I suggest that these scenes depict the feats of a mythical ancestor or culture hero of the Moche, in a manner that is characteristic for this form. Such heroic feats often symbolize the conflict between order and disorder. On a deeper level they represent the dualistic structure of Andean society. We can also confidently interpret other scenes of supernatural combat between different pairs of combatants in the same way, as symbolic depictions of mythic events that relate the confrontation between opposing forces of the Moche cosmos. The Moche hero is often shown in an adversarial setting, and, in the Confrontation Theme, by decapitating the "demon" he carries out the same act that is inflicted on the subdued victims of the Sacrifice Ceremony.

The supernatural struggle of hero and demon, of the victory of social stability over chaos, is evoked and replicated in the physical world by human combatants. I have noted that headdresses, costume, and accompanying accoutrements figure prominently in the symbolic language of Moche elite art. Their form and emblematic embellishment clearly signify their wearer's status and activity. A conspicuous category of headdress is the conical cap crowned by a crescent-shaped crest. This cap is in almost every case accompanied by the armor, weapons, and copper backflap that denote the wearer as a warrior (i.e. figure 4.9). One of the occupants of the Sipán burial platform tombs was an adult male dressed in this way, while other individuals also wore specific items of warrior's regalia, such as the large copper backflap. This association of the symbols of combat with the elite dead immediately suggests that martial status was an important constituent of their high rank. However, we can go further in assessing the meaning of this status. The involvement of these same individuals in the sacred drama of the Sacrifice Ceremony suggests that warriors and their activities cannot be understood solely in terms of political conflict and conquest, although these enterprises may certainly have been involved. In fact warriors performed just as importantly in the religious domain.

While modelled figures of warriors appear throughout Moche ceramic history, they and their activities become frequent subjects of ceramic fine-line painting in the Moche III–IV phases. Various stages of combat are represented. Warriors are shown marching in line, probably to the place of confrontation, wearing conical helmets with crescent-shaped crests, kilt-like tunics, body armor, and backflaps suspended from their belts. Combat itself is usually portrayed as involving single or multiple pairs of warriors engaged in hand-to-hand combat using maces, shields, and sometimes lances or darts. Although in some instances there is a clear distinction between the accoutrements of the combatants, which hints at inter-ethnic warfare (figure 4.10), in most cases major differences are not apparent. More commonly, differences in dress are limited to details of head-dress embellishment or tunic decoration, with overall styles of dress and composition being identical. It follows that these combat scenes usually represent fighting between warriors of the same ethnic group. The minor variations of dress style most likely denote distinctive group affiliation within the Moche world.

With the possible exception of warfare with non-Moche societies, in which on at least one occasion military conquest occurred (see chapter 8), strict conventions of combat were recognized that had as their goal the demonstration of personal courage and the capture of prisoners rather than the seizure of territory. The desert terrain and flora that appear in the combat scenes, together with a total absence of architecture or settlements, suggest that warfare customarily took place outside the settled valleys. Here warriors competed in designated space, in conformity with accepted Moche principles that were grounded in religious belief and ritual requirement.

Defeated warriors were taken prisoner and stripped of their weapons and clothing and, with ropes around their necks, paraded to an assembly area by their captors. Their clothes and weapons were slung from the clubs of their captors (figure 2.12), ultimately to become valued trophies that appear in many ritual and mythic representations (figure 4.3). Following review by persons of high rank (figure 4.8), the prisoners were escorted out of the desert to the occupied river valleys. Here they were ultimately led into the great pyramid complexes (figure 4.11). After being presented to another individual of highest status who received them from his sheltered dais on the summit of the platform, the prisoners were prepared for their central role in the Sacrifice Ceremony. With arms pinioned (figures 4.3, 5.5), their throats were cut and they became the donors of the sacrificial blood that permitted the principal officiant to enter the sacred setting of the supernatural and help renew the bond between the human and spiritual worlds. Subsequently, they were decapitated and dismembered, their limbs and head becoming important symbols of the vitalizing force embodied in the ritual.

Just as representations of the Confrontation Theme directly portray the mythic meaning of combat in Moche society, so do certain mythical signifiers that appear in various depictions of human combat and ensuing events. In the upper right-hand corner of figure 4.11 we see the physical presentation of prisoners associated with a sacrifice scene involving non-human beings. In fact, in this composition there is direct correlation between presentation and subsequent sacrifice, two phases of the wider sequence. Here, a bound and naked captive is having his throat cut by a supernatural actor armed with a *tumi* knife. It is probable that in this single scene an important segment of Moche post-combat ceremony and its mythical inspiration are directly juxtaposed.

The sacred hunt

I have already noted that the hunt, at first glance merely a common Moche recreational activity, upon deeper analysis emerges as a special activity, conducted by a limited elite group and carrying important religious significance (see chapter 4). Moreover, although its connection with the central ritual theme of sacrifice is not as immediately obvious as is combat, a closer examination shows that it was part of the Moche ritual cycle.

There is one transparent correlation between the hunt and the rituals discussed above. Hunting, like combat and sacrifice, results in the death of another, albeit in the Moche case, deer, fox, and felines, instead of humans. The numerous depictions of the hunt offer additional comparisons that further illuminate its meaning and confirm its close conceptual link with the wider sacrificial cycle. First, the hunters are depicted wearing elaborate garb which is generally identical to that worn by warriors in the combat scenes (figure 1.4). The only exceptions are their weapons and headdresses. The hunters carry short darts or lances rather than the maces used in combat, clearly a function of the different activities. They often wear the elaborately plumed headdress, a form that reflected the wearer's social status and was also worn in events of religious significance other than combat (see chapter 4). Hunters are often accompanied by individuals whose plainer garb and smaller stature identify them as retainers. Thus the symbolism of dress and social rank indicates that hunting was an exclusively elite activity that carried religious importance.

We can go further in this examination of the hunt as a metaphor for combat and sacrifice. The vanquished deer is sometimes shown in modelled ceramic art seated upright with limbs trussed and a rope around its neck. This is the identical posture of bound warriors awaiting arraignment and death before their captors in the Sacrifice Ceremony (figure 5.5). Metaphorically, the deer represents the vanquished protagonist of the combat and sacrificial rituals. Such a proposition is supported by analogy with later Andean practice in which deer hunting was largely the monopoly of the rulers, sometimes carried out by specialists on their behalf. Most significantly, animals taken in the hunt in the northern highlands were used in religious feast and sacrificial ceremonies (Paz Maldonado, quoted in Salomon 1986:83). We can be fairly certain that the hunt was not only the subject for the iconographic language of ideology and its mythic source, but was also an actual physical event, conducted by specific members of the ruling Moche elite as part of the ritual cycle that manifested their ideology of power.

Combat and hunting scenes in Moche elite art carried implications far beyond their immediate behavioral confines. When viewed in broad social context, it becomes apparent that these activities were primarily conducted as part of a ritual complex that centered on the Sacrifice Ceremony. The hunt represented a symbolic dramatization of the central ritual events. Combat and its attendant processions and presentations were undertaken as linked and ritualized activities, in order to obtain the substance without which the ceremony could not occur: human blood charged with vitalizing, renewing force, spilt on behalf of society to maintain the prevailing order. There are other less well-identified themes that we cannot yet identify so clearly, for instance Hocquenghem's Game and Dance of Death themes (1979, 1981). But we can assume that their general structure and social significance follow the examples that I have discussed.

The Development of Moche Political Ideology

The history of sacrificial ritual

Our information regarding the Sacrifice Ceremony comes chiefly from the Middle and Late Periods (Moche III–V phases). The absence of the complex scene in earlier phases may be attributed to the fact that the fine-line ceramic painting style that facilitated such depiction is confined to later Moche history. In the earliest phases (Moche I–II), ceramic art emphasized thick-line painting and modelled ceramic forms, media that do not lend themselves to the portrayal of complex scenes like the Sacrifice Ceremony. However, another important factor is involved. Most of the specific participants of the Sacrifice Ceremony do not appear at all in Moche art until Phase III, even as subjects of the molded ceramic style that prevailed in the earlier periods. This situation changes in the Moche III Phase when, in the somewhat abbreviated manner allowed by earlier artistic media, we see the principal officiants of the ceremony together with bound and naked sacrificial victims and the dog companion of the Warrior Priest enter the symbolic inventory.

By contrast, the Decapitator motif, a central element of later sacrificial symbolism, does appear in various (usually non-human) forms in early Moche art of Upper Piura (figure 5.4) and in pre-Moche Cupisnique art (figure 5.8), as do representations of the Confrontation Scene (Bird 1962:201; Cordy-Collins 1992; Jones 1979). Intriguing evidence for human involvement in this early sacrificial activity derives from the oldest of the elite Sipán burials. Here an elaborately garbed and accoutred indi-

Figure 5.8 Cupisnique Decapitator relief image from the body of a turquoise vessel, Lambayeque Valley. The hand to the right of the figure holds a raised knife while a human head hangs from the other. (Redrawn from Roe 1974, figure 34)

vidual is buried with articles that depict the Decapitator. However, the full corpus of objects that designate the Warrior Priest of the Sacrifice Ceremony is not present (Alva and Donnan 1993:167–217). Alva and Donnan suggest that this individual may well be a principal in a sacrificial ritual that antedated the mature Moche III ceremony. In combination these lines of evidence suggest that while sacrifice and combat were already important components of myth and ritual in earlier times, the Sacrifice Ceremony as we see it through later Moche art did not exist prior to the Moche III Phase.

I assume, then, from this extensive artistic tradition, that human sacrifice and attendant combat possessed considerable antiquity in the religious conception of the North Coast. Its Middle and Late Moche expressions are most logically understood as the culmination of an extensive development with roots that actually predate Moche. However, in the light of the current evidence, we must conclude that in earlier periods this important religious act did not stand at the center of the mature ritual complex that is apparent in the later Moche phases. The corollary of this conclusion is, of course, that the formal Moche political ideology whose symbols comprise such a prominent part of the archaeological record also reached its most evolved state in these later phases. This in turn illuminates the evolution of Moche power structure. Thus, in the Moche III period, aspiring elites situated beliefs that had been part of their structural heritage for centuries at the core of an integrated cycle of myths and rituals. Through ritual they played the central roles in events that brought together the physical and supernatural aspects of their cultural experience to renew and maintain social order. We shall see in chapter 8 that this coalescence of ideological authority was matched by an unprecedented move toward territorial conquest, a correlation that appears to be part of the same historical development.

The Moche V ideological shift

Just as the archaeological record traces the rise of the Moche ideology of power in the Middle Moche phases, so it also reflects subsequent radical changes in this system. Drastic changes occurred in late Moche IV society that generated the need for major social reconstitution and reconsolidation. We will see later that the evidence of this change is prominent in all areas of the Moche V archaeological record, attesting to its profound nature. In this final phase, although the Sacrifice Ceremony appears to retain its importance as the central ritual element of the Moche mythic cycle, new accompanying mythic themes appear. Moreover, there appears to be a greater degree of local variation in the symbolic content of political ideology along the North Coast at this time. Although local stylistic variation had always existed, difference in content was minor and appears to have developed around a shared thematic complex. However, in the later Moche IV and Moche V phases it is clear that particular areas developed their own forms, adding or omitting important components of the wider thematic cycle to varying degrees, a development that implies progressive differentiation of Moche ideology.

I will elaborate on the content and meaning of the Late Moche ideological shift in chapter 9. Here it is sufficient to note that at this time many of the key figures of earlier ritual iconography disappear (Berezkin 1980), and are replaced by new ones (Donnan and McClelland 1979). Moreover, the Sacrifice Theme was reinterpreted in innovative contexts (Donnan and McClelland 1979; McClelland 1990). New narrative scenes, termed by scholars the Revolt (figures 5.6, 9.4), Burial (figure 9.5), and Tule Boat (figure 9.6) themes, join the enduring Sacrifice Ceremony in the Moche V mythic cycle (Berezkin 1980; Golte 1994; Quilter 1990). I believe that this cycle represents an example of the ritual form commonly used to reconstitute social renewal (Bloch 1992; Turner 1969). Here the central Presentation-Sacrifice Theme offered important historic continuity and symbolized acquisition of vitality from the defeated forces of disorder as depicted in the Revolt Theme. The Burial Theme depicts a further transformative event which may signify the passage of sacralized officiants between the mundane and supernatural worlds, in so doing acquiring spiritual power that enhanced their authority in Moche society. Finally, the Tule Boat Theme reinforced the common leitmotif of renewal by depicting arrival of beings from exotic maritime sources.

Myth and ritual evolved on various dimensions through the history of Moche society. Although we cannot grasp the full composition or meaning of this society's conceptual system, we can conclude that central elements of this system included a fundamental Andean belief in the power of special individuals to mediate with the spirit world on behalf of their people and the power of sacrificial blood to link the human and supernatural worlds. These beliefs unite the Moche religious complex with that of other Andean peoples in a broad structural stream that transcends time and brings past societies into the realm of present understanding. More specifically, we can see that these basic concepts changed through time. Even before the Moche, the symbolism of complex North Coastal society reveals that the sacrificial theme, and the mythic meaning that this manifested, had been incorporated into a formal and codified belief system associated with the functions of social leadership. The Moche continued this trend. By the middle Moche phases they had combined sacrifice and other ritual themes in a formal ideological complex of power, one sufficiently potent to form the foundations of centralized rule and major political expansion. Finally, in the Moche V Phase we see myth and attendant ritual being structurally adjusted in order to sustain a threatened political order. Here, at the level of political ideology, myth served as the means by which elites could bring order to a disrupted past and underpin their efforts to reconstitute social stability. By eliminating some mythic elements from the formal religious complex as expressions of a discredited political system and re-interpreting the fundamental sacrifice component in the context of newly elevated themes, rulers manipulated basic beliefs on the ideological level to assert their positions in a changing world.

It should be clear that myth and ritual were not just passive expressions of religious belief. By asserting broadly recognized social precepts they played an active role in reinforcing the structural principles upon which North Coast societies depended for their cohesion and identity. In this way they exerted great influence upon the peoples of the region, a quality not lost on aspiring Moche leaders who, in characteristic Andean mode, employed them for their own political advantage. By exploiting Andean shamanistic belief in the wholeness of man and nature and the vitalizing role of blood in this relationship, they constructed an ideology of power upon which to build their dominance. From apparently modest beginnings in the early Moche period, this ideology of power and its ritual manifestations reached its apogee in the complex centered on the Moche III–IV Sacrifice Ceremony, in which leaders acted as sacred shamans with exclusive ability to commune with the supernatural. This

Part II

The History of the Moche

6

The Moche Historical Tradition

The historical context of Moche society was shaped by three factors. The first of these is that every human group is the product of its past. For each group a complex and unique array of events and innovations are embedded in a cultural mosaic that provides its members with the social and metaphysical order that comprises their identity. Second, societies which embrace more than a single social group will be internally diverse, even if they assert common ethnicity, belief systems, and cultural heritage. Third, no human group exists in a vacuum. Just as individuals pass their daily lives in active communion, so societies are in constant interaction with their neighbors, occupying spheres of economy, ideas, and politics that vary through time in their scope and impact. Moche society and its political ideology were the legacy of many centuries of internal development and wider interaction in a large coastal region whose component valleys and their inhabitants possessed their own distinctive characters. In common with all societies, the specific forms and trajectories of Moche history were the product of the structurization of events and processes in time and space (e.g. Giddens 1984, 1990: chapter 6). The archaeological record offers a clear, if incomplete, picture of this complex historical setting.

The Moche Heritage

Earliest coastal ancestors

The ultimate origins of North Coastal civilization in the Moche period can probably be found in the third millennium BC. It was at this time, in the south of the region, that large permanent settlements were first built along the coast (Moseley 1975a). These early maritime societies created and nourished the general principles of coastal Andean civilization. The signs of their presence survive today. During this time, expanding populations clustered around small artificial platforms that were the forerunners of a tradition of monumental architecture that would endure until the coming of the Inka four and a half thousand years later. The construction requirements of these platforms confirm the existence of a leadership that could plan their complex forms and organize the labor needed to build them. The rooms that surmounted these edifices were the loci of social control as were those that topped their distant Moche successors, and clearly reveal the advent of political inequality (Feldman 1985; Moseley 1992b). The beginnings of the formal art styles that later constituted the symbolic media of political ideology, and the system of craft specialization that created them, are visible in unbaked clay figurines and decorated cotton textiles of the period.

However, the direct antecedents of Moche civilization lie in the agricultural communities of the second and first millennia BC. The gradual ascendancy of irrigation agriculture as the basis for human existence brought with it innovations in social organization and settlement that were to persist throughout pre-European history. Most apparent in the archaeological record was the shift of principal settlements from the shore inland. Here, near the points where the Andean rivers tumble out of their mountain courses onto the desert plains, agriculturalists built their great U-shaped platforms – symbols of social cohesion – where they participated in the public rituals that asserted their communal identity (Ravines 1985; Williams 1985). These monuments still stand, surrounded by fertile, canal-watered fields, the legacy of the technological skill of these distant ancestors of modern coastal dwellers. For a thousand years and more the North Coast way of life, based on irrigation agriculture, crystallized and evolved in the coastal valleys.

During this time, termed the Initial Period (figure 1.3), most of the cultural elements that were to characterize Moche society emerged and were incorporated into the cultural experience and history of North Coast people. On the subsistence level, irrigation expanded from a pattern in which short canals fed small fields clustered in the immediate vicinity of inland corporate centers to one that encompassed integrated, valley-wide systems that watered the land along the entire length of coastal rivers. This expansion must have been attended by significant change in labor organization. The early smaller canal systems could have been maintained by relatively few people, probably working in groups of kin. But the later extensive networks with their large perimeter canals and numerous feeder channels would have required a much greater degree of labor organization for their support. Such an increase in the level of irrigation capacity suggests, but does not necessarily immediately denote, the rise of a central organizing authority.

In the realm of architecture, evidence of the expanding capacity for community organization is even more apparent. Even though earlier maritime platforms were of impressive size, some of their Initial Period successors attained truly immense proportions: Sechín Alto in the Casma Valley (figure 6.1) was one of the largest structures ever built in the pre-European Americas (Pozorski and Pozorski 1987). Adding to the significance of this monumental construction is the fact that the Sechín Alto complex was only one of several contemporary structures of this type built in the Casma Valley during the Initial Period. These monuments dramatically express the ability of communities to collaborate over considerable periods of time in order to create vast architectural symbols of social cohesion. Although the architectural achievements of the people of the Casma Valley in the Initial Period surpass those of other North Coast groups, they were not unique, but rather the most impressive expression of a widely shared trend of monumental construction throughout the region.

This trend is further represented in the archaeological record

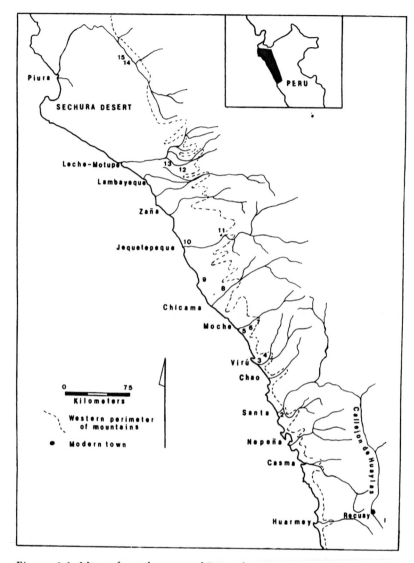

Figure 6.1 Map of north coast of Peru showing principal pre-Moche sites mentioned in text. (1) Chavín de Huantar; (2) Huaca Santa; (3) Gallinazo Group; (4) Castillo de Tomoval; (5) Huaca del Sol; (6) Cerro Arena; (7) Cerro Orejas; (8) Licapa; (9) Cupisnique Quebrada; (10) Pacatnamú; (11) Kuntur Wasi; (12) Chongoyape; (13) Paredones; (14) Ñañañique; (15) Loma Valverde.

by an innovation that introduced a crucial ingredient of later political power – the use of public iconography as a vehicle of ideological authority. During the Initial Period we first see the embellishment of great platform facades by painted and sculptured murals (Bonavia 1985:9–33; Moseley and Watanabe 1974). The often supernatural content and monumental size of these architectural images probably characterize them as manifestations of religious belief. Moreover, their attachment to the great symbols of corporate integration reveals that they were created in order to emphasize the role of supernatural belief in the social domain.

In summary, the achievements of the Initial Period offer the observer enduring evidence of the consolidation of societies integrated on the bases of effective organizational strategies and formal religious precepts codified as political ideology. However, the impressive size of architectural structures of the period does not in itself denote the presence of powerful rulerships or expansive political states as has sometimes been proposed (Haas 1987). Paradoxically, the distribution of the impressive U-shaped platform complexes and the nature of their embellishment suggests that exclusive power systems had not effectively consolidated at this time. In most valleys several centers coexisted, none of them of obviously dominant status. Additionally, with few exceptions, each platform was embellished with a unique imagery which sometimes shared specific motifs, such as the common feline attributes, with its neighbors. However, a cohesive thematic content never emerged during this period. Finally, burials associated with these centers show little evidence of the accumulation of items of high rank that would indicate the presence of an exclusive ruling class.

These factors suggest that the North Coast was characterized at this time by numerous small autonomous societies, each centered on a single corporate center which publicly asserted its distinctive supernatural beliefs. There appears to have been no wider consolidation of political power or religious adherence. Leadership in this context was still largely embedded in the principles of communal ancestry and kinship that form the enduring structural fabric of Andean society. This structure, by requiring that leadership be derived from group-shared supernatural authority, inhibited the formation of a strong ruling elite, qualitatively separated from the populace at large by divisions of class and genealogy. As we shall see with the Moche, this structural pattern created a fundamental tension between the egalitarian force of underlying social beliefs and the attempt of rulers to construct an enduring power base.

Further technological development in the valley societies of the Initial Period occurred in the artistic realm. The various media of portable art, most especially pottery, textile, and metalworking, became extremely important in Moche times as symbols of power. In this earlier era many of the techniques that paved the way for the magnificent Moche artistic achievements entered the cultural repertoire of peoples along the North Coast. In metallurgy this trend is revealed in the origins of a North Coastal tradition centered on copper and gold. The use of alloys to produce gilt copper items (Lechtman 1980), though sparse until the Early Horizon, became common thereafter and formed the technical base for the production of social and political symbolism in subsequent periods. In weaving, elaborately decorated textiles were being manufactured on the backstrap loom, a tradition that continues unabated to this day (figures 3.6, 3.7). In pottery, the other chief vehicle of artistic creativity and iconographic communication, many of the forms and decorative skills that reached their apogee of elaboration in the Moche period were already being used in the Initial and Early Horizon periods. By the middle of the first millennium BC the technological foundations from which the great achievements of the Moche emerged had already been laid.

Some of the imagery incorporated into the portable art of the North Coast was directly ancestral to Moche mythical and ritual symbolism. The Cupisnique archaeological culture that was centered in the Chicama Valley in the later part of the Initial Period is best known for its extraordinary pottery. It has long been proposed that the feline faces and forms that appear frequently on the elaborately formed Cupisnique vessels, sometimes as part of composite human–animal images, represent shamanistic mediums and transformations (figure 6.2; Burger 1992:96). These images strongly indicate the importance to regional religious structure of shamanistic mediation with the supernatural. In addition, the figure of a Decapitator, holding a severed human head and knife, appears in the guise of fish,

Figure 6.2 Cupisnique stirrup-spout vessel depicting paired feline and human half-faces in a composite image that probably portrays the shamanistic experience of cosmological duality and transformation. (After Larco Hoyle 1941, frontispiece)

raptorial bird, spider, and supernatural beings in various media in the later Initial Period, stressing the importance of sacrifice at this time (figure 5.8). Together these various artistic categories suggest that aspects of Moche ritual practice and mythology possessed much earlier ancestry in the underlying structure of North Coast peoples.

In sum, the innovations and developments of the thousand-year period following the first shift of agricultural peoples into the northern coastal valleys laid the social, economic, and ideological foundations for later cultural developments. However, while this long history established the structural base for subsequent developments, the events of a relatively short period in the middle of the last millennium BC provided the catalyst for the emergence of the particular concepts of social and political integration that were used by North Coast elites to create new domains of exclusive power.

Direct antecedents

Crisis in the Early Horizon   During the first half of the first millennium BC the coastal societies were in decline. It appears the vitality that had produced the great Initial Period architectural symbols of authority at Sechín Alto and its gigantic counterparts was on the wane throughout the region and that coastal elites no longer held the reins of power confidently in their hands. Richard Burger (1992) recently summarized the developments of this unsettled period and recognized a general process of decay in the context of determined efforts by local leaders to stem the tide and regain their previous level of stability. While these efforts ultimately failed, their very implementation brought about innovations that were vital to the later sociopolitical organization of peoples of the region.

This crucial period is reflected in the archaeological record by widespread reduction in large-scale building activity throughout the coastal regions of Peru. At this time construction in some centers halted, and they were left unfinished. More decisively, the coastal centers were progressively abandoned and they were usually not replaced by new architectural complexes. The symbols of Initial Period social integration, the places from which social order was implemented and local religious systems promulgated, were left empty except for later squatter settlements that were built in the precincts of several of them. This trend must have accompanied profound disruption in the existing order and, most significantly, rejection of the pattern of ideological integration that supported Initial Period society on the coast.

Two other developments accentuate this picture of social disruption. Although the fishing communities along the shore remained unaffected, their agricultural neighbors in the valleys moved further inland. In leaving the fields that they had previously farmed near the coast, these farmers reduced their food-producing capacity, an occurrence inconceivable in the stable situation that had prevailed previously. Finally, numerous fortifications were constructed in the southernmost valleys, strongly suggesting the presence of inter-group hostility in this zone accompanied by growing insecurity.

Probably no single factor caused such widespread disruption. Burger (1992) suggests that the inherent structural contradiction in coastal society between communally based society and emergent political centralization may have contributed to the problem. This structural stress may well have ultimately led to internal crisis and breakdown, a situation that re-occurs in the Moche period. I would add that the very longevity of Initial Period social order would have promoted such a denouement at some point. However, other factors may well have played a role in the process of decline. There is evidence of invasion from the highlands into the Casma Valley in the south of the region (Pozorski and Pozorski 1987:127–30), an event that would explain the unprecedented increase in construction of defensive works in the south as well as the movement of populations away from the flat coastal plain to less accessible sites further inland. Finally, there are indications of major environmental perturbations, tidal waves, and volcanic action around 500 BC (Bird 1987; Burger 1992:190; Moseley, Feldman, and Ortloff 1981:247) While these events occurred well after the beginning of the decline and therefore did not cause it, they would certainly have exacerbated an already tenuous situation.

Thus, by the middle of the millennium the coastal societies were confronting crises that affected all of the traditional material and conceptual systems that had afforded long-term stability. The local belief systems that provided the ideological foundation for leadership had been discredited, the subsistence base was threatened, and conflict affected at least the southern part of the region. It was at this juncture that a complex of ideological symbols inspired by the important highland center of Chavín de Huantar (figure 6.1) appears throughout the region, at once signalling an end and a new beginning in the continuing history of the North Coast.

Chavín and the Early Horizon The Early Horizon Period (figure 1.3) signalled important change through much of the Andes, highland and coast alike. The term Early Horizon was traditionally applied to the long epoch stretching from 1,200–300 BC. This period designated the entire time-span in which artistic traits believed to have originated at Chavín de Huantar were being created by local societies through much of present-day Peru. This artistic expansion was believed to mark the diffusion of a religious complex that brought with it many of the attributes that, according to the great Peruvian archaeologist Julio Tello, defined mature Andean civilization. The motifs that marked this phenomenon include fanged feline mouths, hooded eyes, snakes, raptorial birds, a penchant for the use of linear decoration on a variety of media, and the practice of building elaborate stone buildings in the highlands (Burger 1992; Roe 1974; Rowe 1962a).

The proposed preeminence of Chavín in this relationship was largely based on the complexity of its art and architecture when compared with its supposed derivatives, rather than on the basis of firm dating. However, now that sufficient radiocarbon dates exist it is clear that this scenario can no longer be supported. Chavín de Huantar itself was probably not settled before 800 BC and its artistic florescence did not occur until after 500 BC. As we have seen, most of the great coastal sites of the Initial Period, together with their embellishment, predated this by many centuries. Thus the original chronological boundaries of the Early Horizon can no longer be correlated with the expansion of a Chavín-centered artistic or broader cultural complex. In response scholars have variously changed their interpretation of the Early Horizon to a simple time-span with no cultural implications, differentiated a late Chavín "horizon" within the longer Early Horizon Period, or compressed the dates of the Early Horizon to match the actual period in which Chavín artistic compositions were adopted elsewhere. In this book I adopt the latter course, regarding the Early Horizon as spanning the period from 500 to 200 BC, the time in which we see the declining coastal centers of Initial Period civilization incorporating the imagery of Chavín and participating in the profound innovations that this signalled.

We have seen that most of the specific categories of material culture that distinguish the Moche are identifiable in the archaeological record of the Initial Period together with, we can assume, the concepts that they manifest. What then was the contribution of Chavín and the short-lived phenomenon that it generated to its successors among coastal societies? The Chavín "horizon" was not important in the generation of any particular cultural feature, although some of these were indeed affected by it. Rather it appears to have created, for the first time, a milieu in which ideas whose significance transcended the interests of the local community became widespread. In turn, these concepts led to the formation of strategies that promoted widespread social interaction. In the Early Horizon these strategies were limited to the arenas of ideology, economy, and technology in which great elaboration of metallurgy and weaving are especially prominent. However, they also laid the conceptual foundations upon which later North Coast societies constructed far-ranging political hegemonies.

The unique iconography of the Early Horizon was inspired by a relatively small corpus of stone carving executed at Chavín de Huantar. Most prominent were the so-called Staff God – a frontal figure with elaborate headdress of rayed snakes holding staffs in each hand – the cayman of the Tello Obelisk, and jaguar and crested eagle forms (Burger 1992; Rowe 1962a). While some of these forms had already appeared in the Initial Period, their distinctively complex Chavín configurations and consistent linear style separate them from the earlier works and comprise a precise artistic and iconographic corpus. These compositions appear in a wide area of the Andes during the Early Horizon, expressed in a variety of media including stone, pottery, precious metal, and textiles.

This phenomenon is generally accepted as signifying the adoption by numerous regional societies of elements of a single ideology whose center was Chavín de Huantar. This took place as a response to the profound social stress that occurred in the late Initial Period; an attempt by local rulers to retain their positions of authority. By adopting Chavín religion as the new basis of their political power local elites achieved two complementary ends. They replaced the now-discredited Initial Period ideologies with one whose transcendental nature related their power to wider supra-community belief. In turn the broad acceptance of Chavín religion created a supportive elite network whose authority was less trammelled by local community-focused precepts characteristic of the earlier North Coast tradition.

It has long been understood that the iconography of Chavín was religious in nature. However, the mechanisms of its diffusion and implications of its widespread adoption have not been well studied. Recent thorough assessment by Richard Burger (1988, 1992) of the entire Initial Period–Early Horizon archaeological inventory has significantly changed this picture by presenting a scenario that conforms well to the material evidence and the parameters of Andean cultural practice. Much of Chavín iconography along the coast was rendered in articles of portable art such as tapestry, small articles of intricate goldwork, pottery, paraphernalia for the storage and preparation of hallucinogenic substances, and ceremonial conch shell trumpets, probably the articles used to embellish the spaces sacred to a dominant religious cult and to conduct its rituals. Significantly, these articles exhibit many local variations of the central Chavín themes. Moreover, they often accompany continuing local traditions of art, or are executed in a mixture of Chavín and local styles. Burger persuasively interprets this variation as the outcome of local adoption of the central highland cult by autonomous polities, each with its own branch center.

In explaining the distribution and constitution of Chavín art, this interpretation accords well with the documented Andean pattern of pilgrimage centers and subsidiary shrines. Further, it helps to explain other broad, interactive features of the Early Horizon Period. The widespread connections established by the expanding cult made possible the diffusion of technologies and the commodities necessary for their realization, resulting in a surge of economic interaction. Rapid innovations in weaving and metallurgy revolutionized the technological capacity of the northern coastal tradition and were later utilized by the Moche. They were stimulated by the need to provide the dominant cult with the ritual items and symbols that fitted its awe-inspiring character and thus to validate its assertions of transcendence and separate it and its principal elite advocates from local control. Prime examples of this development are the remarkable caches of gold crowns, earspools, and other elite items found in

Chavín tombs near the town of Chongoyape in the Upper Lambayeque drainage, and the temple of Kuntur Wasi in the Upper Jequetepeque Valley (figure 6.1; Burger 1992:204). Moreover, the precocity of goldworking adjacent to this area signals the initiation of a strong technological tradition in the northern valleys of the region that was to continue throughout pre-European history and help to differentiate it from the valleys further south in the Moche period.

The Early Horizon had its most consequential effect on North Coast society in replacing the local communal focus with broader concepts of socio-political integration. This was achieved in the ideological domain with the widespread adoption of a formal religious cult to enhance and justify political authority. However, it should be remembered that, in spite of its foreign origin, some key aspects of traditional coastal religion such as the importance of shamanism and the practice of sacrifice were incorporated into the new cult, encouraging its acceptance by the general populace. As an integral part of this process of ideological formation, a conventionalized iconography which visually codified the central tenets of Chavín religious belief in terms intelligible to the various local societies was adopted throughout much of the Central Andes. This development anticipated the establishment of regional symbolic complexes by Moche leaders. Because this new order to a significant extent freed them from local community sanction, North Coast elites were able to distance themselves socially from their subjects to an unprecedented degree, an hierarchical trend that is reflected in the increasing richness of elite burials of the period. Finally, the expansion of conceptual horizons that distinguished this period led to the establishment of formalized long-distance connections to ensure the acquisition of valued commodities, thereby establishing a pattern that was to characterize the economic practice of the region for the rest of the pre-European epoch.

In the third century BC, technological and economic connections that characterized the Chavín expansion declined together with the social order that they had sustained during the Early Horizon. This process affected not only the coastal societies that had suffered prior disruption at the end of the Initial Period, but also the previously stable highland centers, including Chavín de

Huantar itself. While the causes for such widespread change are currently unclear, it is possible that the inherent paradox in Andean social structure between its basic holistic tendency to place the interests of the community above that of the individual, and elite aspirations of exclusive power, were again involved. Early Horizon rulers clearly based much of their authority on religious ideology – indeed it is this quality together with its material symbolism that defines the Chavín phenomenon. By contrast, there is little evidence for similar development of administrative and coercive institutions that would have ensured long-term consolidation of power. We shall see in the following chapters that this general structural property of Andean culture also deeply affected the history of Moche political formation and similarly contributed to its relatively short-lived florescence.

By around 200 BC Chavín centers had been abandoned and the strong bonds that had connected societies throughout the Andes had broken. The archaeological picture shows a resurgence of regional isolation with local art styles rejecting the formal and iconographic unity of the Early Horizon for a diversity of local expressions. In addition, trading declined drastically. The immediately succeeding period brought deeper disruptions to the coast than the abandonment of Chavín ideas and art and commercial interaction. The disruptions are vividly revealed by an upswing in the construction of defensive architecture unparalleled in regional history. The end of the Early Horizon, then, clearly marked a major transition in Andean and North Coast history.

The Salinar transition   The two or three centuries that followed the disintegration of the Chavín interaction sphere constitute a relatively short phase in which the peoples of the North Coast, along with their contemporaries in other regions, experienced rapid change. On the basis of ceramic style and settlement study scholars have ascribed two components to this quite brief initial segment of the Early Intermediate Period. These have been termed the Salinar and Gallinazo archaeological cultures (figure 1.3). However, on the actual human level, these "cultures" merely reflect conspicuous material products of indigenous people of the North Coast during a transitional phase of their history. The actual chronology of these cultural phases is unclear as is the precise relationship between them. It appears that Salinar commenced around 200 BC while Gallinazo emerged a century or so later and continued as a North Coast cultural presence through much of the Moche sequence.

Salinar and Gallinazo are usually distinguished on the basis of their ceramic styles, which essentially represent regional derivations of earlier Chavín period pottery. Significantly, recent work by Peter Kaulicke (1992) has raised the possibility that they actually represent divergent stylistic manifestations of largely contemporary North Coast peoples, not successive stages of an historical sequence as often assumed. Both Salinar and Gallinazo contributed significantly to Moche artistic and social forms. In fact it is the Salinar style that established the strongest thread of continuity between earlier Chavín-related Cupisnique ceramic decoration and imagery and the rich Moche tradition of modeled and bichrome painted wares.

Salinar social evolution also offers some precedent for succeeding Moche development. The phase, at least in its early period, was characterized by considerable social disruption, probably a continuation of the events that ended the Early Horizon. Settlement distribution survey tells us that the inhabitants of the Moche, Virú, and Santa Valleys (figure 6.1; Brennan 1980; Willey 1953; Wilson 1988) lived under the threat of attack and we can assume that similar circumstances afflicted people further to the north as well. In most of the region this unrest probably involved local groups raiding their neighbors in the same or adjacent valleys. The single exception was farther to the south where there is good evidence that people of the culture termed Recuay or their immediate predecessors from the nearby highlands descended the natural corridor from the Callejón de Huaylas into the upper parts of the Santa, Nepeña, and Casma Valleys (figure 6.1) where they settled as farmers, creating an avenue for cultural interaction and the transmission of various artistic images that were adopted by coastal peoples and subsequently appear in Moche iconography (Proulx 1985:281–8). Whatever the source of unrest and violence, it brought great insecurity to the farming communities of the coastal valleys, forcing them to leave some of their lands and move to the relative safety of fortified hill ridge locations or to aggregate in large villages where their numbers afforded a measure of protection.

The most conspicuous example of this initial Early Intermediate Period response to unrest is the large settlement of Cerro Arena in the Moche Valley (Brennan 1980). Cerro Arena is by far the largest known Salinar site and is located along the top of a large ridge that juts into the middle of the valley affording at the same time protection through its strategic location and through its large population. Significantly, the settlement is the earliest example of a phenomenon that was to recur during a time of stress in the same valley at the end of the Moche period. This phenomenon was the North Coast version of urbanism. Cerro Arena possessed the densely-clustered architecture, stratified population, corporate administrative, religious, and economic facilities, and overall planning that characterize urban life. Significantly, this social formation seems to have occurred in the North Coast region in the context of social unrest. I believe that the wider pressures of this period that encouraged populations to congregate for mutual benefit also necessarily encouraged the development of new strategies of social management in order to meet the challenges of urban life. Some of these new organizational strategies introduced at Cerro Arena were incorporated into the political inventory of North Coast elites at this time and appear in modified forms with a long-lasting effect over the next half millennium or more.

Gallinazo and the origins of Moche   The inheritors of the Salinar innovations were their slightly later counterparts, the North Coast peoples of the Gallinazo culture (figure 1.3). Gallinazo is primarily known for a distinctive elite pottery style that emphasized "negative" painting, in which the areas of vessels to be decorated are shielded by wax during firing, then highlighted with carbon coloring. This style has recently been described in three developmental phases (Fogel 1993:6) and was one component of the complex of material symbolism generated by the rulers of Gallinazo society to proclaim their identity. In the Middle Gallinazo Period the earlier settlement configuration with its emphasis on inland defensive location was replaced by a more dispersed pattern. This trend probably reflects the emergence and ascendancy in the Virú Valley of a

Gallinazo authority from the previously fragmented local situation. After consolidation in the Virú Valley Gallinazo influence, associated with the distinctive ideological symbols that further indicate consolidation of its central political system, extended to contiguous valleys (Fogel 1993).

With the region again in a state of general stability, its inhabitants were free to live their lives largely free of threat and to develop further the skills that many centuries of history and experience had taught them. The fruits of this stability are evident. Agriculture flourished as never before. Farmers extended their canals to areas that had not previously been watered, cultivating new lands to produce unprecedented yields of maize, fruits, and vegetables in the rich soils and temperate climate. Now that protective locations were no longer needed, these farmers built their homes in small villages scattered throughout the valleys. Many of the most prominent Gallinazo settlements are located in the sections of the valleys near the sea, a pattern that contrasts with Salinar emphasis on more easily defensible inland zones, and one that dramatically demonstrates the new sense of stability. The rural villagers lived in close proximity to their lands, to the fishing communities of the coast which provided them with the products of the sea, and to their centers of religious and political life. Community centers were again dominated by great towering platforms – the enduring symbols of North Coast civilization – whose re-emergence signalled the end of the period of social unrest.

Stability is also seen at this time in the increased number and size of settlements. Typical of the largest is the huge terraced settlement of Cerro Orejas in the Moche Valley (figure 6.1) which extended along the southern side of the valley for several kilometers and housed several thousand inhabitants (Moseley and Mackey 1972). Other similar sites were built in the Chicama Valley at Licapa (Moseley 1992a:165) and at Huaca Santa in the Santa Valley, where several square kilometers of residential homes housed the population of the area's largest settlement (Wilson 1988:160–1). In the Virú Valley the extensive Gallinazo Group, to which I will return later, was a town of several thousand inhabitants (Bennett 1950). However, the Gallinazo occupation of Cerro Blanco in the lower Moche Valley was to play a more important role in subsequent history.

Here, on the lower slopes of the hill and the flat plain below, the Moche Valley people established a settlement contemporary with Cerro Orejas further inland (Hastings and Moseley 1975). This Gallinazo site was probably of significant size but has been largely obscured by dune sand and later construction. But it marks the foundation of the town that would in a short time evolve into the most grandiose manifestation of Moche civilization, capital of a large polity, and location of the Huaca del Sol, one of the largest structures built in pre-European South America.

The well-studied Virú Valley is representative of what was occurring throughout the region during the Gallinazo phase (for an account of the Virú Gallinazo occupation see Willey 1953). Here, in a relatively small valley, the land under cultivation reached its greatest extent in pre-twentieth century history with related growth in settlement density and population size. These trends can be regarded as partly the cause and partly the consequence of consolidation of effective political strategies through which leaders capitalized on the stability and prosperity of the period to enhance their power. During the Gallinazo phase in the Virú Valley, not only did the number of occupation sites and area of irrigated land reach their maximum extent, but the composition of many settlements changed in a way that denotes the growth of central political authority. The most obvious signs of this are the great adobe platforms of the Gallinazo settlements. After the interruption of such monumental building programs during the Salinar phase, this renewed platform construction dramatically marked the re-emergence of the time-hallowed symbol of social integration in the North Coast in its dual political and religious aspects. Gallinazo platforms are located throughout the valley, standing on the flat coastal plains where they overlook the fertile fields and, like the impressive hilltop Castillo de Tomoval (figure 6.3), tower over the valley communities below, vividly projecting the grandeur and authority of their builders.

Through their very size, these Virú Valley monuments of the Gallinazo phase reflect the power of leaders to command the obedience and mobilize the labor of their wider communities; moreover, in their technique of construction they allow us a more precise glimpse into the actual strategy used to implement

*Figure 6.3 Castillo de Tomoval, Gallinazo Culture, Virú Valley.
(Courtesy Michael Moseley)*

this authority. Early Gallinazo structures were built of *tapias* (large slabs of tempered mud). The later platforms used mold-made adobe blocks which were to become the building material of the Moche. These later Gallinazo platforms also used the segmentary building technique that was to typify later Moche monumental architecture (see discussion on pages 104–5; figure 3.11). This constructional pattern with its suggestion of labor taxation reveals that Moche leaders and their Gallinazo counterparts were able to mobilize the work of several communities concurrently and to direct it to serve the interests of central social authority.

Until recently the sparse amount of information available from valleys to the north of the Chicama River precluded any detailed understanding of the pre-Moche situation in this important part of the region. Heinrich Ubbelohde-Doering, who worked in the Jequetepeque Valley a half century ago, noted the presence of Gallinazo burials at the impressive late city of Pacatnamú which stands on a bluff overlooking the Pacific

Ocean (figure 6.1; Ubbelohde-Doering 1967:22–4, 1983). He also made an observation the implications of which have not been fully explored until now: these burials contained both Gallinazo and Moche grave goods, indicating that the two cultures were contemporaries. I will return to a fuller discussion of this and other evidence for contemporaneity later.

For several decades Ubbelodhe-Doering's work provided virtually all knowledge of Gallinazo in the great complex of northern valleys that extends from Jequetepeque to Piura where Larco Hoyle (1965:9–10) had during the same period noted the presence of pottery of Gallinazo form and decoration. However, recent work in this part of the region is changing this picture dramatically. Izumi Shimada, who has conducted surveys here over the past decade, has to date detected only sparse Gallinazo occupation in the middle Lambayeque drainage, although the lower valley situation may change this picture (Shimada 1994a:69–71; Shimada and Maguña 1994). By contrast, he identified an extensive Gallinazo occupation in the middle La Leche Valley, including impressive residential clusters and monumental platform mounds. The entire zone was served by an extensive canal system. The apparent center of this area, Paredones, on the south bank of the La Leche (figure 6.1), is dominated by the impressive Huaca Latrada platform, its sides measuring 100 by 60 meters, standing over 20 meters in height. Further north in the Upper Piura River Valley, recent research has confirmed Larco's earlier observation of similarity between the Vicús and Gallinazo pottery styles (Kaulicke 1992). Most significantly, the site of Loma Valverde (figure 6.1) presents a platform mound built in characteristic early Gallinazo architectural style with large *tapias* as the chief construction material, associated with pottery of similar affiliation (Kaulicke 1992, 1994). This work has provided convincing evidence of the broad extent of Gallinazo cultural traits as an expression of North Coast tradition from the Santa Valley in the south to the present-day borders of Ecuador.

In summary, Gallinazo occupation of the North Coast region signalled the emergence of a pattern of political society that was to persist through much of the Early Intermediate Period. In addition to the dominant visual impact of the great Gallinazo corporate centers and the power that they embodied, the con-

temporary residential settlements testify to the growing authority of elites in the earliest centuries of the Christian Era. It is
again in the Virú Valley that this aspect of political consolidation is most apparent. Here the so-called Gallinazo Group
(figure 6.1; Bennett 1950; Fogel 1993), a huge town with an
area of over 8 square kilometers, flourished on the open plains
inland from the coast surrounded by extensive agricultural
fields. Consisting of many dense clusters of homes separated by
courts and alleys, the town was dominated by numerous platforms that accommodated the administrators and their retainers. Some of these were attached to elaborate residential
structures and probably comprised the homes of the leaders of
Gallinazo society. Individuals of high rank were buried in the
precincts of these complexes; their funerary possessions reveal a
richness rarely seen in earlier times and attest to their superior
position. The accumulated information of the Gallinazo period
strongly suggests to some recent researchers (Fogel 1993) that at
this time the first North Coast multi-valley political state was
formed in the same territory that would see the Moche build an
even greater power.

7

The Emergence of Moche Society

The cultural milieu that we usually associate with the Gallinazo Phase, itself expressing the persisting legacy of human occupation on the North Coast, formed the historical setting for the developments of the Moche period. Here I will examine the emergence and consolidation of Moche culture in both its historical and geographical dimensions. In addition, I explore the particular social and political constituents of Moche culture. By examining Moche archaeological and artistic manifestations within their historical and social contexts I refine their interpretation. The brilliant artistic complex that has long been accepted as the hallmark of the Moche period and traditionally used to characterize its culture, appears instead as a distinctive manifestation of North Coast political ideology. By contrast, the broader archaeological residue of North Coast life during the Moche period is not nearly as distinctive. This is because it represents the long historical continuity of regional culture from which Moche ideology, together with its predecessors and descendants, derived its meaning.

Problems of Time and Space

Traditional understanding of the emergence of Moche culture and its Gallinazo and Salinar heritage has depended heavily on ceramic analysis (e.g. Collier 1955; Ford 1949; Larco Hoyle

1938, 1939, 1944, 1945, 1948, 1965). In common with most culture historical research in archaeology, the study of ceramic decoration and form, in their temporal and spatial aspects, has played a central role in identifying the origins and tracing the subsequent evolution of Moche culture. As I noted in chapter 1, Rafael Larco Hoyle, the great Peruvian scholar, devised the universally used Moche ceramic typology. He identified a series of five stylistic classes of the distinctive Moche stirrup-spout vessels, using excavated grave materials for this purpose (Moche I–V: figure 3.8). This formal series was based on changes in the shape and size of the spout, the shape of the vessel body and stirrup, and the relative proportions of all three major elements. In summary, the vessel body became progressively taller through time, a trend echoed by the stirrup, while the spout evolved from a straight-sided element surmounted by a rim to a rimless form in which the top is narrower than the base. Decorative elements also evolved. Moche I–II vessels emphasized thick-line drawing of bold, simple motifs. This technique gave way to fine-line representational and narrative scenes in the Moche III–IV phases and to exceptionally complex, crowded imagery in Moche V, the final stylistic phase.

This Moche stylistic sequence has been further refined following intensive analysis of the grave-lots originally excavated by Max Uhle at the Cerro Blanco site at the turn of the century. On the basis of changes in stirrup, spout, and vessel body shape Christopher Donnan was able to subdivide the Moche III Phase (1965). Today three stylistic subphases (IIIA–C) have been identified for this phase. This refinement both demonstrates the great emphasis traditionally placed on the analysis of fine ceramics in Moche studies and the precise understanding of stylistic development now possessed by scholars of the Moche. However, as we shall see, significant problems attend the use of this sequence for illuminating wider social dynamics in the region during the Moche period.

An initial difficulty pertains to the chronology represented by each phase. At present, with the possible exception of the Moche V Phase, there are insufficient dates available to permit confident correlation of these stylistic phases with an absolute chronology. Consequently, the stylistic sequence can only in the most general way be used to investigate issues concerning the

duration of the events and processes reflected in the archaeological record. Any dates preceding the end of the Moche IV
Phase around AD 600 must be accepted with this clarification in
mind and regarded at best as informed estimates.

Another problem with the Moche stylistic sequence concerns
its utility for accurately dating non-funerary contexts. The sequence is based almost entirely on excavated grave-lots. Almost
by definition, items used as part of mortuary ritual possess
special significance in the realm of religious belief. It is often the
case that such items are manufactured or adorned specifically
with this meaning in mind and are not used in the more mundane settings of daily life. It follows that they may not occur in
residential contexts and therefore cannot routinely be used to
date or understand settlements. However, it is precisely the
settlement that contains information crucial for understanding
social organization and broader processes of change. While
Moche settlement excavation reveals that at least the forms used
in burials often occur in residential contexts, it also demonstrates that there was considerable variation in decorative content between elite objects employed for funerary ritual and
those used in other settings. Consequently, care must be taken
to recognize the likelihood of such functional variation when
using the Larco sequence to study wider aspects of Moche
society.

As with most style-based chronologies, the Salinar-Gallinazo-
Moche sequence tends to highlight the integrity of each stylistic
phase. Conceptually this method emphasizes the differences
between, but not within, the phases. This is even the situation
when, as in the Moche sequence, there is considerable sharing
of features. Consequently transition from one phase to the next
appears rather abrupt, assuming change in the entire diagnostic
complex of formal and decorative features. This approach unavoidably conceals gradual stylistic evolution in favor of transformation. Therefore when such a series is used to identify
wider historical developments in the archaeological record, it
will bias interpretation toward the sequential occurrence of
major transformations which correspond to observed changes
in style, which are themselves the results of somewhat arbitrary
selection of diagnostic traits.

This approach has certainly distinguished traditional views of

Moche history. Here cultural development has largely been understood within a framework characterized by transformations separated by static interludes. In fact, while the several sets of attributes that identify Larco's five phases may be valid as general categories, there is considerable overlap among them that is often regarded as unimportant. Thus potential continuities are largely disregarded when stylistic change is emphasized. In the Moche sequence shared features are especially marked between contiguous stylistic phases. Even in the case of burial pottery it is at this juncture extremely difficult to discriminate between either the Moche I and II or the Moche III and IV phase ceramics except by subtle formal features. This situation suggests that although individual phases may be useful tools for artistic analysis, they possess limited relevance as measures of social change. The primary purpose of this book is to examine Moche culture from a broad historical perspective. I therefore treat each of these pairs of stylistic phases, together with Moche V, as the smallest segments of social reality that can be identified by ceramic correlation. For convenience I term the Moche I–II phases the Early Period, the Moche III–IV phases the Middle Period and the Moche V phase the Late Period (figure 1.3). I would stress, however, that within each of these temporal segments society was not static but constantly underwent change that is either observable in the material record or can be confidently assumed from this record.

The wisdom of adhering to this broader framework is underscored by examining the geographical implications of Larco's temporal scheme. As I noted previously, Larco based most of his research on excavated ceramic lots from burials in the Chicama Valley and its neighbors immediately to the south. The five-phase sequence was assumed to represent a fine-grained chronological scheme, equally applicable in all parts of the region. While since Larco's time numerous additional burials have been excavated and, unlike most of his, carefully described, they predominately represent the Moche and Jequetepeque Valleys (over 75 percent of published burials: see Donnan 1995:118 for exact tabulation). The huge Lambayeque complex remains largely unrepresented in the published burial literature, with the dramatic exception of the Sipán burials, a situation repeated in the important Upper Piura drainage. Thus from the beginning major distributional inconsistency has existed, together with the problems that this raises for wide regional applicability of the related chronological data.

Another source of difficulty derives from Larco's (1965, 1967) identification of another source of Moche ceramics far to the north in the Vicús area of the Upper Piura drainage (figure 1.1). Separated by a considerable distance from the principal area of Moche material culture, the Moche ceramics of Vicús, representing an entirely looted sample, displayed both close similarities to and intriguing differences from their southern counterparts. For years the Vicús material remained an enigma in Moche studies. Recent research elsewhere in the northern valleys suggests that its distinctive stylistic character was not so exceptional. It now appears that there was considerable geographical variation in Moche ceramic stylistic developments on the North Coast, and that different "phases" of Larco's sequence actually existed at the same time in separate areas. Thus, for overall chronological study it is currently better to use more inclusive temporal categories rather than the precise phases that may well only possess local significance with reference to their valleys of origin.

The prevailing view of cultural transition from Gallinazo to Moche has similarly been affected by the primary location of field excavation in the Moche and Virú Valleys. From the time of the Virú Valley Project, this restricted area has been the center of intensive settlement examination as well as ongoing ceramic study. It should be no surprise that the Chicama-Moche Valleys came to be regarded as the "core area" of Moche cultural emergence. It was only in these valleys that there appeared to be a clear succession from Gallinazo to earliest Moche ceramics. Moreover, it was in the Moche Valley at Cerro Blanco that the largest Moche settlement was built on Gallinazo foundations around the great Huaca del Sol. All this pointed to the Moche and Chicama Valleys as the heartland of Moche culture and its social and political accomplishments, a central tenet of the dominant scenario of Moche origins.

This scenario, summarized in my introductory chapter, sees Moche as a new "culture" which emerged on the North Coast around AD 100 (although in accord with the chronological problems that I have discussed above, dates as early as 100 BC and as late as AD 200 have been proposed). Moche inherited many of its material and cultural features from its Gallinazo and earlier North Coast predecessors, yet at the same time was distinct. The chief center of earliest Moche emergence in Phases I and II was its so-called "core area," the Moche and Chicama valleys. It was from here that invasion of the Virú Valley and its southern neighbors was believed to have originated in the Moche III Phase. The apparent absence of earliest Moche remains to the north or south of the core zone (except in the Piura area) led researchers to believe that these valleys were brought into a political state by conquest during the Moche III Phase around AD 400. It was then that a single centralized state was created and Moche cultural and political boundaries embraced the entire North Coast region.

This scheme of Moche origins and initial development suffers from its single source inspiration. The absence until recently of any considerable settlement work north of the Chicama Valley meant that direct information from this important area was under-represented in the information-base. This, in turn, has imposed an illusory pattern of regularity on ideas regarding the spatial development of North Coast society during the Moche period. Historical process is interpreted within a mechanistic diffusionist model of cultural origin in a single "core area," followed by local political consolidation and subsequent conquest radiating symmetrically from this core area to the north and south until the entire region was united under a political capital at the Cerro Blanco site.

Moreover, the ceramic style-based Moche model of social change imposed a transformational element on this spatial pattern. In this model, Moche culture appears as an abrupt replacement of Gallinazo in the core valleys. This transformation occurred later elsewhere, with equally abrupt conquests of the coast that were assumed to have taken place in the Moche III Phase. In general, this scheme over-emphasized consistency and diffusion and concealed local variation and differential evolution. As I have already intimated, recent research, especially in the northern valleys, reveals a much more complex situation. Specifically, the unresolved issue of the Early Period remains in the Upper Piura region, which had long remained dormant, has now broadened to include other northern valleys from which

similar material is now emerging. It is becoming increasingly
evident that we can no longer interpret Moche archaeology or
that of its underlying cultural tradition purely by reference to
developments in the "core" valleys, or by a simple concept
of socio-political evolution. A brief survey of Moche emergence throughout the North Coast underscores this essential
conclusion.

Unity and Diversity

Early Intermediate Period cultural continuity   The archaeological record of Moche emergence demonstrates that most
categories of daily life remained essentially unchanged. At the
centers of administration and religion the formal character of
the monumental architectural complexes persisted from earlier
times; the great flat-topped edifices were approached by frontal
ramps in the southern valleys and by zig-zag ramps mounting
the platform sides in the north. Similarly there is continuity of
construction technique. The segmentary construction system
suggestive of community-based labor organization is shared
by Virú Valley Gallinazo platforms such as the Castillo de
Tomoval (figure 6.3; Bennett 1939:27–8), the Castillo de Napo
(Willey 1953:177), the Castillo de Sarraque (Willey 1953:172)
and, by the Moche period, the Huaca del Sol (figure 2.14;
Hastings and Moseley 1975; Moseley 1975b). Moreover, with
the possible exception of the extensive Gallinazo Group site in
the Virú Valley, almost all major Gallinazo and Moche architectural complexes display the configuration that has usually been
described as a "ceremonial center." In this arrangement the
platforms dominate a relatively dispersed settlement in which
some accompanying specialized architecture is present but without the associated dense population densities that developed in
some locations at the end of the Moche period.

  In the rural villages where most people lived, there was similar continuity of the material expressions of daily life. The
houses themselves maintained the basic North Coast plan with
rectangular rooms containing kitchens, living areas, and small

domestic storage rooms. Houses were enclosed by plastered cane walls set into adobe or stone foundations and roofed by thatch. This easily available vegetal material also served to shade the adjacent courtyards where many of the daily chores took place in the tropical climate. These tasks are reflected in the red-fired pottery vessels, wooden tools, and weaving and sewing implements so commonly found at such sites. Overall the archaeology of Gallinazo and Moche settlements reflects a picture of cultural stability at the level of daily domestic life. In most areas this picture is repeated in patterns of settlement distribution. Indeed many important sites were occupied in both Gallinazo and Moche periods. Significant settlement disjunction between the two cultural phases was limited to the southernmost valleys where clear evidence of re-orientation accompanies the appearance of Moche during the Moche III Phase. This unique situation was due to conquest, an event specific to the southern part of the region that I shall discuss more fully in the next chapter. Finally, the large-scale agricultural systems with their extensive irrigation systems that supported Moche period populations derived from major Gallinazo phase construction.

To a significant degree continuity was also embodied in other, more exclusive and specialized domains of culture. Thus, not only are common cooking, storage, and serving vessels identical in the two periods, but more ornate items share many formal and decorative features. Heidy Fogel (1993) has recently conducted an intensive study of Gallinazo pottery and concluded that most of the more elaborate vessels that have been used to characterize the Moche culture actually derived their formal and, in many cases, decorative origins in the Gallinazo period. The many decorated forms with distinctive handles, bridges, and spouts, most especially the stirrup-spout vessel (figure 2.7), hallmark of Moche culture, together with molded animal and human forms, all occur in Gallinazo. Many of these in turn derived from much older regional ceramic traditions. Likewise in metallurgy, copper-gold alloy, the technological basis for the brilliant Moche complex of precious metal artistic production, became popular in the Gallinazo period.

I should again note here that in many specific details of decoration, construction, and shape, the other initial Early Intermediate Period ceramic style – Salinar – also closely resembles Moche forms. Thus, Peter Kaulicke (1992) has documented most of the features mentioned above for Gallinazo and suggested that, given the somewhat greater antiquity of Salinar, this style may more feasibly be regarded as a Moche progenitor than the Gallinazo style that co-existed with it through the remainder of the Early Intermediate Period. However, the currently uncertain nature of the relationships between the three styles is less important than the broader social context that they reveal. It is clear that they are all expressions of the common cultural tradition of North Coast peoples. It is also becoming clear that they do not represent a simple chronological sequence. In fact, although Salinar may have appeared first, it probably overlapped in time with Gallinazo, the latter ultimately outlasting it to become a full contemporary of the Moche style (figure 1.3). Thus continuity and shared heritage characterizes the Moche legacy. Its unique quality is to be found in the ideological realm rather than in any dramatic historical transformation.

Even in the realm of ideas, as we glimpse them through their material symbols, there are striking continuities throughout the Early Intermediate Period on the North Coast. Mortuary ritual, almost by definition religious in meaning, exhibits several important features that linked Moche, Gallinazo, and Salinar practice (Donnan and Mackey 1978; Fogel 1993:280–90). Each buried the deceased, accompanied by multiple pottery vessels of identical shape and decoration, in an extended position within a rectangular underground chamber that was often lined by stone or adobe blocks (for elaborate examples of this burial style see figures 4.2, 4.4). In addition, the placement of pieces of copper over the mouth, in the hands, or near the feet of the dead, was shared. Finally, both Moche and Gallinazo high-status burials were usually placed in locations of importance, such as platform mounds and their architectural precincts.

These numerous close similarities clearly define cultures that were very closely related. Indeed some recent scholarship has suggested that Moche and Gallinazo cannot be separated in any way and that they were simply successive phases of a single development encompassing all aspects of material culture (Fogel

1993) and ideology (Makowski 1995). I am in sympathy with this view in as far as it recognizes that both were products of a single North Coast tradition with the strong affinity that this implies. However, we must at the same time acknowledge that they differ markedly in the material manifestations of political ideology. Moreover, as we shall see below, there is increasing evidence for their contemporaneity through much of the Early Intermediate Period, a situation that precludes any possibility of simple cultural succession.

Only in the area of elite art is there discontinuity between the material culture of Moche and Gallinazo. At the time of the emergence of Moche, it appears that the Salinar style had already disappeared as a major component of North Coast ceramic production and use. Of the two persisting styles that dominated the remainder of the Early Intermediate Period, the complex and formal Moche iconography contrasts with the much plainer Gallinazo elite style. Various scholars have described the religious content of Moche art, the chief motifs and themes of which I have discussed in chapters 4 and 5 of this book. This iconography was restricted to status symbols such as fine pottery, textile, and metal, and used in broadly ceremonial contexts – elite burials and great platform complexes. Exclusive use of religious iconography in contexts of corporate authority and formal religion clearly identifies it as a symbolic component of power. However, there was overwhelming continuity in most other areas of North Coast culture including all levels of basic domestic life and work, and even including significant aspects of religious belief and governmental practice, as demonstrated by the stable funerary practices and configuration of the great architectural centers of authority. Material difference, then, between Gallinazo and Moche was confined to the iconography and artifacts of power. It follows that Moche iconography was the manifestation of a belief system that emerged from the existing conceptual tradition of North Coast people. It was not the consequence of cultural replacement as often assumed. Moche material culture has its greatest significance as the symbolism of a political ideology which, for a time, dominated the cultural tradition that formed its continuing context and gave it meaning.

The shape of Moche genesis in the "core"   The archaeological record indicates, then, that the Moche and Gallinazo phases were both the cultural creations of indigenous people of the region. Their only significant difference was in the realm of political ideology. Although the reasons for the formation of the Moche ideological system with its great emphasis on elaborate material symbolism and ritual display remain to be explained, we can assume that its founders shared a single cultural tradition with their Gallinazo counterparts but based their power on very different conceptual bases. The traditional scenario of Early Intermediate Period development would see this difference as due to historical change, with Moche succeeding Gallinazo in the Moche I Phase in the central valleys, in Moche III elsewhere. However, a further survey of the North Coast in its entirety demonstrates that the relationship between the two cultural phases cannot be explained by simple chronological succession and diffusion as the term "phase" might suggest, but was actually much more complex. Two chief revisions must be made. First, it is now clear that many regional groups, north as well as south, continued to utilize the characteristic expressions of Gallinazo material culture throughout the entirety of the Moche period. Second, it is equally clear that Moche culture did not emerge solely in the "core" valleys but possessed a much broader origin than previously accepted, with ramifications that reach to the extreme borders of the North Coast region.

It has, of course, long been understood that Moche and Gallinazo cultural complexes co-existed in the southern part of the region, the former consolidating its position around the great Cerro Blanco site during the Early Moche Period while Gallinazo culture flourished in the Virú Valley and its southern neighbors (figures 1.1, 7.1). This situation persisted until around AD 350 when the conventional view assumes that Moche armies conquered the valleys both to the south and north of the Moche River in the Moche III Phase (figure 7.1). Although Moche III appearance in the southernmost valleys is well documented by both ceramic and settlement data, the same is not true for the extensive northern area. Here only sparse information has been available until recently and the assumption of invasion from the south was largely based on the fact that all known Moche architectural complexes appeared to be

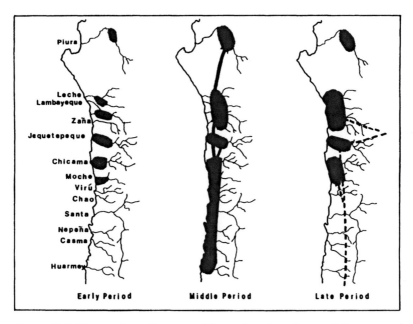

Early Period   Middle Period   Late Period

Figure 7.1 Maps of north coast of Peru showing the spatial course of Moche development. Left-hand map shows emergence and consolidation in the Moche I–II phases. Center map shows political expansion in the Moche III–IV phases with consolidation of the southern polity from the Chicama to Huarmey valleys in the south and the posited conquest of the north in the Moche IV Phase (shown by arrows). Right-hand map shows Moche V developments with loss of the southern valleys and expansion of the Pampa Grande polity to the sea. Dotted arrows show the chief sources of outside influences (Central Coastal Wari-related influence from the south and Cajamarca from the Northern Highlands).

of late date. Moreover the situation has always been complicated by the far northern Vicús area, where earlier pottery and metal materials of Moche I–II affiliation were found long ago by Rafael Larco Hoyle (1965, 1967).

Scholars now recognize that the traditional scenario of Moche emergence and expansion is based on less than firm foundations. No one seriously contests the fact that interpretations associated with the northern valleys have long suffered from an absence of good information. However, under scrutiny, the picture in the south also appears to be far less secure than usually supposed. This can again largely be attributed to the research methodology. While it is true that until recently Moche pottery of Phases I and II had only been found in the Moche Valley – with the conspicuous exception of Vicús – there has been little discussion of the implications of the actual quantities of this early material or its settlement associations in the valley.

To date, only one burial containing pottery of certain Moche I affiliation has been found in the Moche Valley. This burial was associated with the early construction levels of the Huaca del Sol (figure 7.2; Donnan and Mackey 1978:59–61). The pioneering work of Max Uhle at the same site produced three Phase II burials and an additional example, seemingly transitional between the first two phases (Donnan and Mackey 1978:63). However, Heidy Fogel, in her recent analysis of Gallinazo pottery and settlement (Fogel 1993:237), documents many other vessels that share formal and decorative features of the Moche I–II stylistic phases and incorporates the entire corpus, including the small Moche Valley inventory, into a single transitional category. According to this analysis only a single site – a small settlement near Cerro Blanco – can be ascribed to the earliest Moche period in this "core" valley (Topic 1982:265–6). It should be noted that recent work by Peruvian researchers from the University of Trujillo suggests that the origins of the Huaca de la Luna may also date to this period (Uceda et al. 1994:293). By contrast to the sparse Early Moche occupation, Gallinazo presence is quite widespread, encompassing the earliest phase of the Cerro Blanco site (Topic 1982) and a variety of settlements scattered throughout the Moche Valley. As I noted above, the Gallinazo occupation includes numerous residential settlements and several sites containing public architecture such as Cerro Orejas and possibly a Gallinazo occupational component at the Huaca del Sol. Furthermore, Fogel documents much of this extensive Gallinazo occupation as contemporary with that of the neighboring Virú Valley which I and most other scholars would see as persisting throughout the Moche Early Period. Only in phases III and IV did a distinctive Moche presence become widespread even in the Moche Valley.

This confusing information raises a serious question as to the actual status of the earliest Moche occupation in its eponymous

Figure 7.2 Moche I Phase burial exposed at the base of the Huaca del Sol, Moche Valley, 1972. (Chan Chan-Moche Valley Project)

valley and the nature of its emergence. Fogel, in the most radical revision of the traditional view so far, carries the implications of Gallinazo-Moche cultural continuity to their logical conclusion by regarding Moche I and II Phase pottery as merely transitional stylistic entities that apparently carry no significance whatsoever as markers of change in the existing social order. Their appearance in the Moche Valley and elsewhere is interpreted as taking place within the existing late Gallinazo cultural milieu. I agree with much of this in as far as it further confirms the reality of the historical tradition that produced both Gallinazo and Moche and rejects a transformational model in which earliest Moche ceramic style is viewed as signalling the emergence of a new culture. However, I would not repudiate the significance of Moche I–II pottery as an indicator of change within the wider context of cultural continuity.

In the light of this Moche Valley information, it seems likely that, although Moche ceramic styles of the Early Period were indeed a formal outgrowth of existing artistic practice, they also symbolically foreshadowed the emergence of new ideological concepts. Restriction of these few early examples to burials, almost always contexts of religious significance, supports this view. I suggest, then, that in the Moche Valley, new religious beliefs were emerging within the North Coast conceptual tradition. Whether the origins of these beliefs were local or foreign cannot be known at present. Still, as we shall see, there are grounds for positing some external roots.

It is probable that at the time of the earliest Moche burials at the Huaca del Sol the influence of these new concepts was small. They either formed a small element of the wider Gallinazo religious system, or they reflected localized beliefs of the inhabitants of the important Cerro Blanco settlement. In either case the simple imagery of the earliest Moche pottery gives no indication of the codified thematic iconography and related formal ideology that appeared later. In my scenario, the Cerro Blanco site by Phase III became the first Moche Valley center of a new consolidated political ideology. For some time this center of Moche ideology may have co-existed with the traditional Gallinazo system that it gradually replaced in the other settlements of the Moche Valley. Given the general lack of fortifications at either Moche or Gallinazo sites in the Moche

Valley, this expansion may well have occurred through peaceful diffusion.

This reading of the archaeological record in the Moche Valley leads me to a much more gradual and differentiated view of the emergence of the Moche cultural phase in this important area. This perspective assumes fundamental ethnic and cultural unity in this area and recognizes that there was differential acceptance of Moche ideology by various local groups, especially in the earliest phases. In sum, Moche ideology emerged, not as a full-blown conceptual system, but initially as a set of unconsolidated ideas that only later were incorporated into the coherent and organized structure of the Middle Moche Period.

Diversity in the northern valleys   It has long been assumed that Moche did not appear until late in the Early Intermediate Period in the valleys north of the Chicama River. In the absence of substantial data to the contrary, the prevailing view saw the region brought into the Moche political sphere in the Middle Period Phase III or IV through conquest of existing non-Moche societies by an expansionist "core valley" polity. Walter Alva's demonstration of a powerful Moche III presence at Sipán in the middle Lambayeque Valley forces significant rethinking of this scenario given that the associated "Royal Burials" (see chapter 3) far outstrip any of the burials at the Cerro Blanco site in complexity and richness. Clearly this is not the expected pattern for a subordinate center. Still, given the paucity of excavated settlements of the period, the earliest phase of Moche occupation and the pattern of its emergence remains unclear.

The scenario of Moche-Gallinazo co-existence that I outlined for the Moche Valley appears generally valid for the northern part of the region as well. As I noted, Heinrich Ubbelodhe-Doering long ago recorded the inclusion of Gallinazo and Moche vessels in the same funerary architecture at Pacatnamú in the Jequetepeque Valley (figure 1.1). More recent surveys in the northern valleys by Izumi Shimada and his colleagues (Shimada and Maguña 1994) reveal further evidence of this pattern of early Moche-Gallinazo co-existence. However, an elaborate, partially looted tomb recently excavated at La Mina in the Jequetepeque Valley clearly indicates that, although Moche communities may not have dominated the entire valley,

their rulers had already developed characteristic trappings of
Moche power (Narváez 1994). The La Mina tomb was large
and massively walled with adobe bricks (figure 7.3). Its entire
interior was painted with polychrome murals containing geometric motifs. The remains of five individuals, mostly young
and of both sexes, were found but due to looting damage their
relative status could not be ascertained. Nevertheless the presence of a large quantity of superbly modeled and painted ceramic vessels clearly indicated the importance of the interred
individuals. This tomb and its counterparts elsewhere in the
region strongly indicate that basic Moche ideological tenets

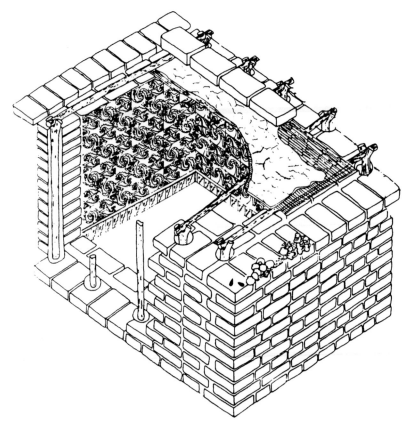

*Figure 7.3 Moche I Phase burial chamber at La Mina, Jequetepeque
Valley. (Redrawn from Narváez 1994, figure 2.5)*

centered on funerary ritual were coalescing in the Jequetepeque Valley at this early phase.

Moche occupations of the Early Period are located in the middle sections of the Zaña, Lambayeque, and La Leche Valleys, while Gallinazo occupations of apparently contemporary date appear in the same valleys (Shimada 1994a:69–71; Shimada and Maguña 1994). This would indicate, just as in the Moche and Jequetepeque Valleys, that local communities were adopting the new Moche ideological complex during the early centuries of the first millennium AD while many of their neighbors adhered to the still-strong Gallinazo tradition.

It is at the extreme northern perimeter of the region that factors involved in the emergence of Moche can best be observed. The present-day Department of Piura in northernmost Peru (figures 1.1, 2.6) possesses characteristics that at once set it off from the coastal areas to the south and help to explain its significance in pre-European history in general. Recent archaeological field research in the area, by US scholar James Richardson III and his colleagues (Richardson 1987, Richardson and Heaps de Peña 1974) and by an international program sponsored by the Pontifícia Universidad Catolica del Peru (Kaulicke 1991), has contributed greatly to an understanding of the emergence of Moche society. The zone comprises the Sechura Desert, the broadest and most inhospitable section of the arid Peruvian coastal plain and several rivers lying immediately to its north. Of these, the Piura drainage is the most significant for our purposes. The Piura zone represents an important geographical cross-roads between the northern equatorial regions of Ecuador, the Peruvian coastal valley zone, and the Andean highlands. The Piura has always served as the corridor through which commodities and cultural influences from these diverse sources have flowed. Such items as cinnabar, turquoise, *Spondylus*, and conch shells were transported south from Ecuador in exchange for finished metal objects, dried fish, and agricultural produce of the Peruvian north coast. This situation offered the region's occupants the strategic opportunities for brokering commodities and exchanging ideas that regularly made them important players in the affairs of the regions around them. On a more fundamental level, the archaeology of the Upper Piura convincingly demonstrates that the history of

the North Coast region cannot be understood in isolation
from the wider interactive social sphere of which it formed
part.

Although the Sechura Desert has always represented an obstacle to direct communication between surrounding areas, the
Piura River which circles the desert on three sides offers natural
corridors across this diverse region. The river's lower course
provides access between the coast and the highlands, while the
upper course, parallelling the rampart of the Andes, forms the
vital inland connector between the coastal La Leche and
Lambayeque drainages and their adjacent highlands and the
equatorial zones further north (figures 1.1, 2.6). This well-
watered inland corridor supported abundant irrigation agriculture that could even be supplemented by dry farming in rainy
years, in contrast with its less productive lower course. Consequently the inhabitants of the Upper Piura had easy access to a
generous local subsistence base while their strategic position
permitted them access to the benefits of long-distance traffic.
Because of these social and natural resources the Upper Piura
sustained a long course of human occupation that reveals its
history as an ecological and cultural cross-roads. It is becoming
increasingly clear that the zone played an important role in the
developments of the Early Intermediate Period that generated
Moche society and its distinctive ideological system.

In the cultural domain scholars from the time of Rafael Larco
Hoyle have recognized that the Upper Piura, and indeed the
region as a whole, embodied a combination of Ecuadorian and
Central Andean traits (Lumbreras 1979). The Vicús ceramic
style, developing in the period prior to the Early Intermediate,
displays close similarities to such southern Ecuadorian styles as
Chorrera (Amaro 1995), and related Tumbes Valley cultures.
Indeed, we can reasonably assume that the entire Piura region
fell largely within the northern equatorial cultural sphere for
much of its early history (Hocquenghem 1991). Significantly,
for the initial Early Intermediate Period of the Upper Piura
drainage, the period of immediate Moche origins, the recent
program of research has identified a sequence of ceramic and
architectural developments that largely corresponds to those
seen further south along the Peruvian coast (figure 7.4). Thus,

Figure 7.4 Vicús stirrup-spout vessel from Upper Piura Valley sharing Early Moche stylistic features. (Courtesy James Richardson III. Photo: James Richardson III)

while northern Andean influences remain, they are incorporated into a complex of styles that are closely related to late Cupisnique, Salinar, Gallinazo, and Moche.

Recent investigation of the settlement history of the Upper Piura is shedding valuable light on the emergence of Moche in the region. For the early period the U-shaped ceremonial center of Cerro Ñañañique with its Chavín Horizon features (figure 6.1) represents a northern occurrence of the far-flung ideological complex that dominated the North Coast region in the middle of the first millennium BC (Guffroy 1989). In addition, the contemporary occurrence of a diverse set of stylistic traits in the pottery of the site clearly demonstrates the geographic importance of Cerro Ñañañique in its location at the crossing of communication and exchange routes. Moreover, the appearance of monumental architecture at this date in the Upper Piura

strongly suggests that local elites had already seized the opportunity opened by their strategic location to appropriate superior
power on a combined base of economic control and Chavín
ideological authority.

The pattern represented by Cerro Ñañañique prevailed
throughout the subsequent Early Intermediate Period and is
well illustrated by the important Nima/Valverde ceremonial
complex at Vicús (Kaulicke 1994). The principal structure,
Loma Valverde, was built in several segments which incorporated construction styles typical of the North Coast region
cultural sequence. Thus, the oldest section was built largely of
rubble-filled walls, characteristic of Salinar construction further
south, while the principal, latest phase, used large blocks of
tapia. Recall that this latter style characterizes Gallinazo platforms in the Virú Valley much further south. Underscoring its
affiliation to the wider North Coast regional sequence of material culture, this large Gallinazo structure was accompanied by
ceramics of like association.

The subsequent occupation of the Nima/Valverde complex is
represented by a group of platforms and walls which were built
with mold-made adobes. I have stressed that the use of these
building materials distinguishes monumental construction of
the late Gallinazo and Moche phases in the "core" valleys. It
appears that the same association applies to their appearance in
the Upper Piura. Moche-style pottery, probably of the earliest
phases, occurs in these structures, clearly revealing the source of
the new modes of technological and decorative usage and the
ideas that they express. However, the context of Moche emergence is one in which continuity is equally apparent. The inves-
tigator of Loma Valverde posits contemporaneity between the
later Gallinazo and Moche occupations of the Upper Piura area
(Kaulicke 1992), a situation which suggests that some local
communities were adopting the new customs while others retained their traditional ways.

Elsewhere in the Piura-Tumbes region the situation is very
different. Local cultural traditions continued undisturbed
throughout the Early Intermediate Period with little evidence
of any Moche contact. This has led to a recent suggestion
(Makowski 1995; Makowski, Amaro, and Eléspuru 1995) that
the Upper Piura region participated in the development of a

multi-ethnic state. In the initial phase, conforming to the early Moche periods, societies producing ceramics of the Vicús and other local styles co-existed with an emerging Moche presence. However this ultimately gave way to full hegemony in which Moche ideology with its related artistic and architectural symbolism was adopted by a dominant elite while their subjects continued to produce their traditional material forms. It was this ideology that transcended ethnic diversity as the integrating bond of a single political state.

This scenario reflects an archaeological record in the Piura region indicative of broad cultural diversity. While more pronounced than elsewhere in the North Coast region, this situation is similar to the Moche-Gallinazo pattern that I have detailed further south. It is likely that the Moche presence in the Upper Piura similarly represents the appearance of the same prominent political ideology. However, at present I see no convincing archaeological evidence for asserting that this was associated with an extensive political state. Indeed the Moche archaeological presence in this area is more limited than in most other areas of the North Coast. This record suggests that Moche acceptance by local societies was more restricted and that it never attained the dominance over other political systems that it achieved in some other valleys.

Turning now to portable material culture, the picture is complicated by the contexts from which much of the associated artifacts were recovered. Until recently almost all Vicús and Early Moche ceramics derived from looted cemeteries in the Upper Piura Valley. The same situation applies to the impressive works of precious metal fashioned in Moche decorative style that were looted from the Loma Negra cemeteries (figure 5.4; Disselhoff 1972; Jones 1979). Appearing on the antiquities market in the 1970s, the magnificent metal items from Loma Negra drew immediate attention to the Moche presence in the Upper Piura and made the world aware of the technical sophistication and artistic creativity of Moche metallurgy. Unfortunately the absence of good archaeological context for these items precluded access to their original cultural associations and contexts.

The Upper Piura Moche metal and ceramic inventories possess yet another puzzling dimension. They do not appear to be stylistically compatible with Rafael Larco Hoyle's five-phase chronological typology for the Moche ceramic sequence. Many of the Loma Negra ceramics were assigned by Larco to his Phases I and II on grounds of style and form (figure 7.4). But the gold and copper objects, ostensibly from the same cemetery, display features that most closely resemble the fine-line decorative style of the later Moche periods. Complicating the picture even more, some of the ceramic vessels incorporate features from various Moche phases. In the light of these confusing features, Luis Lumbreras, in his study of the extensive Semenario Collection housed in the Central Reserve Bank of Peru Museum in Lima (Lumbreras 1979, 1987; see also Kaulicke 1992), suggests that the Upper Piura ceramics represent two different contemporary origins. These include a Vicús/Moche corpus that incorporates much stylistic diversity and was produced by the local inhabitants of the Upper Piura area, and a component that more closely resembles the typical Moche style of the northern Peruvian valleys, and probably represents a colony established by intruders from the Lambayeque region.

An alternative view, and one with which I personally have considerable sympathy, sees the distinctive nature of early Moche material culture in the Piura region as the product of local development. Larco's typology may be applicable to the central valleys of the region, but it cannot be indiscriminately applied elsewhere without taking into account the factor of local variability. Earlier I noted the differences in Moche architecture between the northern and southern parts of the region. Other material symbols also vary by location in form, style, and content. Thus, the slip paints of Moche northern ceramics predominantly use orange and purple hues, contrasting with the brown and cream of the south (Klein 1967). Moreover the complex narrative iconography of the southern Moche ceramics does not appear in the Upper Piura (Makowski, Amaro, and Eléspuru 1995:238). We will see that iconographical differences also characterize metallurgical art of the various zones and separate the Upper Piura Moche presence from its southern counterparts. The distinctive character of this early Moche cultural expression is entirely understandable as adoption of a new ideology by local elites. The material symbols of this ideology were, of course, manufactured in accordance with existing technological and aesthetic modes which were largely influenced in the Upper Piura by unique geographical location, natural resources, and cultural links.

Moche metallurgy from the Upper Piura bears iconography that differentiates it in content, though not in style, from work produced in other North Coast areas. Moreover, it is unique in its level of sophistication for the early Moche period. Despite their lack of good cultural context, Moche metal objects from the Loma Negra burials both support the view of independent adoption of Moche ideology by certain ruling elites of the Upper Piura and provide insight into the nature of this emergent ideology.

At the outset it is important to note a most important feature of the Loma Negra metals. Although the iconography of the Vicús and Moche metallurgical inventories of the Upper Piura differ, their technologies are the same (Diez Canseco 1995). This continuity strongly suggests that they are products of a single cultural milieu and that the Moche style was produced by local people, not colonists from further south.

Further support for local manufacture of Moche material culture from the Upper Piura derives from the chronological relationship between its metal and ceramic art and the availability of ores required for metallurgy. The superb quality of Moche metal objects from the area, including many of gold, gold alloy, and copper, has persuaded some scholars that they date to a later period than the much less elaborate pottery of the region. This view is not supported by archaeological evidence and, in fact, is unnecessary if the context of production is examined. The area has easy access to the abundant metal ore sources that are located in the highlands adjacent to the upper courses of the northern Peruvian coastal rivers, a resource that was not readily available to the societies of the southern part of the region which highlighted ceramic art. This natural mineral resource was most probably an important factor in the formation of the northern tradition of metalworking which produced the impressive Chavín Horizon caches of golden objects from Chongoyape, and much later the contents of the Moche Royal Tombs of Sipán. Both of these sites are, of course, located in the Lambayeque drainage not far south of the Sechura Desert (figures 1.1, 6.1). Given the role of the Upper Piura as a natural inland corridor through the Andean foothills of this area, the acquisition of metal ores by local elites and their emphasis on the production of fine metal objects of prestige at the expense of ceramics is quite understandable. Indeed we see a similar emphasis by the Moche elites of the Lambayeque Valley. Moreover, by the Moche period the region had already supported a considerable tradition of centralized authority as manifested in the monumental platforms of Ñañañique and Loma Valverde. It is therefore not surprising that by the dawn of the Moche epoch, local rulers should have developed the organizational and technological skills to fashion metal into the symbolism of their new ideological complex as represented by the Loma Negra objects.

There is a second reason that metal, where available as in Upper Piura, should have been used rather than pottery as the preeminent vehicle for ideological symbolism. This reason (Lechtman 1979:30–4, 1980; Sallnow 1989) is based in fundamental Andean values. First, the inherent qualities of gold imbued it with profound cultural significance in Andean thought, its incorruptibility suffusing it with sacred importance. Inka rulers used this sacred quality in the realm of political ideology. They regarded gold as a fitting symbol of the supernatural origin and permanence of their power. Accordingly, they monopolized all gold production for use as an active manifestation of their status. Lechtman has suggested that this essential nature of the commodity shaped Andean metal technology and explains its significance even when painted or interred.

Moche metal items in all probability also acted as symbols of divinely sanctioned power, a role that would explain their active use in exclusive contexts of ritual, ceremonial, and funerary activity. This role would also explain the technical priority of gold relative to pottery in the early Upper Piura complex. Moreover, their funerary context would have associated the deceased with sacred properties, at once separating them from the general populace and according them supernatural status. In this the Loma Negra materials, much more than their counterparts in the Moche and Chicama valleys, are related to the even more elaborate Sipán and San José de Moro tombs as central elements in the emerging Moche political ideology.

However, the Loma Negra funerary inventory also possessed

more particular ideological significance. The metal inventory included masks and other items that repeated specific themes, reflecting the process of symbolic codification that is vital for communication of a well-defined ideological system. Further, headdress emblems iconographically linked their wearers to representations of specific rituals, marking the beginnings of the Moche practice of interring powerful individuals in the regalia of their rank and ritual status, practices that again are seen at their full level of development in the Sipán and San José burials of later Moche phases. Although several rituals are suggested, the best defined includes a figure holding a trophy head in one hand and a knife in the other (figure 5.4; Jones 1979:95–8). Given its association with execution this ritual composition undoubtedly portrays an early version of the Sacrifice ritual that I described in chapter 5 as a focal element of Moche ideology. Although the representational iconography, and possibly the ritual that it depicts, became much more complex in later time periods, the appearance of the "Decapitator" as a central component of ideological symbolism in the Loma Negra metal complex graphically illustrates the early origin of this essential ideological element. It is significant that this subject, together with the frequently-depicted condor and the numerous relief plaques of fully accoutred warriors (Disselhoff 1972:44; Jones 1979:96–100) appear much more often in early Upper Piura Moche iconography than elsewhere on the North Coast, again suggesting its local character.

The Loma Negra metal iconography also underscores the origins of emergent Moche ideology in the wider historical tradition of the North Coast region. Thus the "Decapitator Theme" itself clearly derived from earlier Chavín-related Cupisnique religion (figure 5.8; Cordy-Collins 1992) that was widely adopted by elites throughout the North Coast in the middle of the first millennium BC. Moreover, a recurrent motif associated with the decapitation theme is the so-called "Moon Animal," a four-legged animal with clawed feet, a long tail, and open mouth with head surmounted by a crest (figure 7.5). This figure, incorporated into early Moche religious symbolism in the Upper Piura, is believed to have been borrowed from the Recuay culture (Benson 1985; Menzel 1977:62–4) that charac-terized the people of the highlands adjacent to the southern part

Figure 7.5 Early Moche stirrup-spout vessel bearing drawing of a Recuay-derived "Moon Animal" motif. (Redrawn by Rebecca Bawden from Menzel 1977, figure 39)

of the region. These two examples help to place Moche ideology in its historical, temporal, and spatial context. On the one hand, adoption of the Cupisnique/Chavín Decapitator Theme suggests the intentional manipulation of powerful symbols of an earlier pan-Andean ideological system that had been dominant in the history of the region. On the other hand, the "Moon Animal" represents incorporation of the material signifier of ideas from a non-local belief system as an adjunct of power.

Moche as Ideological Innovation on the North Coast

In this chapter I have sought to reconstruct the emergence of Moche society on the north coast of Peru. The traditional picture of simple and homogenous Moche origins was largely based on undue reliance on a stylistic sequence drawn from a restricted archaeological area – the Moche and Chicama "core area." This has encouraged a transformational view of Gallinazo-Moche transition and a unitary picture of North Coast cultural integration during the Moche era. While these ideas adequately explained the restricted information-base of earlier decades, recent work is clearly indicating that they can no longer accepted in their traditional form.

Although much work remains to be done, especially in the northern part of the region, the essential qualities of early Moche society are now emerging. It is now apparent that in most respects Moche and its Gallinazo counterpart were identical in their cultural composition and their geographical distribution throughout the North Coast. Indeed there appears no reason to assume that significant ethnic or demographic replacement marks the appearance of Moche society. The only apparent difference lies in the realm of the material symbols of ideology. Even here, many basic religious customs continued unchanged. However, the Moche inventory of ritual items and related iconography does reveal significant innovation. This change signals the emergence of a new ideology, closely associated with the contexts of authority and elite status, as the principal basis of a new political order. It is this rather circumscribed category of symbolism that has traditionally been regarded as the mark of broader Moche culture. Knowledge that it operated in a more limited social context allows us better to understand the nature of Moche society and its historical development.

The Loma Negra funerary material of the Upper Piura drainage, although unique in its local geographical and cultural setting, illustrates the general character of early Moche ideology. Here, its sacrificial quality already appears to be a central component of the ideological system. With its roots in earlier North Coast ritual, expressed in a distinctive iconographic form with unique associations, this important element foreshadows the mature later system that I described in chapter 5. Elsewhere in the region specific referents to the structure of emergent Moche ideology are less evident. Only a relatively small quantity of ceramic vessels, recovered from localized contexts, constitute the Early Period cultural corpus from the Moche to the La Leche Valleys. These items in their modeled representations of animal, bird, and warrior figures that were to become common in Moche art, anticipate the more formal and complex ritual content of later phases. However, their technological limitations and restricted numbers inhibit full correlation with the intricate iconography of the Loma Negra metal complex.

On the basis of the information presently available, it appears that in the early first millennium AD, in the extensive region bounded by the Moche and Piura rivers, the rulers of various North Coast groups began to adopt a new ideological basis for their authority. The prevailing social order at this time, as represented by the Gallinazo cultural phase, had already developed the social institutions necessary to integrate large societies and to establish and sustain the extensive hydraulic agricultural systems essential for their subsistence, thereby creating a context in which power could be further developed. The specific factors that initiated Moche ideology and the historical period which it denotes are largely unknown although in the Piura region it immediately followed a major flood whose destructive impact is apparent in fallen walls of the Gallinazo-associated Cerro Ñañañique architectural complex.

The new Moche ideology was incorporated into the continuing cultural tradition and probably took somewhat different forms according to the dictates and social textures of the pre-existing local societies. The Upper Piura societies expressed the new system particularly through symbolism in the medium of metallurgy, some of the content of which was unique to the area. In terms of pottery style the region incorporated attributes of the northernmost coastal valleys. By contrast, the localized Early Period Moche society of the Moche River Valley and its immediate neighbors to the north expressed their new affiliation through the medium of decorated pottery, in a bichromatic style distinctive to its region. The advent of Moche, then, is characterized by multiple rather than single source emergence, selective adoption of cultural traits, and a varied symbolic expression that probably reflects distinctive local content.

Finally, I would stress that many North Coast communities did not at first adopt the Moche ideology. Indeed it is quite possible that in some areas, especially in the valleys north of the Chicama River, societies persisted in their adherence to the older Gallinazo tradition throughout the Early Intermediate Period. This factor is most obvious in the south where, while the population of the Moche Valley was progressively adopting the new forms through the Early Period, the valleys of the south solidly resisted this change. Only in the Moche III Phase was this large area brought into the Moche sphere, probably by conquest. Elsewhere, the early pattern of Moche societies, probably located in the middle segments of the coastal valleys, co-existing with Gallinazo societies in the lower courses, persisted for most, if not all, of the Moche period. As with the other factors relating to the emergence of Moche, the relations between Moche polities themselves and between Moche and enduring Gallinazo societies were complex. We have evidence both for prolonged peaceful co-existence and various levels of conflict from small-scale raiding to major territorial invasion. These considerations, however, more properly belong to the next phase of Moche history, to which I now turn.

8

Moche Florescent

History and Structure in Middle Moche Society

We have seen that in the Moche Early Period a new ideology, manifest through elaborate symbolism, emerged from its North Coast cultural base and was differentially adopted by elites throughout the region. This process heralded a period of social consolidation. By the end of the Moche I–II phase it appears that all communities of the central valleys adhered to the Moche ideology, although its acceptance was more restricted elsewhere. The following phase of Moche history, which I term the Middle Period, represented by the Moche III and IV stylistic phases of Larco, lasted approximately from AD 300 to AD 600. During this period Moche ideology was progressively adopted throughout the North Coast. However, not all societies accepted its tenets. Some populations, probably comprised of people of the same ethnic identity, continued to adhere to the older Gallinazo forms of social integration. The relative strength of these different political realms varied according to local area and, as we shall see, the diverse strategies of the rulers of the different societies. This local variation is reflected in the imagery of political symbolism, a quality that becomes increasingly significant to an understanding of the major developments that dominate the later course of Moche history.

I stated at the very start of this book my intent to use the material record as a window through which to glimpse the motives and actions of the people who shaped North Coast society in the Moche period. Although our ability to perceive the precise motives of the rulers who created early Moche society is still largely inhibited by the sparse nature of the available information, in the succeeding period the picture becomes considerably clearer. Here, the archaeological record reveals that the rulers of the various Moche III–IV societies evolved different ideological strategies and political policies to expand their dominant positions. Their success was such that this period saw Moche political domination of the region reach its apogee, accompanied by a similar florescence of Moche civilization with its magnificent technological and artistic achievements. Yet, this very success established the conditions for the social and political breakdown that characterized the end of the Middle Moche period. I examine these trends from the central viewpoint of this book – historical exploration of North Coast development in the context of its distinctive Andean social structure. By seeing the Moche elites and the people that they ruled as the products of their specific long-term history and the cultural tradition that this embodied, we can identify and understand their accomplishments in their own conceptual terms rather than those inspired by universal models of social evolution.

The structure and evolution of Moche power

At this juncture it helps to reiterate the chief structural tenets that to a large extent directed the course taken by North Coast elites in their quest for power. Andean social structure is loosely characterized by what have been termed "kinship principles." Inhabitants of the North Coast region shared with Andean peoples generally a holistic conception of the human universe in which such factors as affinity to the mythical founder of the community, ancestral reverence, and emphasis on community membership define status, strengthen social cohesion, and impede inter-group political integration. At the community level, authority is exercised more through consensus than according to the decisions of a formal governing agency. Consequently, elite power, by definition exclusive in nature, must be constructed within a context that innately resists it, creating a structural paradox between the wider social conception and the striving of leaders for individual power (Bawden 1995). The greater this contradiction, the greater the potential for disruption should social stress imperil the ability of elites to sustain their position.

A brief summary of wider Andean political structure illustrates this point. In order to justify their seizure of power over a wider variety of peoples, the Inka presented themselves as a senior lineage group, exploiting principles of genealogy and descent to create an ideological basis for their dominant position (Bauer 1992; Conrad and Demarest 1984; Urton 1990). Nevertheless, in many cases local societies were left to administer their own affairs within the greater Inka realm. Netherly's ethnohistorical study of the Chimú successors of the Moche on the North Coast (1984; 1990) suggests that they were organized according to an extended segmentary system within which two primary groups – moieties – of unequal social and economic status were nested hierarchically according to principles of asymmetrical dual organization. While integrated by a single political system, these moiety segments maintained their internal integrity, and thus their capacity for independent existence. Given the persistence of Andean social strategies, it is likely that, despite the impact of conquest, this pattern generally reflects earlier North Coast organizational techniques. In both of these examples the foundations of social integration embodied contradiction between the conflicting forces of holistic Andean structure and central political power. The ensuing structural tension inhibited the formation of stable, enduring political entities and ensured that their component parts would revert to autonomous existence with the removal of their political superstructures.

I assume that the structure of earlier societies was also grounded in traditional Andean principles and that Moche elites faced the same challenge as their Chimú successors of creating exclusive power within an holistic social milieu. They met this challenge by creating a political ideology based on the authority of myth and public ritual whose composition and means of symbolic communication I examined earlier. Moche elites manipulated this ideology successfully in the Middle Period to mediate the conflicting forces of traditional social structure and individual political enhancement. By assuming central, shamanistic roles in the enactment of myths of communal order and projecting these roles into the timeless supernatural domain through funerary ritual, rulers identified themselves in life and in death with omnipresent sacred authority. They thus placed themselves at the axis of traditional communal belief and the daily world of human organization as the arbiters of Moche society. However, the archaeological record clearly tells us that, while Moche rulers achieved great success in their quest for power, the paradox inherent in North Coast social structure ultimately generated stress too great for them to overcome, leading to profound disruption.

The conception that lay at the core of the Moche power structure both determined the nature of its evolution and shaped its limitations. Moche rulers, in common with their counterparts throughout history, aspired to formalize their social separation from the general populace. I believe that in the Moche instance this was achieved by the manipulation of ideology. Exclusive control over the manufacture and use of the material symbols of social preeminence drove political and economic development. Creation of the vast quantities of elaborate items that fill entire museums and whose production sites are prominent in the archaeological record demanded a huge specialist labor force. The resulting need to feed these vital specialists and the extensive elite that they served in turn dictated the maintenance of an intensive agricultural system, effective procurement networks, and the agencies to control them. Most Moche polities controlled large northern valleys where local resources were sufficient for their sustenance. However, in the small Moche Valley the situation was different. Here demands of the ruling system for large-scale human and natural resources could not be met locally. The response was southward expansion and the establishment of the only multi-valley territorial domain of the Moche epoch. However, as we will see, the continuing dependence of leadership on a non-material base created an innate weakness that could not be permanently surmounted by progressive elaboration of the existing structure, and the polity collapsed.

It should be clear from the above that although broad structural principles provided the conceptual context and persistent internal logic for Moche political formation, they did not determine its specific strategies or course. Shared social structure constrains but does not determine action. Within these constraints individuals always have alternatives open to them. Their chosen course of action is given meaning by structure, but also reflexively alters it, creating a force for change. The variation in the form and content of Moche ideological symbols across space and through time, together with the distinctive courses taken by various polities, was not simply the passive product of cultural diversity. In fact it expressly reveals the calculated application of policy-making agencies operating at the institutional centers of power. This purposeful management was aimed at realizing the precise political goals dictated by local exigency. In a broader sense this process represents the active construction of discrete historical trajectories through the engagement of short-term contingencies and persisting structural tradition. The potentials for change generated by these intersecting forces were actively exploited through the decisions of local elites who manipulated them in their own interests. The natural consequence of this process was the development of diverse local political strategies and histories within the greater Moche ideological sphere.

In this and the following chapter we shall see that the tendency toward divergent development was one of the most important characteristics shaping Moche society. The differences that we first identified in the emergent societies of Phases I and II continued to develop in the Middle Period. The ultimate consequence of these trends was that the divergent historical pathways taken by the various local Moche societies created their own momenta for further development and differentially shaped their active responses, whether to the successes of the Moche Middle Period or to the misfortunes that came later. Clearly, then, the history of Moche culture cannot be treated as a unitary whole but must be seen as the interconnected evolution of a group of closely related societies whose specific interests dictated distinctive courses and outcomes. Consequently, in the following sections I shall discuss each area that can be identified as a distinct social entity in terms of its own development before summarizing the overall trends of the period.

The Southern Moche Polity of the Middle Period

The setting   By around AD 300 the communities of the central valleys had accepted the new social order. There is no indication that this process initially involved any other agency than peaceful adoption of a new religious movement whose substance derived from the familiar cultural heritage of the North Coast. However, it seems certain that by the commencement of the Moche III Phase the early religious tenets had been consolidated into the formal ideological foundation of a central ruling elite that had politically unified the people of the Moche and Chicama valleys. This aspect of Moche period religion centered on traditional rituals now reinterpreted by the leaders to support their political power. The attendant material symbolism that formed a potent element of this religious complex attests to the strict organization of Moche ideological structure during the Middle Period. The physical center of power in this polity was located at the greatly expanded settlement of Cerro Blanco. Dominated by its two great architectural complexes, the Huaca del Sol and the Huaca de la Luna, this expanding settlement accommodated the agencies of Moche power.

To the south of the Moche domain, the Virú Valley and its neighbors remained the domain of vigorous Gallinazo societies. The most northerly of these societies was centered at the extensive Gallinazo Group in the lower Virú Valley and probably encompassed its entire drainage together with its rich agricultural lands and the large population that extended from the Andean foothills to the Pacific Ocean (Bennett 1950; Fogel 1993). Gallinazo societies similarly flourished in the Santa Valley (Wilson 1988), dominated by the large ceremonial platforms that towered above the productive fields. Further south the dominant populations of the Nepeña, Casma, and Huarmey valleys do not appear to have participated in the Gallinazo sphere, maintaining instead strong relations with the adjacent highlands. Indeed they may have been part of a regional highland polity that had incorporated these coastal areas toward the end of the Initial Period (Pozorski and Pozorski 1987:128).

North of the Chicama Valley the picture is less straightforward. Here, as we have seen, the material expressions of Moche society appeared in the early period in contexts similar to those of the central valleys. However, whereas in the Moche and Chicama valleys the process of political unification was complete by the beginning of the Moche III Phase, this was not the case further north. There is growing evidence that in the coastal valleys from Jequetepeque north many societies continued to resist the adoption of Moche religious tenets and persisted in their adherence to traditional forms. The resulting pattern was one of in which Moche and Gallinazo societies co-existed in the same valleys (e.g. Shimada and Maguña 1994). Thus, the current information indicates that by about AD 300 a complex patchwork of political and ideological allegiances existed among North Coast peoples. Only in the central valleys are there clear indications of the existence of a political entity that incorporated an entire valley, its people and material resources. This polity was flanked to the south by a solid block of Gallinazo societies that extended at least as far as the Santa Valley and to the north by a mixture of autonomous Moche and Gallinazo groups. This complex pattern was significantly altered by the events of the Middle Period in the southern part of the region. At this time a polity based on conquest of the southern valleys was established with its religious and governmental center at the Cerro Blanco site in the Moche Valley and its political dominion ultimately reaching as far south as Huarmey.

The center of southern Moche political power   Located six kilometers inland at the southern edge of the Moche Valley on the lower slopes of Cerro Blanco, a settlement that had originated as a small Gallinazo establishment in the Middle Period became the most impressive Moche site in the region. As it is now visible (figure 2.14), the Cerro Blanco site comprises two huge architectural structures – the Huaca de la Luna and the Huaca del Sol – and the flat plain between them in which are located irregular architectural features and the remains of cemeteries (the following discussion draws chiefly on the following research: Donnan and Mackey 1978; Hastings and Moseley 1975; Moseley 1975b; Topic 1982; Uceda et al. 1994). Although still imposing in size and architectural composition, the Cerro Blanco site has suffered greatly over the centuries from both human and natural forces. Sporadic flooding has destroyed many of the smaller architectural components on the plain, while windblown sand has deeply buried large portions of the settlement. In addition the site has been the target of some of the most intensive looting in the Andes, a process that reached its apogee in 1602 when the Moche River was diverted into the Huaca del Sol in an attempt to mine the platform hydraulically in order to reveal the treasure believed to have been buried in the interior of the structure.

The surviving settlement is still impressive. The Huaca del Sol comprises a vast solid pyramidal core with huge attached terraces. The central platform measures 380 meters in length and 160 meters in width and at its highest point stands 40 meters above the present land surface. It is estimated that 143 million adobe bricks were used in its construction. The smaller Huaca de la Luna stands 500 meters to the east across the plain on the lower slopes of Cerro Blanco and comprises a complex of courts and three platforms measuring in ground area 95 meters in length by 85 meters in width; the complex is roughly 25 meters tall. The great size of these edifices and their segmentary construction method (figures 2.14; 3.11) vividly demonstrates that the rulers at the site controlled the labor of a large regional work force over a long period of time. We shall again see this ability dramatically manifested in the demographic and agricultural re-organization imposed in the valleys further south during the same period.

Significant Moche construction began on the two Huacas during the Early Period (although the origins of the Huaca del Sol can probably be placed earlier, in the period of Gallinazo hegemony of the Moche Valley). However, the majority of construction took place during the Middle Period when the Cerro Blanco site constituted the political center of the southern Moche sphere. While the size and construction requirements of the great edifices that dominated the Cerro Blanco site in themselves clearly testify to the operation of a strong central authority and suggests its Andean foundations, other features help to understand further the nature of this power. The Huaca de la Luna, with its elaborately decorated series of platforms enclosed by high walls, its interior courts and corridors and scarcity of residential occupation, projects an aura of formal exclusivity that has led researchers to regard it as a temple or residence of supreme Moche rulers. While its purpose cannot be confirmed at present, the complex certainly contrasts in form and probably function with the Huaca del Sol, indicating that they possessed quite different roles. A series of murals adorn the walls of the Huaca de la Luna (figures 8.1, 8.2; Bonavia 1985; Mackey and Hastings 1982; Uceda et al. 1994). Although the several scholars who have studied the murals do not agree on their chronology, recent work by scholars from the University of Trujillo under the direction of Santiago Uceda (Uceda 1995) suggests a more complex sequence which spanned much of the Moche period, the earliest construction dating from the Early Period Phase II while the latest extends into the Moche V Phase (Uceda et al. 1994).

Figure 8.1 Drawings of two polychrome mural panels from the Huaca de la Luna, Moche Valley, discovered by the Chan Chan-Moche Valley Project in the early 1970s. (Chan Chan-Moche Valley Project)

Figure 8.2 Polychrome reliefs, south side of the principal platform of the Huaca de la Luna, Moche Valley, recently discovered by the Huaca de la Luna Archaeological Project of the University of Trujillo. (Courtesy Santiago Uceda)

In their content the murals reveal their ideological purpose and historical context. The earliest mural contains the frontal depiction of a figure holding serpents in both hands, a theme with a long history in North Coast iconography and, indeed, throughout the Andes. Specifically the motif was a prominent part of the Chavín iconographic corpus. It thus possessed historical importance in the ideological sphere of the regional tradition. In its specific Huaca de la Luna form this motif has been regarded as similar to Late Gallinazo architectural examples discovered at the Castillo de Tomoval in the Virú Valley (Uceda et al. 1994:292). This suggests an early date for this mural and the edifice itself. A later mural depicting a battle between Moche warriors and anthropomorphized objects, originally described by Alfred Kroeber in 1930 (figure 5.6), conforms to the later Moche period, where it also appears on fine-line painted pottery. Finally, a sequence of murals uncovered from the 1950s to the 1970s, containing various mythical and natural themes, including another version of the serpent figure, may well range in date from the Middle Period through the Moche V Phase (figure 8.1). Painted in vivid colors on the walls of this imposing architectural complex, these murals attest to the central importance of visual communication as an active agent of the ideology of power that supported Moche elite authority at the core of the southern polity.

In addition to shedding further light on the long mural sequence at the Huaca de la Luna, the recent University of Trujillo work has offered additional testimony to the nature of Moche authority at its center. The remains of two adult males were recently recovered buried in substantial stone-walled tombs, accompanied by a rich set of objects of funerary ritual (Uceda et al. 1994). These included superb ceramic jars and, significantly, copper cups of the form replicated in the Sacrifice Ceremony. The possession of central accoutrements of Moche sacrifice by the occupants of the two tombs suggests that they were important participants in the principal Moche ritual of power. This identification is further supported by the wider archaeological context. The wall murals adjacent to the burials include depictions of a figure wearing the serpent belt of the principal officiant in the Sacrifice Ceremony. In addition, the very recent discovery of a group of 35–40 skeletons in the complex further supports the growing certainty that the Huaca de la Luna and its occupants were closely associated with sacrificial ritual (La Industria 1995:1). These skeletons are the remains of individuals who had apparently been buried without formality. In almost all cases their necks show signs of trauma associated with cutting. They have been identified as sacrificial victims. It appears, then, that the occupants of the two elaborate tombs were intimately involved in ritual activities of similar sacrificial character to those conducted at Sipán far to the north. They are further instances of the centrality of the Sacrifice Ceremony and its elite officiants to Moche power.

The Huaca del Sol presents a very different though no less imposing aspect. The huge structure was the single most prominent symbol of Moche power ever erected. The Huaca del Sol was raised in at least eight stages, most of them probably completed during the Middle Period, the time of southern conquest. In form the edifice appears to represent a huge example of the structures frequently depicted in Moche art at which the activities of social control took place. Here in full view of the population, ceremonies of continuity and renewal created a forum for the proclamation and assertion of elite power. The religious importance of the Huaca del Sol is underscored by the placement on its terraces of elaborate burials of high-status individuals. However, in addition to these exclusive qualities, the practical exigencies of power evidently required the daily performance of more mundane administrative activities whose residue covers the platform terraces. The discovery of abundant domestic refuse on and around the huaca indicates that it was the focus of the everyday activities of community integration, not merely a dominant symbol of power.

Other less readily visible features at the Cerro Blanco site also give evidence of the prevailing strategies of social integration employed by the southern Moche polity. Scattered throughout the settlement is evidence of formal craft production. This includes the tools and products of bead production; the lapiz lazuli associated with this work was probably imported from the southern Andean area. There is also evidence for ceramic manufacture, metalworking, and possibly shell working using *Spondylus* imported from Ecuador. This range of activities largely pertains to the production of sumptuary goods and marks the presence of a considerable body of specialist craftsmen working in formal, controlled settings. At the behest of the rulers of the polity, these specialists produced objects that functioned as symbols of superior position. We shall see that there are other hints in the archaeological record of the Middle Moche Period in valleys further south that the great ceremonial centers of power were associated with controlled craft production of this type.

The residential settlement at the Cerro Blanco site gives important information regarding the social organization of the related community and, by projection, that of wider Moche society in the Middle Period. Buried by windblown sand on the level plain between the two great huacas lies the remains of a substantial residential occupation while other habitational architecture covers part of the lowest slopes of the Cerro Blanco near the Huaca de la Luna. Theresa Topic, the most recent excavator of this portion of the settlement, has described this architecture as representing a three-tier social hierarchy (Topic 1982:268–70). This trend toward social differentiation was to become significantly more rigid at the later, Moche V town of Galindo (see chapter 9). The hillslope structures together with an area of architecture midway across the plain were built of stone and adobe bricks and contained carefully constructed storage bins and niches, attesting to a considerable degree of residential storage. They also contained domestic items of high quality, elaborately decorated pottery, beads of various materials, small copper tweezers, and knives. Other nearby structures were of similar though less elaborate form and content, while those structures nearest the Huaca del Sol were even less substantially constructed and accoutred. These structures consisted of small rooms of irregular shape whose walls were built of cane superstructures set into stone and mortar foundations. Topic suggests that the highest elite – namely the ruler of the settlement – dwelt in the Huaca de la Luna in isolated grandeur. From here the paramount leadership developed the policies that commanded the destinies of the southern polity and its peoples. While the pattern of social stratification discussed here is based on limited architectural investigation and a relatively small burial sample and thus may not reflect the precise structure operative during the Middle Moche Period, there can be little doubt that it reflects the development during this time of a powerful elite who separated themselves from their lower-status neighbors through exclusive living areas, elaboration of residence, and richness of possessions.

Finally, the burial data from the Cerro Blanco settlement is the most extensive from any Moche site to date. We have noted how few burials dated to the Early Period, the time of the introduction of Moche ideological forms at the settlement. In the succeeding Middle Period the picture is very different, with numerous burials having been discovered from various parts of the site. Indeed the vast majority of the burials were of Moche III and especially Moche IV vintage. This should reflect the fact that the settlement reached its highest population and political importance at the center of the southern polity during the Middle Period. The most elaborate burials are those located in the Huaca de la Luna complex. In addition to the two burials associated with the Sacrifice Ceremony which I described earlier, an even richer example was probably looted late in the last century (Jones 1979; Seler 1912). From this tomb came a number of gilt copper items including a three-dimensional fox head and several masks. No other grave assemblage approaches this in richness of metal, and it is tempting to regard its occupant as a senior member of the power hierarchy that controlled the southern polity and either resided or held court at the Huaca de la Luna.

In addition, Max Uhle long ago excavated burials that were richly endowed with Moche ceramics and some of which contained small precious metal pieces from the Southern Terrace of the Huaca del Sol and from his Site F just below the Huaca de la Luna. More recent work has located on the plain between the huacas an elite funeral platform whose burials contain comparable material, and another elaborate burial on the Huaca del Sol itself, as well as numerous burials of lesser status in various locations adjacent to the more elite cemeteries and in the residential areas (for summary see Donnan and Mackey 1978). From these burials come examples of the impressive "portrait heads" – stirrup-spout vessels bearing the realistic depictions of Moche persons, mostly of high status, vessels that only occur in the central and southern valleys (i.e. figures 4.6, 4.7). These vessels raise implications regarding the nature of Middle Moche political leadership on which I shall elaborate later in this chapter.

The trend toward progressive social differentiation of the elite, the expanding capacity of the elite to mobilize labor, and the situation of this power in the traditional yet dynamic Moche ideology, is visible in varying degrees elsewhere in the central valleys during the Middle Moche Period. First, the exploitation of the principle of reciprocal work obligation that has its origins deep in Andean social history and that is apparent in the construction of Gallinazo and Moche architecture, was probably also utilized for agricultural expansion in the Moche Valley during the Middle Period. Michael Moseley and his colleagues have determined (Moseley and Deeds 1982) that during the Moche III and IV phases all existing main irrigation canals were extended and elevated to beyond the limits of present-day cultivation. This resulted in the expansion of the agricultural production capacity on both sides of the river to a level never again attained on the southern side of the river, while in the north it was not until the heyday of the Chimú polity that this Moche expansion was surpassed. Accompanying this development in agriculture was a large increase in the numbers of small rural villages, mostly the homes of farming communities that bordered the cultivated land. My own work in the area upstream of the valley neck indicates the intensity of small-scale Middle Period occupation in this area. Indeed, the slopes that flank the narrowing valley bottom are lined with small clusters of residential structures with occasional small platforms representing the rural nodes of central administration.

Recent work in the Moche Valley has also given a glimpse of the other important group of food producers whose settlements have not generally been the target of archaeological research. Located just south of the modern fishing village of Huanchaco, a much earlier Middle Moche counterpart straggled along the beach and the edge of the bluffs that parallel the shore (Donnan and Mackey 1978:189–201). Abundant Moche habitation residue accompanies clusters of rooms whose walls were built from beach cobbles fixed by mud mortar. Numerous subterranean pits were set into the floors of the houses, attesting to a significant domestic storage capacity, perhaps concerned with the preservation and distribution of marine resources. The Huanchaco fishing village is a rare physical reminder of the important role of marine specialists in Moche society, a role prominently depicted in ceramic art.

This pattern of corporate centers, rural villages, and specialist fishing and craft communities also characterized the Chicama Valley in the Middle Period. This giant neighbor of the Moche Valley has produced most of the vast corpus of ceramic material from the period, recovered by Rafael Larco Hoyle. A large quantity of the Chicama funerary material represented finely decorated sumptuary material manufactured at controlled workshops like the recently discovered Cerro Mayal site (Russell, Leonard, and Brirceño 1994). Located near the religious center of Mocollope, the specialist craftsmen resident at this site mass-produced a variety of elite ceramic goods that probably served the ceremonial needs of the lower Chicama Valley. This implies the presence of a significant body of Moche elite in the vicinity at this period. Moreover, Mocollope was just one of a large number of platforms spread throughout the Chicama Valley dating to the Moche III and IV phases, a situation that indicates a large and varied rural hinterland and consolidated political system. This evidence of an extensive Moche occupation contrasts with that of the subject valleys to the south and emphasizes the role of the central valleys as the heartland of the southern polity.

One important recent investigation elaborates on this picture in the Chicama Valley. A conglomerate consisting of the National University of Trujillo, the Regional Institute of Culture – La Libertad, and the Augusto N. Weise Foundation has recently supported a major program of excavation at the large Huaca El Brujo complex in the lower valley under the direction of Regulo Franco (Franco, Gálvez, and Vásquez 1994). With occupation ranging through many centuries from the preceramic era to the Early Colonial, the complex offers an important record of the vast span of human occupation in this location. A major platform, Huaca Cao Viejo, measuring 170 by 130 meters in area and standing 30 meters tall, dates largely to the Middle Moche period.

Significantly, the principal facade of Huaca Cao Viejo is adorned by several tiers of impressive polychrome friezes, the best preserved of this genre yet uncovered (figures 8.3, 8.4, 8.5; see also figure 4.9). The friezes represent several phases of construction and include motifs that are central to Moche ideological symbolism and represent the rituals that took place at the site. Thus, the familiar figures of warriors engaged in hand-to-hand combat, and a line of naked and bound captives, repeat two of the most common Moche themes of the Middle Period. These depict the initial phases of the ritual series that included the taking, arraignment, and sacrifice of captives. The climax of this ritual series is indicated by a dramatic depiction of the anthropomorphized executioner holding a sacrificial captive and ritual knife. In its role as a symbol and place of power, the Huaca El Brujo complex is only one imposing example of the great platforms that dominated the land throughout the southern Moche polity in the Middle Period.

Conquest of the Virú Valley   In his pioneering settlement study of the Virú Valley, Gordon Willey (1953) long ago observed

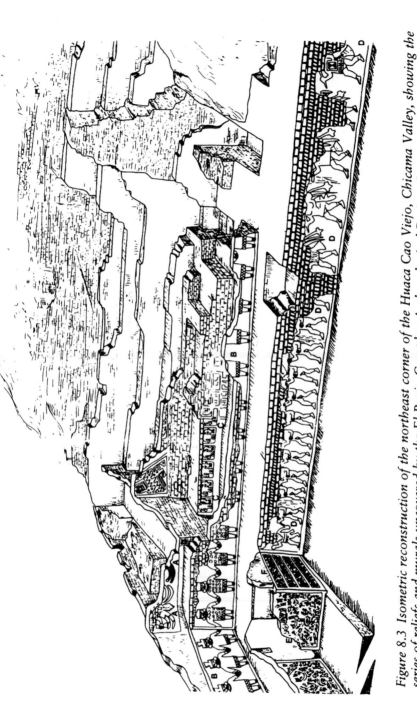

Figure 8.3 Isometric reconstruction of the northeast corner of the Huaca Cao Viejo, Chicama Valley, showing the series of reliefs and murals uncovered by the El Brujo Complex Archaeological Project. Images include A: Bottom portion of Decapitator holding a tumi knife in the right hand; B: Frieze of frontal figures, possibly portraying a ceremonial dance; C: Panels showing a sacrifice scene; D: Procession of warriors and bound naked prisoners; E: Scenes from Moche cosmology; F: Warriors in combat. (After Franco, Gálvez, and Vásquez 1994. figure 4.12)

Figure 8.4 Work in progress at the Huaca Cao Viejo, Chicama Valley, 1995. Visible are two walls bearing Moche cosmological scenes (E in figure 8.3), and registers of warriors in combat (F in figure 8.3), with the Decapitator (A in figure 8.3) above the procession of prisoners and warriors (D in figure 8.3). (Photo: Garth Bawden 1995)

Figure 8.5 Conservation in progress, July 1995, of high-relief polychrome figures from the facade of Huaca Cao Viejo, Chicama Valley. Figures probably depict ritual dancers. (Photo: Garth Bawden 1995)

that the rich material tradition and widespread settlement pattern of the Gallinazo cultural phase was abruptly replaced by intrusive forms that correspond to the Middle Period inventory of the neighboring Moche Valley. It is universally accepted by students of this period that the rather abrupt and widespread appearance of Moche III ceramic and architectural material in the Virú Valley indicates intrusion from the north. The most generally agreed scenario views this development as the successful subjugation of Gallinazo societies by their Moche neighbors, and the incorporation of their valley into an expanding polity whose center of government was the great Cerro Blanco settlement.

A brief review of the available information sheds light on the basic character of Moche political domination of the southern valleys during the Middle Period. Even though such factors as small-site destruction and the difficulty of confirming the date of sites that present no decorated pottery unavoidably biases the interpretation of settlement surveys, Willey's work does indicate a considerable Moche presence in the Virú Valley during the Middle Period. This presence is reflected by an archaeological record that ranges from considerable, though shallow, residential refuse, to large numbers of Moche III and IV burials, including one of the most elaborate elite examples ever found in the south (Strong and Evans 1952). These sites are accompanied by numerous monumental architectural complexes that, as elsewhere, are the most visible indications of Moche occupation.

Willey noted that, although in overall occupation the Moche settlement pattern of Virú generally corresponded to that of Gallinazo in its valley-wide distribution, the new Huancaco (Moche III) phase displayed some significant internal reorganization that reveals the nature of the transition. Thus the great Gallinazo Group site, the town that may well have been the center of government of a quite extensive polity, was largely abandoned following the Moche III intrusion. The Gallinazo Group was replaced in this preeminent administrative role by the Castillo de Huancaco, a large Moche complex of adobe platforms and walls centered on a monumental five-stage platform. Several other large platform complexes, believed to be subsidiary to Huancaco, were built in other parts of the valley at this time, presumably as secondary centers of Moche control.

Tall adobe walls of a type found at Huancaco and believed to be defensive in nature also occur elsewhere in the valley. A final Moche period change involved agricultural management and production. Thus, there appears to have been a significant shift of agricultural emphasis from the north side of the lower Virú Valley to the south, with accompanying expansion of the irrigation system in this zone. Although it appears very probable that force accompanied these imposed changes, there is little indication that this resulted in the establishment of a permanent military institution. Indeed, there is insufficient architectural evidence here or elsewhere in the southern valleys to suggest the presence of complex bureaucratic, military, or corporate storage infrastructure of the type that became conspicuous in the latest Moche period and that accompanied the expansion of the Wari, Chimú, and Inka polities.

These Moche III innovations in the Virú Valley tell us much about the nature of socio-political process in the southern part of the region in the Middle Period. First, and most obvious, the displacement of the Gallinazo Group as the focus of political control in the valley eloquently denotes the nature of the transition. Huancaco, the new center, represented the imposition of power from an external, Moche Valley source. More importantly, its great terraced platforms mark the establishment of the dominant architectural symbolism of Moche ideology in the new setting. The Virú Valley representatives of Moche power were ultimately accountable to the rulers who manifested their authority through the ceremonies of power at the Huacas del Sol and de la Luna. However, they themselves appear to have exerted their local control through subsidiary centers scattered through the Virú Valley and distinguished by smaller, but still impressive platforms such as the Huaca Verde and Huaca Carranza.

We have more vivid expressions of the presence of the ruling Moche elites in the newly subjugated valley. As part of his survey report (1953:215–18), Willey reported the discovery of a Moche "throne." The throne was placed on the summit of a small isolated platform, believed to be of Moche construction. Located within a room whose walls were covered with white plaster, the structure consisted of a pedestal, circular in cross-section, standing on a rectangular base, and approached by a flight of seven steps. In its form the feature replicates another example at the Huaca de la Luna, now destroyed, that was originally noted by Alfred Kroeber (1930:72). Similar structures were portrayed in fine-line painted and modelled ceramic vessels. By studying these depictions scholars have concluded that the throne was used by Moche leaders as they participated in ceremonies of power.

An even more dramatic expression of Moche rule was uncovered by Duncan Strong and Clifford Evans during excavations in Virú in the 1940s (Strong and Evans 1952). Until the recent discovery of the Royal Tombs of Sipán, the so-called Tomb of the Warrior Priest was probably the most elaborate Moche burial ever studied. It contained the body of a mature male wearing the lavishly embellished nose ornament and copper face mask that we have noted as symbols of superior status in Moche society. This individual was wrapped in fine cotton textiles and interred in a burial chamber which also contained the bodies of sacrificed male and female retainers and llama offerings.

The rich burial goods included numerous ceramic vessels, among them portrait vessels of the type found at the Cerro Blanco site, and gilded metal images of fox and bird heads. In addition, several wooden staffs of office had carved representations of a fanged deity, probably one of the mythical beings that appear regularly in Moche art, and an owl – a bird associated with supernatural powers in modern North Coast belief, that is sometimes portrayed in sacrificial contexts in Moche art. The accoutrements of the carved figure on the staff are quite similar to those of the actual deceased individual and it is quite logical to assume that, like the rulers of Sipán, in life this individual portrayed a mythical being in the ritual performances, including sacrifice, which enhanced his personal status while demonstrating the power of Moche ideology to the subject population of Virú.

Other indicators of the nature of Moche III intrusion are the adobe walls that are so conspicuous at the site of Huancaco itself. Made of adobe bricks and still standing to a height of over 9 feet in places, these walls were located so as to defend the main platform complex from access from the hillslopes above. Similar walls appended to other Moche sites of the period also prevent easy passage through side valleys leading from the hills into the occupied plain. Willey reasonably suggested that these walls were defensive constructions, an indication that the Moche occupation was not peaceful in nature.

Finally, the re-organization of agricultural land that accompanied the Moche intrusion marked another important feature of the southern political expansion. It appears that a considerable area of land that had been cultivated by the Gallinazo on the north side of the Virú Valley was abandoned with the coming of the Moche (Willey 1953:365). However, a new agricultural zone south of the river was brought into cultivation at this time, a development that involved the construction of new feeder canals under Moche supervision. What is important here is not that there was any substantial increase in productive land but that the new ruling authority initiated re-organization of the agricultural system following its seizure of control. We shall see that this process was carried much further when the Moche polity conquered the Santa Valley further south.

By around AD 300, a time marked in the archaeological record by the emergence of the Moche III stylistic phase, the polity that encompassed the Moche and Chicama Valleys expanded into the Virú Valley. Here it suppressed the native Gallinazo societies and imposed a new political order. The intrusion was accompanied by a group of changes that supported the new hegemony. First, these changes involved alteration of existing agricultural patterns to permit greater control over economic resources, an adjustment whose effects we shall more clearly see in the Santa Valley. Second, modification of residential patterns involved some relocation of indigenous population and the settlement of people from the Moche and Chicama region to serve the administrative and economic needs of the newly acquired territory. Third, and most conspicuous in the archaeological record, the expanding Moche polity brought with it the trappings and mechanisms of power. In the Virú Valley, the Middle Period saw the erection of the platforms that were the dominant symbols of Moche authority and the sites of the activities that supported it. In addition, the Tomb of the Warrior Priest clearly shows that the new rulers of Virú adhered in all basic regards to the tenets and material manifestations of Moche political ideology. By using this ideology to identify themselves directly with traditional and supernatural North

Coast Andean origins of authority, Moche III leaders were able to create a core of political power that for a time held a considerable territory under their dominion.

Expansion to the far south   The archaeological evidence of change in the Middle Period seen in the Virú Valley is generally repeated further south. It appears that the southern Moche polity ultimately wielded hegemony as far south as Huarmey, 150 miles from the Huaca del Sol and the center of the government (figure 1.1). However, it is clear that in the valleys south of Virú, Moche occupation in Phases III and IV was more limited. In the Santa Valley and its neighboring Nepeña Valley, the bulk of Moche occupation was restricted to the lower valley segments, the upper valleys either being relatively depopulated, in the case of Santa, or occupied by non-Moche societies in Nepeña (Proulx 1985; Wilson 1988). Further south the situation is less clear. It has only recently been established that any Moche settlement existed in the Casma Valley (Wilson 1991). However, a modest occupation has now been confirmed on the basis of still incomplete survey, including both habitation and administrative sites. A similar situation is present in the Huarmey Valley 60 miles to the south (see summary in Shimada 1994a:91). Before confirmation of the Casma occupation, the Huarmey Valley was frequently regarded as a distant enclave established in the political domain of non-Moche people. In the light of recent discovery, however, the valley more feasibly appears to have represented the furthest Middle Period Moche penetration. Huarmey was in fact an integral part of the southern Moche polity, and its frontier with the societies of the Central Peruvian Coast.

Given the lack of firm scientific dating and the imprecision associated with using ceramic style for this purpose, the actual chronology of this expansion is at present uncertain. Thus there is no way of knowing whether the entire southern area was subjugated during a single episode of conquest or by intermittent thrusts during the course of the three centuries of the Middle Period. Neither can we be certain of exactly when during Phases III and IV these southern valleys were conquered, nor of the length of their Moche occupation. Certainly the sparse Moche presence in of the southernmost Casma and

Huarmey Valleys indicate an occupation of rather short duration, a situation that contrasts with the Virú and Santa Valleys
with their large number of settlements and impressive administrative centers. As more work is completed in the southern
valleys and a more exact stylistic analysis is available, it will at
least be possible to place any short-term occupation within its
relative chronological phase during this quite extensive period.
This, in turn, will permit a better understanding of the history
of the southern Moche polity in its peripheral provinces.

If we turn now to what is known of the nature of Moche rule
in the south, we will see that while in some basic qualities this
conforms to the Virú situation, there are also some significant
differences. First, the manifestations of Moche political domination are quite similar, again underscoring the importance of
Moche ideology at the center of political power. Thus, the Santa
Valley contains an impressive number of Moche platform
mounds, ranging in size from the massive central structure at
the Pampa de Los Incas complex, through smaller local examples scattered throughout the valley. David Wilson, who has
conducted the most recent survey of the area, has described the
Pampa de Los Incas site as the chief locus of political control in
the valley (figure 1.1; Wilson 1988:207–12). This extensive
complex of platforms, adobe walls, habitation areas, and cemeteries covered an area of over 2 square kilometers and was
approached by the main road that entered the Santa Valley from
the north. Also in the immediate environs of this site Wilson
identified what was probably a pottery production workshop –
the center of a formal craft workshop controlled by the polity.
In this regard Wilson also noted that the pottery of this period
from Santa, while displaying typical Moche characteristics,
includes only a restricted number of types, a feature that
Wilson ascribes to the formal dictates of a controlling central
administration.

When one looks at the demographic and economic structure
of the Santa Valley during its Moche occupation, it is clear that
much greater re-organization was imposed than in the Virú
Valley. Wilson estimates that the overall population of the area
fell from 30,000 to 22,000 individuals, possibly due to the
effects of military conquest and resettlement. However, at the
same time, the surviving population whose Gallinazo-affiliated

predecessors had been thickly spread throughout the valley, were now concentrated along the bottom lands in its lower course. In this restricted lower valley zone the population actually increased by 500 per cent. At the same time the productive land in the lower valley experienced a drastic expansion with the construction of new canals and fields. Wilson regards this area with its abundant water supply as a major food supplier for the southern Moche polity. The causes of this radical adjustment were probably twofold. They reflected the desire of the conquering Moche to maximize the productive economic potential of the valley with the least expenditure of effort while at the same time permitting the easy control allowed by accessible populations who could no longer live on the defensible hilltops and ridges as in earlier times. This Santa Valley evidence indicates more strongly than that of any other valley that economic concerns played an important role in the events that led to the expansion of the southern Moche polity. These major changes also imply, at least in the period of initial intrusion, the presence of coercive military presence. However, there is no architectural indication that this became a permanent part of the Moche regime.

In the Nepeña Valley, directly to the south of Santa, the situation during the period of its control by the Moche is somewhat different. Two important factors distinguish this Nepeña occupation. First, the Moche presence in the valley appears to have been much smaller than in the valleys to the north. The Nepeña settlement corpus numbers 37 sites in all, of which only a puzzling 5 habitation sites are confirmed (Proulx 1985:277). The Santa totals, by contrast, include 84 habitation settlements in a total of 205 sites. While the extremely small number of habitation sites in the Nepeña area may be misleading due to erosional or identification factors, nevertheless it is clear that the Moche occupation of this valley was meager compared with the areas further north. This fact might well suggest that the Moche presence was of shorter duration in the southernmost valleys. Moreover, most Moche sites cluster around the major center of Pañamarca in the middle part of the valley adjacent to the most likely access roads from the north (figure 1.1). There are virtually no sites near the coast and only a few in the upper valley, one of which Donald Proulx regarded as a fortress. I shall discuss the implications of this site and its upper valley affiliations later in this chapter.

First, however, it is useful to review the focal point of Moche control in the Nepeña Valley. The Pañamarca site (figure 1.2; Bonavia 1985; Proulx 1968; Schaedel 1951b) is located in the largest concentration of Moche settlements in the valley at the hub of a network of habitation sites, subsidiary ceremonial centers with associated cemeteries, and irrigated fields. The site is centered around a major terraced platform mound which, like the Castillo de Huancaco in the Virú Valley, rises in five stages above the surrounding land surface. The summit of this main edifice is approached by means of a ramp that ascends its side. Adjoining the chief Pañamarca platform is a series of walled enclosures in which a number of burials were placed.

Painted on the walls of the main compound at Pañamarca are several unusually well-preserved murals depicting rather complex scenes of ceremonies involving numerous participants which vividly manifest the nature of Moche dominion in this peripheral area. The largest of these, commonly known as "the frieze of warriors and priests" (figure 8.6; Schaedel 1951b), contains a line of eight figures. These figures are richly dressed and accoutred in the characteristic style of the Moche elite with elaborately decorated tunics and sashes. The centrally located individuals in this scene are attended by figures whose small size, deferential attitudes, and plain garb indicate their subsidiary status. Most of the principal figures wear the large metal backflap that Donnan has suggested is a distinguishing mark of warrior status and which was worn by the Lord of Sipán, occupant of the richest of the Lambayeque Valley Middle Pe-

Figure 8.6 "Frieze of Warriors and Priests" from the Pañamarca Complex, Nepeña Valley. (Redrawn from Kosok 1965, figure 10)

riod Royal Tombs. This particular item also usually accompanies the central officiant of the Sacrifice Theme which, as we have seen, was one of the most widespread and persistent rituals of power of the entire Moche period. Although the precise meaning of this mural escapes us, it clearly depicts a ceremonial event in which representatives of the Moche ruling elite are portrayed in a context that emphasized their status and communicated their authority to observers clustered in the plaza.

Another impressive mural is one of the most replicated and discussed artifacts of Moche art. Described by various scholars (Bonavia 1985; Donnan 1978; Schaedel 1951b), this mural is a monumental representation of the Sacrifice Theme. Although severely damaged, the surviving portions of the mural portray several of the central figures of the Sacrifice Ceremony in details so exact as to confirm its narrative theme beyond any reasonable doubt (see chapter 5). Flanking the ritual scene are large-scale examples of the Moche mace and shield emblem, a design that routinely occurs in Moche elite art and probably signifies in an abstract sense the presence of Moche formal authority. Interestingly, another such mural was found by David Wilson on one of the secondary platforms in the Santa Valley, indicating that this class of architecture generally asserted the symbolism of Moche power throughout the southern Moche polity.

It seems certain, then, that Pañamarca fulfilled its role as the center of intrusive power by being the site of the symbols and rituals of power that I regard as the vital signifiers of Moche political ideology. At Pañamarca local populations, congregated in the open plazas of the complex, were regaled by impressive representations of the power of the Moche while acting as participant-observers in the actual rituals that these murals depict. By projection, and on the basis of mural fragments found elsewhere in similar architectural centers, we can confidently assume that Moche ideology was a potent agent of political expansion in the south and a pervasive presence in the everyday social scene.

Foreign interaction on the southern frontiers   I noted above that the bulk of Moche occupation in the Nepeña Valley was restricted to the lower part of the drainage. Further inland, while there are a handful of sites in which Moche pottery was found, only one appears to reflect a formal, though brief, occupation (Proulx 1985:277–81). This site is a stone-walled fortress that stands on a plateau overlooking the valley. The site probably represented an attempt by the Moche to establish a presence in the upper valley prior to the expansion of their control into the area. Given the absence of any signs of habitational settlement, the attempt seems not to have been successful. The reason for this failure is revealed at the same site where pottery of very different, though contemporary, affiliation is mixed with the Moche material. This foreign pottery was the product of a highland-centered society commonly known as the Recuay Culture. Its occurrence in an otherwise Moche-controlled valley is an indication of relationships that existed between the societies of the greater region.

As I have already noted, one of the prominent motifs of early Moche artistic design in the Upper Piura region – the Moon Animal (figure 7.5) – was derived from a common Recuay theme. This motif, possibly given new meaning by the receptor society, was to become a fixture of its art. The archaeological record suggests that little formal economic or political interaction occurred between the essentially self-sufficient coastal Moche peoples and their highland neighbors. But this does not mean that they were isolated from each other. The very appearance of the Moon Animal in the context of Moche ideological iconography signifies the familiarity of coastal societies with Recuay art and probably implies their general knowledge of the associated cultural beliefs. Of course, in this instance, the Moche were only following the example of their ancestors who incorporated the Chavín ideological complex from the same general highland source centuries earlier and probably engaged in significant economic interaction with their highland neighbors.

The people of the Recuay Culture, then, were the Early Intermediate Period successors of highlanders who had earlier shared elements of Chavín ideology with the nearby coastal groups. The creators of a distinctive kaolin-based decorative pottery that emphasized modeled human and animal figures, the Recuay Culture appears to have had its core in and around the Callejón de Huaylas in the fertile uppermost intermontaine reaches of the Santa River where an abundance of stone habitation and hilltop defensive sites attest to the large population and high degree of social organization (Gero 1988, 1990; Grieder 1978). To the west, the Recuay highlanders met the peoples of the plains in the upper valleys of the coastal rivers from Virú at least to Nepeña, and possibly farther south. Recuay sites and pottery are especially abundant in the upper Santa Valley since this was the best natural corridor between its highland heartland and the coast. Prior to the advent of the Moche in the area, the relations between the Gallinazo and Recuay societies were largely peaceful (Wilson 1988:355). However, after the Moche conquered the Gallinazo, it was probably inevitable that the two polities would come face-to-face in the Andean foothills in a setting of mutual distrust, if not outright hostility.

Thus, while peaceful ideological borrowing apparently marked the early Moche adoption of the Recuay Moon Animal, the situation was different during the Middle Period in the Moche south. Here, the settlement record strongly suggests encounter of a more hostile nature. The general settlement pattern reveals that Moche control of the valleys subjugated during the Middle Period was checked in the mid-valleys and largely confined to the areas near the sea. A fairly intensive Recuay occupation in the upper valley areas, contiguous with its highland hegemony, represents the physical evidence for this settlement delineation. Moreover, the presence of fortifications like the Nepeña fortress at the boundary of the two occupations implies that the nature of the interface was not always peaceful and that the upper valleys were an area of competition. Another line of evidence for this view, though difficult to confirm, interprets the fine-line Middle Period pottery depictions of combat in which some warriors are dressed in garb of distinctively non-Moche character as representing conflict between the Moche and Recuay (figure 4.10; Proulx 1982). Consequently it appears probable that Moche expansion to the south replaced the existing Gallinazo hegemony and confronted an already strong Recuay presence that may well have aspired to direct access to the sea. Moche occupation of the lower segments of the coastal valleys would have prevented this access, leading to uneasy peace punctuated by more overt hostility between the two polities.

Thus, the relationship of the southern Moche polity with its most powerful neighbor was in large part shaped by the need to ensure its new lands with their high economic potential against invasion from the highlands. However, other important, though less demonstrable considerations were probably involved in the foreign relations of the southern Moche. These concern the sustenance of even more distant connections. Earlier I emphasized the importance to coastal dwellers like the Moche of the distant resources represented by the offshore islands with their guano deposits and of their ability to trade with other regions both north and south of the Moche region. The otherwise insignificant Huarmey Valley represented the southern frontier of the Moche polity and its gateway to these distant resources. Inland, beyond the limits of Moche control to the south, the vast uplands of the Central Peruvian Highlands would have been a plentiful source of wool, obsidian, and salt. On the coast, finds of Moche pottery in the area occupied by contemporary Nasca society hint at contacts with the Central and Southern Coast peoples (Proulx 1994; Shimada 1994a:91).

Although none of these remote connections can be fully substantiated at present, the demonstrated endeavors of North Coast peoples to traffic with other Andean peoples throughout their history make it probable that the Moche presence in the agriculturally poor Huarmey Valley was intended to further such activity. In any case, the foreign interactions of the southern Moche polity make it clear that in spite of the natural bias in the archaeological record toward the remains of direct intrusion, Moche expansion also took the form of significant long-distance exchange with multiple neighboring societies.

The Northern Valleys in the Middle Period

We saw in the last chapter that the Early Moche Period data from the north suggested a process of differential adoption and manipulation by local elites of the emerging tenets of Moche ideology, a process best reflected in the distinctive ceramic forms and the imagery that adorns the precious metal items from the Loma Negra cemetery of the Upper Piura. This process conforms to that of the central valleys in Phases I and II and reflects the emergence and slow consolidation of the new political ideology. The archaeological record shows that the Moche III Phase brought a drastic interruption of this local developmental pattern in the south by initiating a process of unification, accompanied by displacement of the local political order. However, this was not the case in the north.

While the traditional view of Middle Moche history accepted, in the absence of data to the contrary, that a wave of political conquest swept northward from the Moche Valley and ultimately incorporated the entire coast in a single powerful state, this view can no longer be sustained. The accumulating material evidence from the north suggests that its Middle Period history was quite different from that of the valleys south of the Jequetepeque (Castillo and Donnan 1995). Interestingly, this geographical division parallels the linguistic pattern observed by the early Spanish traveller, Fr. Antonio de la Calancha ([1638] 1976), who described Muchic as the language or dialect of the north and Quingan as that of the south. Differences in architecture and pottery also conform to this geographical division. These internal cultural differences accompanied and perhaps facilitated the different courses taken in the Middle and Late Period in the two parts of the region. In commencing this discussion of the northern valleys, two important features must be addressed – persistence of Gallinazo societies throughout the Middle Period and variation among the Moche societies themselves.

Moche and Gallinazo in the northern valleys   In contrast with the situation further south, societies using Gallinazo material cultural forms persisted throughout the Middle Moche Period in the northern valleys. In general Gallinazo settlements are located in the lowest parts of the valleys, where they form a coastal band of occupation between the ocean and the inland Moche settlements (Shimada and Maguña 1994). A partial exception to this pattern is the La Leche Valley (figure 1.1), where a major Gallinazo occupation in the middle valley persisted at least into the Moche IV Phase. It appears that the relationship between Moche and Gallinazo was peaceful for much of the Middle Period. Shimada recently posited a new version of the expansionist scheme, arguing that the Cerro Blanco-centered polity conquered the entire region in the Moche IV Phase (Shimada 1994a:89–90). But this scenario is largely based on ceramic data for which stylistic and absolute dating associations are far from assured. We shall see that there is also strong evidence that local autonomy characterized the region throughout the Moche period.

In fact, evidence from the northern valleys suggests that relations between contemporary Middle Period Gallinazo and Moche societies were at times very close. At the town of Pacatnamú in the Jequetepeque Valley, Heinrich Ubbelohde-Doering discovered Gallinazo and Moche ceramics used as burial offerings in the same burials (1967:22), radiocarbon dated to the fifth or sixth centuries AD. This juxtaposition would indicate the co-existence of the two styles and their related social forms in the Jequetepeque Valley during at least part of the Middle Period.

Even more interesting is the situation documented by Shimada and Maguña in the middle La Leche Valley (1994). Here, in what was arguably the most extensive area of Middle Period Gallinazo settlement in the entire northern region, the common appearance of Moche and Gallinazo occupation at both ceremonial and ceramic production sites suggests a level of co-existence that transcends uneasy stand-off. Instead there is considerable evidence of close cultural and economic collaboration. This relationship is not so surprising, however, if one remembers that in all probability the various Gallinazo and Moche settlements were inhabited by people of similar ethnicity and shared North Coast history who were separated only by the political aspects of their respective religious beliefs.

Moche diversity in the north   A brief review of information on Moche settlement in the northern valleys during the Middle Period suggests a condition of considerable local diversity, again contrasting with the contemporary situation further south following the establishment of the southern polity. One important factor that must be addressed at the outset is the utility of ceramic style for tracing northern spatial connections and chronological development. I have already discussed in detail the problems associated with Larco's five-phase developmental

scheme of Moche ceramic style. While this scheme may generally reflect wider historical process in the Moche-Chicama
region, it is less accurate elsewhere, both because of major
stylistic difference between north and south and because of
variation within the northern coastal expressions themselves
(see Kaulicke 1992 and Castillo and Donnan 1994 and 1995 for
good recent discussions of this issue). Thus there is little evidence of the Moche IV Phase in the northern stylistic sequence.
More specifically, flaring bowls and portrait vessels, common
in the central and southern valleys, occur rarely further north,
while the converse is true of modeled figure vessels and the large
accumulations of almost identical vessels found in the Sipán
burials.

We have already seen that in the Upper Piura region, the
picture is extraordinarily complex. Not only does the style of
the Loma Negra metal objects differ from that of apparently
contemporary ceramics, but the stylistic sequence itself does not
neatly replicate Larco's scheme (Kaulicke 1992). Thus the Upper Piura Moche society incorporated various features from its
Ecuadorian and highland neighbors into its material inventory,
utilized the already ancient metallurgical tradition of the far
northern area to display Moche ideological imagery rather than
the ceramic medium preferred in the south, exhibited this imagery with distinctive iconographic treatment, and made its
pottery with structure, form, and decoration that differed from
pottery of the central valleys. While in part this discrepancy may
be ascribed to insecure data, I suggested in the last chapter that
there are other, more important, contributing factors. These
derive from the particular locational and historical attributes of
the area. In the absence of any convincing signs of conquest and
given the distance of the Upper Piura Moche societies from their
counterparts, it would be surprising if their cultural forms were
not distinctive. This local society adopted Moche ideology and
developed it locally in the Middle Period according to its specific cultural norms. Consequently, it is unreasonable to project
the central valley stylistic sequence to the Piura region with the
expectation that they can accurately define social trends.

The limited archaeological picture suggests that other northern valleys also developed independently. One particular feature
of the Upper Piura stylistic complex – the scarcity of the Moche

IV Phase in the region (Guffroy, Kaulicke and Makowski, 1989:12) – is especially pertinent. Luis Jaime Castillo and Christopher Donnan found a similar absence of Moche IV stylistic material in their stratigraphic work at the site of San José de Moro in the Jequetepeque Valley in the context of long Moche occupational continuity (Castillo and Donnan 1994). This contrasts with Izumi Shimada's assertion of a major Moche IV occurrence in the intervening Zaña, Lambayeque, and La Leche valleys, a circumstance that he uses to posit invasion from the south (Shimada 1994b). However, if each of the elements of this complex distributional picture proves to approximate reality, then two important implications arise (figure 7.1). First, there was no uniform developmental sequence of Moche style, a situation already suggested by the Piura and Jequetepeque material. Instead the Moche style reflects differential local evolution. Second, such diversity must reflect a pattern of parallel, but distinct cultural traditions within the wider Moche sphere. It follows that the political and social histories of these northern valley societies also followed separate, if related, courses.

Several isolated pieces of settlement information support this scenario. At Pacatnamú, a huge city overlooking the sea, Donnan (1986:23) recently confirmed earlier conclusions of Ubbelohde-Doering by identifying an extensive Middle Moche occupation. However, Doering's idea that Pacatnamú was a supra-regional pilgrimage center now seems unlikely for the Moche period; the extensive cemeteries of this time mostly hold individuals buried with simple goods characteristic of a purely local population. Moreover, contrasting with the extensive ceremonial character of later times, there was probably only a single platform associated with the Moche occupation.

Elsewhere, at San José, the Middle Moche occupation includes several of the most elaborate Moche burials ever discovered, of elite women who served as the "Priestess" in the Sacrifice Ritual (figure 4.4; Castillo 1993; Donnan and Castillo 1992, 1994. See also chapter 3 above). While San José occupation associated with these burials persists throughout the Middle Period, and thus is contemporary with Phases III and IV further south, the latter phase does not occur at the site, indicating a distinct development. Adding to its uniqueness, San José presents abundant evidence for adoption of foreign ceramic features from North Highland Cajamarca and Central Coast Nievería and Pachacamac cultures, into the Moche ceramic tradition. Moreover, it seems clear that the Jequetepeque settlements conducted intensive commercial activity with their highland Cajamarca neighbors. The magnitude of this interaction is not replicated in any other valley. These data suggest an independent development of Jequetepeque society which included formal long-range contacts and a unique level of cultural borrowing.

Further north in the large hydraulic complex composed of the closely contiguous Zaña, Lambayeque, and La Leche Valleys, the current archaeological evidence suggests yet another distinct historical course. By the Moche III Phase local development in the Lambayeque Valley created the magnificent funerary monument of Sipán with its dramatic revelations of the nature of Moche political leadership and its ideological meaning (figures 4.1, 4.2; Alva and Donnan 1993). Clearly the rulers of Sipán shared with their Upper Piura counterparts the tradition of northern metallurgy, using this for explicit projection of ritual symbolism. In contrast, ceramics are relatively coarse with simple embellishment. No other examples of such elaborate centers of social integration are presently known in these valleys. However, Moche occupation has been established by surface survey and we can tentatively posit the existence of one or more local Moche III polities in the area similar in form to that of Sipán.

Largely on the basis of surface survey, Izumi Shimada has suggested that this localized Moche III political pattern changed in the Moche IV Phase. He believes that extensive political unification was established at this time by the southern Moche polity whose forces advanced north along a coastal trunk road from the Moche-Chicama area to conquer the middle segments of each valley (figure 7.1; Shimada 1994a:88–90, 1994b). This invasion left the coastal areas largely in the hands of Gallinazo societies while the highland Cajamarca culture, whose ceramics occur commonly in the region, dominated the upper valleys. In the supposed subject valleys there is as yet no evidence to compare with that of the south for demographic or agricultural reorganization. Architectural evidence of political conquest is sparse. In the Lambayeque Valley the Gallinazo occupation at

Huaca Soledad in the Batan Grande complex was replaced by Moche IV occupation. Elswhere, the imposing ridge-top fortifications at Cerro Boro in the same valley may represent the seaward boundary between expanding Moche IV and residual Gallinazo domains.

Another scenario of political Moche consolidation in the Middle Moche Period, albeit more localized, has been presented by Makowski in his view of the evolution of Moche political power in the Upper Piura drainage. He has most recently (Makowski, Amoro, and Eléspuru 1995) suggested that Moche political domination culminated in this region in the formation of a Moche IV state. It is somewhat unclear whether this merely represents the northernmost aspect of much wider northern consolidation as in Shimada's scheme, or an autonomous Upper Piura formation. Moreover, this position appears to fly in the face of the sparse evidence for Moche IV occupation in this area that I have noted above. Consequently, I believe that resolution of this issue in the Upper Piura must remain open for now.

Lack of evidence for invasion in the Jequetepeque Valley which would have stood solidly in the path of southern political expansion, together with the perplexing situation in the Upper Piura drainage and uncertainty regarding the utility of Larco's stylistic sequence for tracing northern developments, leave the conquest scheme rather tentative at present. However, if Shimada's assertion of the diffusion of Moche IV ceramics in the areas between the Jequetepeque and Upper Piura Moche settlements (where they are mostly absent) should prove to be correct, then the Zaña, Lambayeque, and La Leche Valleys illustrate yet another distinct historical course in the Middle Period.

Regardless of the eventual outcome of this rather confusing evidence for the northern area in the Middle Period, its history differed significantly from that of the central and southern valleys (Castillo and Donnan 1995). It is most likely that the northern valleys contained a number of autonomous small polities, ruled by the successors of elites who adopted Moche ideology in the Early Period and evolved their political strategies according to their own local interests (figure 7.1). By contrast with the south, these Middle Moche polities appear to have peacefully co-existed with their Gallinazo contemporaries in the Moche III period with only minor encroachment later. No northern political upheavals appear to have approached in magnitude those of the south and there is no evidence for the intensive political and economic organization that followed establishment of the southern polity.

Political Ideology in the Middle Moche Period

Having described the different pathways taken by the various Middle Period Moche polities, I return now to the theme that opened this chapter, the role and nature of ideology in this process. I noted early in this book that political ideologies are never static. They exist in a state of dialectical tension with antagonistic forces within their wider societies. Through active engagement with these forces, they continually adjust, thereby reflexively affecting social structure and stimulating wider change. The Middle Moche archaeological record illustrates this dynamic aspect of ideology. Traditionally, the well-known central valley "core area" has been used to characterize Moche III–IV society as a whole. However, we have seen that the archaeological picture is one of variability among the Moche societies. While regional trends certainly existed, political strategies and ideological beliefs varied locally and displayed this difference symbolically. This variation carries implications for understanding the further history of Moche societies in the final Moche V Phase and thus is a valuable tool for investigating the dynamics of change inherent in Moche political ideology.

The context of various material expressions of the southern Moche polity show the extreme growth of individualizing ideology and the distance that this would have opened between rulers and a general populace whose social conception was grounded in the holistic social structure of Andean peoples. Various developments in the manufacture of fine ceramics testify to this trend. First, on a general level, the numerous instances of intensive pottery production that are associated with the Middle Period corporate centers of authority in the south suggest the presence of a body of specialists working under supervision of the elite. The existence of such specialists was probably also a necessary precondition for the advance in technological and decorative skill required to produce the intricate fine-line styles of the Middle Period and the unusual southern form that I shall discuss shortly. The establishment of such a controlled body of specialists, working solely to make elaborate status goods for severely restricted elite circulation, accompanied and affirmed the intensification of centralized power by Moche rulers.

However, another attribute of elite ceramic art in the south allows a closer view of the actual nature of their power. Moche portrait vessels (figures 4.6, 4.7), variously interpreted as realistic depictions of individuals or symbolic images of shamans, are among the best-known and admired expressions of New World indigenous art. They portray persons wearing headdresses that bear distinctive emblems. Two important points provide the geographical and social contexts of their meaning: almost all known vessels were recovered in the central valleys, and they were used exclusively in funerary settings. Portrait vessels repeat basic Moche practice of visually using headdress signifiers to relate individuals to specific ritual activity of the kind depicted on monumental architecture of the southern polity.

However, the portrait vessel was not just another symbolic signifier. It actually reflects an extension of the earlier Moche ideological system and its meaning. The question of whether or not these vessels were actually portraits is less significant than the fact that symbols of social position were now strongly individualized, a development that suggests progressive elevation of an exclusive elite group, if not of actual persons. I believe that in the Moche-Chicama area, Moche III political leaders succeeded in acquiring a greater degree of exclusive power than either their Early Period predecessors or their northern counterparts. This in turn marked the emergence of a domain of power less constrained by community action, together with its structural corollary – increased potential for social tension between individualizing and holistic ideology.

We have seen that this unprecedented consolidation of power accompanied coercion of the southern valleys into a Moche Valley-centered polity that displaced Gallinazo hegemony in this part of the region (figure 7.1). This process of coercion generated the need to govern a dispersed territory occupied by subdued and probably hostile peoples. However, there is little evidence that the intrusive Middle Moche southern ceremonial centers initiated increased managerial differentiation. With small resident populations, they lacked the highly controlled corporate storage facilities, elaborate administrative complexes, and military housing that formed such a conspicuous part of Moche V and Chimú administrative centers. Also, Moche narrative art usually depicts the hand-to-hand combat between Moche warriors that I have earlier identified with ritual combat, and lacks any suggestion of large permanent armies. Instead, whether through the products of the craft workshops of Cerro Blanco, Pampa de los Incas, and Cerro Mayal, the thrones of Huaca de la Luna and Virú, or the great murals of the Huaca de la Luna, Huaca El Brujo, and Pañamarca, emphasis was overwhelmingly on the symbols and imagery of status.

It appears that southern leaders primarily enhanced their authority by manipulating beliefs shared by all North Coast people rather than by creating new institutions of government. By so doing they appropriated an exceptional personal aura that was capable of constituting the integrating force of their extensive territorial realm in the absence of permanent armies. The viability of the southern Moche polity depended chiefly on the personal ability of its rulers to articulate in their own persons the combined authority of high social position, ritual status, and supernatural affiliation through the codified symbolism of Moche ideology. Ironically, their triumph was both the result and cause of internal flaw. It was initiated by the inability of the small Moche Valley to provide the resources required to support its economic and political needs. It resulted in the need to maintain control over a far-flung territory without the integrated agencies of differentiated political organization, an ultimately impossible task.

While in the south Moche ideology actively accommodated the enhancement of individualized power at a time of territorial expansion and centralized political consolidation, in the northern valleys it served somewhat different interests. Here, with the possible exception of the Lambayeque area in the tentatively identified northern Moche IV Phase, the conquest of territory seems not to have been a priority of Moche leaders. Instead we can assume that the generally large agricultural potential of the northern valleys sufficed to support a number of thriving, politically separate, societies in close contact with each other, with their Gallinazo neighbors, and, in the case of the Upper Piura and Jequetepeque Valleys, with areas far distant. Therefore, there was no need to create a power structure to dominate remote and diverse subject peoples. Consequently, northern leaders never attempted to merge the supernatural power central to Moche ideology with individualized power. Their authority remained embedded in their ability to assume the roles of the figures of Moche myth in rituals like the Sacrifice Ceremony, where they acted as shamans, entering the sacred world and manipulating it on behalf of their societies. In this role their individuality was subsumed by their ritual position even while they promoted their power as a ruling elite.

Thus portrait vessels, signifiers of the individualization of power, were not produced north of the Chicama Valley. They had no meaning in the context of northern Moche ideology where power remained linked more closely to its traditional community base. For the same reason the northern polities eschewed introduction of fine-line ceramic art as the most important vehicle for the communication of ideological iconography during the Middle Period. The highest status funerary symbols, as in the preceding period, were of precious metal. While many generations of separate history produced considerable variation among the northern societies, it appears that they retained closer links to their traditional ideological origins than did their southern counterparts.

The Middle Moche world

Several autonomous polities existed in the Middle Period on the North Coast of Peru, some Moche, some Gallinazo. These were dominated in size by the southern Moche polity, formed as the result of a systematic process of conquest, the only such instance that can yet be determined. Elsewhere hostility was probably confined to the ritual combat that appears so frequently in Middle Moche ceramic art as the initial phase of the ritual cycle that culminated in the Sacrifice Ceremony. The increased demands on central authority generated by the Moche conquest of the south were addressed, not by administrative differentiation, but by ideological adjustment. This process was dependent on further enhancement of elite power through funerary and political ritual whose fullest material symbol was the portrait vessel. The accompanying individualization of authority would have further separated the ideology of power from its holistic cultural origins, a process never as marked in the northern polities where the political system did not have to meet the challenge of widened territorial or demographic responsibilities. Progressive alienation of rulers from their subjects in the south would have unavoidably raised the potential for social tension in times of stress. In the late sixth century AD in a context of regional crisis, the efficacy of Moche political ideology was so tested, precipitating profound structural crisis and transformation.

9

Collapse and Reconstitution in the Late Moche Period

Major change affected the North Coast towards the end of the Middle Moche Period. Indeed the modifications of the archaeological record that can be dated to this time comprise a diagnostic framework within which to identify the Moche IV–V transition. In the broadest sense these changes entailed elimination of Moche occupation from the southern valleys and abandonment of large areas of previously cultivated land in the central and northern valleys (figure 7.1). More specific features included abandonment of much of the Cerro Blanco site, the erstwhile center of the southern Moche polity, establishment of various inland urban settlements in the valley necks, and major changes in the iconography of elite art. In absolute chronological terms, the last decades of the sixth century AD initiated a relatively brief era in which the Late Moche Period societies of Phase V to a large degree set the stage for the subsequent history of peoples of the North Coast.

At the outset we should address the nature of the Moche IV–V transition. It has often been assumed that the rather dramatic events subsumed into this process were manifestations of a single, pan-regional phenomenon that culminated in the collapse of the Moche polity. However, in this chapter I shall make two arguments that oppose this simple view. First, the changes imprinted in the archaeological record were actually differential expressions of local responses to stress. Thus the various Moche polities that we have seen following their separate courses in the Middle Period adjusted to the pressures that initiated the Moche V Phase in their own ways, drawing on the resources created by their particular historical experiences. A second, related point is that there was no overall "collapse." Although in the south profound interruption of the Middle Period society did occur and left permanent and damaging effects, further north the impact was not as powerful nor were its results so negative. The Late Moche IV–Moche V Phases can undeniably be regarded as representing a period of rapid change. However, it would be wrong to equate this simply with decline. In the light of its imposing achievements, it would be more accurate to discuss the Late Period, especially in the northern valleys, as cultural reconstitution that bridged the transition between North Coast society of the Early and Late Intermediate Periods.

The Sources of Social Change

Environmental catastrophe   I have stressed the fact that the Andean physical world is among the most active on earth. The great Pacific ocean plates constantly press upon each other in their quest for the stability that comes with geological maturity, prompting responsive movement along the continental ranges of the Andes. This endless process enters the realm of human experience through the primordial media of the earthquake, volcano, tidal wave, and flood. These transcendental forces continually confront people with the chaos threatening social life, inspiring the rich textures of Andean myth and ritual that orders and makes them comprehensible. These forces enter Andean cultural conception, shaping religious beliefs and the content of artistic imagery through which they are manifest in daily life. There are times when the delicate relationship between humans and the natural world breaks down. From an Andean perspective this usually happens because of human disregard of the religious tenets, resulting in natural disaster. Such calamities as the 1970 earthquake that devastated the Callejón de Huaylas, and the extended El Niño episode of the early 1980s are recent examples of phenomena that have ravaged the human world intermittently through history, leaving human society temporarily devastated and its members spiritually demoralized.

Still, we must be careful not simplistically to ascribe Andean social change to environmental agency. Although there can be no doubting the fearsome power of the natural forces that pervade the Andes, Andean peoples have acquired a resilience from their millennia-long familiarity with these forces that allows them to surmount all but the most extreme cataclysm. After all, it is the same world that provides Andean peoples with their physical and spiritual necessities, promoting interdependency between human and supernatural spheres. Thus in most instances the impact of natural disruption, though sometimes profound, is temporary. Rarely, if ever, can such events be demonstrated to have caused by themselves the total breakdown of society.

There is growing evidence that the physical environment of the North Coast experienced unusually extended disruption during the sixth century AD. During recent decades a great deal of research has been directed toward understanding the impact of climatic phenomena in the Moche IV–V transition. This work has identified both drought and violent flooding as possible contributing factors. The work of Michael Moseley and his colleagues in the Moche Valley in the 1960s and 70s generated strong evidence of abrupt environmental change. At the Cerro Blanco site they uncovered the summit of a low platform that stood in the plain that extends between the Huacas del Sol and de la Luna (figure 2.14). This platform had been used in Moche IV times for the interment of several individuals of high status (figure 8.3; see chapter 8). The platform showed little weathering or post-Moche IV use and had been buried with windblown sand that was itself sealed by a thick layer of water-borne silt, attesting to the occurrence of a serious flood sometime after establishment of the cemetery (Moseley 1978; Moseley and Deeds 1982:37–8). Elsewhere on the plain an extensive residential area was also deeply covered by sand, probably during the late Moche IV Phase (Topic 1982). This stratigraphic information, together with the absence of Moche V occupation on and around the Huaca del Sol, suggests that the Cerro Blanco site was largely abandoned by the end of the Moche IV Phase in the context of active sand-dune formation. However, the Huaca de la Luna and its immediate environs appear to have survived this abandonment and continued in use for a considerable time (Bonavia 1985:85–97; Uceda et al. 1994).

The events at the Cerro Blanco site were only one part of a much broader process. During the late Moche IV Phase, a period that we can reasonably correlate with the end of the sixth century AD, sand encroached on the entire south side of the Moche Valley. This destructive advance was in all probability vigorously opposed, the rural farmers of the area and their Cerro Blanco supervisors struggling for years to keep the waterways open and the land clear. Their efforts at stemming the tide ultimately proved in vain. Eventually the life-giving canals were clogged, the fields that they served were abandoned together with the homes of the families that had worked them, and the terrain gradually acquired the barren, desert-like appearance that it presents today. The focus of occupation then moved north of the Moche River, where it has remained ever since.

Further north the situation is less well known. However, the end of the Moche occupation in the imposing Huaca El Brujo complex in the Chicama Valley appears to have been associated with a massive pluvial event (Franco, Gálvez, and Vásquez 1994). In the Jequetepeque Valley recent survey suggests that the south side of the river suffered similar encroachment by windblown sand toward the end of the Moche IV Phase (Eling 1987). If these associations are correct, they distinguish the developments of the Chicama, Jequetepeque, and Moche valleys as parts of a wide environmental phenomenon. Further, in the light of additional lines of evidence that I present below, they suggest that this phenomenon affected other valleys of the North Coast to varying degrees. The consequence of what was probably a long period of sand intrusion was the progressive loss of agriculturally productive land with resulting hardships for the valley populations. Moreover, given the prevailing oceanic wind pattern, the areas closest to the sea would have been most strongly affected, forcing displaced families to move inland to zones where the land was still relatively protected from the onshore winds.

A second type of environmental problem affected Moche societies during the later part of the sixth century: excessive rainfall and consequent flooding of the desert landscape. While Santiago Uceda and his colleagues (Uceda and Amico 1993) have rightly cautioned against causal association of social collapse with the well-documented El Niño phenomena, there are strong suggestions that exceptional inundation played a role in late Moche IV events. We have seen the evidence of deep flooding at the buried platform at the Cerro Blanco site, an event which may be even more dramatically marked by the clear signs of flood damage on the base of the Huaca del Sol itself and related removal of several meters of soil from much of the low-lying parts of the settlement (Moseley 1987). Although the stratigraphic location of the flood deposit above the Moche IV cemetery in the buried platform indicates a later date, this configuration still allows for the inundation to have occurred late in this same phase. If this terminal Moche IV dating for the flood is confirmed, it would add considerable weight to views of the Cerro Blanco site as a settlement that was undergoing extreme environmentally induced stress that resulted in its partial abandonment.

In the Upper Piura drainage Peter Kaulicke (1993), on the basis of geomorphological investigation, has detected several phases of exceptional rainfall. These inundations caused major damage to the monumental architecture of the Nima/Valverde Complex, site of a Moche occupation of the Middle Period (figure 1.1). Kaulicke believes that one of these events occurred in the later sixth century and was a significant factor in the abandonment of the site by the Moche. Thus while a considerable Moche presence persisted in the Upper Piura region (Matos 1965–6: figure 1), the Nima/Valverde data suggests that it was severely interrupted at a date corresponding to the late Moche IV Phase of the central valleys.

A final and most important body of climatic information establishes a framework within which the various lines of evidence can be correlated and interpreted. Izumi Shimada and colleagues have recently summarized the results of extensive analysis of cores from the Quelccaya ice cap in the southern Peruvian highlands and the La Garganta Glacier on the Huascarán Col in the northern highlands (Shimada et al. 1991). Their results have dramatic implications for an understanding of Andean climate in the sixth century. This analysis permits the identification of climatic cycles and, more important for our purposes, distinguishes annual seasonal variations in moisture content. It has thus become possible to compile a long-term precipitation record that extends from AD 500 with only a 20-year range of possible error. This data clearly indicates that the climate of the sixth century was dominated by a series of droughts, smaller ones in the first half of the century and, significantly, a 30-year event encompassing its last third. This drought has been characterized as one of the longest in history and would have caused severe problems in the already arid coastal region.

There are several consequences of such an event. Although farmers can withstand short-term droughts by a variety of irrigation and crop adjustment techniques, persistence of dry conditions for an extended period cannot be countered by these means. Over time, the decline of water in the coastal rivers would have lowered the available water flow, making irrigation of peripheral areas difficult, then impossible. At the same time the lowered water table would allow soil in these areas, especially near the coast, to desiccate, heightening the possibility of erosion by the constant onshore winds or by rare El Niño episodes that may have punctuated the otherwise arid period. This result would be especially probable if the climatic events were of the great magnitude indicated by the Cerro Blanco and Nima/Valverde episodes. We must then accept the strong possibility that persistent climatic disruption afflicted northern coastal societies towards the end of the Middle Period.

This persistent adverse situation would have damaged the economic infrastructure of North Coast societies and exerted pressure on leaders to respond in some fashion to alleviate the accompanying hardships to the population. However, we must realize that even general episodes of environmental trauma affect various areas to different degrees, depending both on local climatic variation and on the level of vulnerability specific to each particular economic system. Moreover, we must recognize that in a situation of social and political diversity like the North Coast in the Middle Period, responses will vary in nature from valley to valley, bringing major change to one area while leaving another relatively unaffected. We cannot place sole reliance on transformations in the physical world when searching for explanations of the large-scale and general cultural changes that are clearly manifested in the Late Period archaeological record. Andean history provides us with evidence of several socially constituted agencies of change.

Foreign pressure: the Wari phenomenon In my discussion of the history of the pre-European Andean regions, I mentioned the intermittent impact of aggressive polities. The Inka built a vast empire through military force, while the contemporary North Coast Chimú, successors of the Moche, similarly conquered a large coastal realm. I also discussed the more direct role of aggression in the history of the Moche and their predecessors, whether in the unrest of Salinar times, the Moche III conquest of the Gallinazo, or the probable conflict between the southern polity and its Recuay neighbors in the south. Disturbances with human origins were therefore another source of threat to societies of the Andes. In fact, there is little doubt that more permanent social disruption can be ascribed to successful conquest by an expansionist polity rather than to accidents of nature.

One of the most complex issues in Andean archaeology is the nature of the Middle Horizon. This relatively brief period, usually presumed to have commenced in the late sixth century AD, has long been associated with the expansion of a highland-centered empire with its capital at Wari in the Ayacucho Basin. Even before the identification of the importance of Wari itself or the invention of the Middle Horizon as a chronological concept, it was recognized that an unusual phenomenon of artistic sharing occurred through much of the greater Andean area beginning at the end of the Moche Middle Period. First labelled the "Tiahuanacoid" expansion by Kroeber, Larco, and their contemporaries, this epoch was marked by the rapid diffusion of a distinctive set of iconographic motifs largely inspired by the imagery of the Gateway of the Sun at Tiahuanaco in Bolivia. This complex was, and still is, believed to have communicated religious meaning. Later, following the realization that another center for the radiation of this imagery existed at Wari, the urban characteristics of this settlement were seen as inspiring those of other large towns, coastal as well as highland, and the concept of an expansionist polity developed with these architectural and artistic traits representing its most obvious material residue.

Although changes in settlement configurations, especially the assumed introduction of Wari-like walled enclosures, have been used as evidence of imperial conquest of the coast in the early Middle Horizon, the most systematic evidence has always been ceramic patterns. Dorothy Menzel, in a series of supremely thorough stylistic studies (1964, 1969, 1977), unassailably demonstrated the occurrence of super-regional sharing of ceramic styles in the Middle Horizon. The period of active dissemination of Wari-related iconography appears to have occurred during a two-century period commencing toward the end of sixth century AD, after which regional societies continued to use attributes originally derived from this phase of innovation in their own separate traditions independent of further outside influence.

According to Menzel's scenario, the period of active Wari expansion was itself composed of two distinct phases. During the initial phase, in Middle Horizon Phase 1B (figure 1.3), Wari influence spread as far north as the Callejón de Huaylas in the highlands and encompassed the southern and central valleys of the Peruvian coast. The expansion was in the form of military conquest accompanied by the establishment of regional administrative centers that contained architectural elements of the capital and a formal state art style that emphasized the religious iconography of Wari. This advance, of course, affected the areas bordering the conquests of the southern Moche polity (figure 7.1). While, on the basis of existing archaeological evidence, and counter to earlier ideas, there appears to have been no direct foreign intrusion into the North Coast region, it is precisely at this time that Moche hegemony collapsed in the southern valleys. David Wilson, who most recently researched this issue in the Santa Valley, suggests that Moche domination of the southern valleys was replaced at the end of the Moche IV Phase by a locally based polity, defined by the distribution of its characteristic black, white, and red decorated ceramics, possibly with its center in the Casma Valley (figures 1.1, 7.1; Wilson 1988:334).

According to Menzel's position, the initial Wari expansion was followed by retrenchment and re-organization of the empire during which the provincial Central Coast center of Pachacamac became prominent as a center of religious ritual, pilgrimage, and political power (see also Shimada 1991 for further discussion of the Middle Horizon coastal chronologies). This was followed by a second phase of expansion in Middle Horizon 2A (figure 1.3), which Menzel believes to have encompassed the northern Peruvian regions.

On the North Coast, Wari-related features, often incorporated into local ceramic or mural decoration, appear in Moche V contexts in the Late Period. In addition they also occur throughout the North Coast in contexts of religious and ceremonial significance that immediately post-date the end of the Moche epoch. These two intrusions may well correspond to the two phases of Wari expansion. Nevertheless it must be stressed that, contrary to Menzel's position, there is no evidence of direct Wari occupation of the North Coast in either period. However, the close chronological correlation of these wider Wari-connected Andean disruptions with Moche retreat from the southern valleys and the later introduction of Wari elements into the region pose the question of linkage.

Internal social stress   There is a third possible source of social disruption that is less visible in Andean history than either natural calamity or external invasion. This is internal social conflict. In the Andean world the civil war that ravaged the Inka Empire prior to the Spanish Conquest provides the only clear example of such structural breakdown (Conrad and Demarest 1984; Patterson 1991). Fought between Huascar and Atahualpa, the conflict was grounded in an unsolvable ideological dilemma that tore the fabric of Inka imperial structure apart and contributed to the easy triumph of Pizarro. Although there can be little doubt that other such examples of internal tension were instrumental in driving social change in earlier Andean history, it is more difficult to reveal their presence through archaeological research. However, we must attempt to do so if the real scale and complexity of social transformation are to be identified.

Every human society exists in a state of tension between the various interest groups composing it. Indeed this very tension promotes the negotiation between individuals and groups that is an active agency for change. The varied and often conflicting ideologies that give groups their identities promote the religious, political, or economic interests of their members. They exist in a state of dynamic tension, always possessing the potential for overt conflict and breakdown but rarely reaching this extreme state of disruption. Usually the institutions of political and social integration prevail through compromise and adjustment to maintain the existing social order. Through this process they not only preserve their own existence but necessarily experience structural change. However, on occasion the prevailing system can no longer accommodate the pressures placed on it within society. This most often occurs in the context of extreme economic or political pressure when the system no longer serves the basic interests of society as a whole or, more importantly, is perceived to have failed in this responsibility. At this point internal tension turns into overt conflict and social breakdown ensues, usually involving rejection of the dominant order.

I suggest internal stress as another possible source of change in the sixth-century Moche world. I have fully described my belief that there was an inherent paradox in the civilizations of the North Coast between the Andean structural principles that ordered the social, economic, and religious systems of indigenous New World peoples in general and the aspirations of their elites to exclusive power (Bawden 1994a, 1995). I discussed this paradox within the theoretical framework of Louis Dumont's thesis of basic tension that exists between holistic and individualizing ideology. An important point to re-emphasize here is that such dichotomy does not mean that exclusive domains of power cannot exist in holistic societies, merely that the field of conflict changes. In Andean society individualizing power was itself couched in principles of communal belief – shamanism, kinship, reciprocity, and ancestral reverence. This did not, however, lessen the impulse among elite groups to separate themselves from the populace at large and exclusively to command access to the ideological and economic sources of political power. They achieved this by manipulating the very principles that underlay holistic social order into the tools of restrictive power. Thus the myths and associated rituals that underscored North Coast social identity and order were transformed into a formal agency of authority, asserted and supported by symbolic codification – the language of power – and its social manifestation through ritual.

In this way the leaders of the various societies that adopted Moche ideology paradoxically achieved their goal of elevated status and power while at the same time separating themselves from the ultimate basis of this power – shared Andean holistic conception. This internal tension would have inevitably raised the likelihood of social conflict, especially at a time of stress. Moreover, this potential would have been heightened in those societies in which the paradox of power was most pronounced. I have described how this extreme degree of internal stress developed in the southern Moche polity. Here in the single instance of wide territorial conquest, leaders used their ideological identification with the traditional sources of structural order to conquer and maintain control of a far-flung, variegated, and hostile domain. They did this without creating new institutions of political authority such as standing military forces and complex administrative structures that would have augmented their personal authority. Clearly, then, the political system that controlled the southern Moche polity was inherently unstable relative to its northern counterparts which did not confront the challenges generated by political expansion. Historically derived sources of social stress, specific to the various local polities whose archaeological manifestations I described in the last chapter, must thus be regarded as a major factor when the causes of Moche V transformation are considered.

There are thus a variety of natural and human forces that can lead to social disruption. When any of these occur in isolation, it is most probable that the leadership of the threatened society can respond through internal adjustment or external defense to prevent structural breakdown. Certainly, there is little evidence to suggest that environmental disruption by itself has ever caused socio-political collapse in the Andes. However, if these pressures occur simultaneously, the chances of the society surviving unscathed are much lower. The challenge of combating foreign pressure at a time when economic and communication infrastructure has been severely weakened is one that will tax the resources of even a well-integrated society to the fullest extent and collapse may well occur.

This combination of circumstances occurred on the north

coast of Peru in the late sixth century AD in the context of prolonged drought, damaging flood, and the rise of Wari power beyond the borders of the region. Compounding these tangible external threats, Moche political structure, with its reliance on individualized power, possessed innate instability. By the end of the sixth century AD Moche rulers lost their ability to manipulate traditional belief systems to sustain their power. The rituals which in Moche belief had for so long ensured fecundity of the land ceased to be effective and people experienced progressive hardship. Traditional Andean societies typically respond to profound disruption by regarding it as punishment for failure to maintain the fundamental religious tenets and practices that underlie all human social life, a pattern recently reflected in the widespread belief that the huge 1970 earthquake was caused by abandonment of traditional religious belief for reformist practice, with ensuing cosmological imbalance (Bode 1989). In the Moche instance, increasing disruptions would have led to the perception that the rulers had offended the deities and ancestral spirits upon whose support depended the security of the human world. Ironically, at this critical juncture the very success of earlier Moche elites in persuading their subjects that social well-being rested on their omnipotence as shaman-leaders maintaining cosmological balance would have acted against them and resulted in their being blamed for the deteriorating situation. Alienation of power from its structural base and absence of mature administrative infrastructure only exacerbated this predicament. The result was rejection of the failed ideology together with the political system that it sustained.

The effects of this development would have been especially severe in the southern polity because of its need to administer a large, discontinuous territory with a potentially hostile population. Here, unlike other areas, the Moche political system was unable to fend off either political disaster or total disillusionment with the traditional religious system, and transformation occurred in both spheres. While this loss of confidence and its related instability was greatest in the south, it affected all areas to some extent, initiating a series of complex and varied impacts that collectively initiated major change throughout the region in the Late Moche Period.

The archaeological record of these diverse phenomena is

uneven. Settlement information largely consists of site data from three important sites – two large towns and an elite burial complex – minor additional survey and excavation data, and negative evidence in the abandoned southern valleys. This field data is complemented by the Moche V ceramic record, formal and iconographic characters of which have been the subjects of various studies over the years. Together these data comprise a body of material culture that enables us to recognize both the effects of the diverse pressures discussed above and the different ways in which Late Moche societies confronted them.

The Form of Change in the Moche Late Period

Transformation in the iconography of power

Ceramic art is again a principal means for identifying and interpreting Late Moche social dynamics in the ultimate phase of Moche history – the Moche V Phase. Pottery vessels bearing the Moche V style are largely missing from the valleys from Virú south. These are the valleys that had previously been conquered by the southern polity at the outset of the Moche IV Phase. Elsewhere, although significant innovations occurred throughout the region, the basic ceramic inventory remains solidly in the Moche tradition. This pattern clearly suggests that the southern valleys were abandoned by the Moche at this time and that retrenchment occurred in the central and northern valleys. The settlement and architectural modifications that accompanied this process allow us better to understand the related social and political changes that occurred in the Late Period.

Changes in the formal and iconographic qualities of elite Moche painted pottery provide important information regarding the nature of social transformation in the Late Period. In technical terms the chief innovation consists of the widespread appearance of blackware vessels alongside the more traditional brown and cream wares (Bawden 1987, 1994b; Shimada 1994a). These black surfaces characterize a variety of vessel forms ranging from conventional stirrup-spout jars and bowls to new forms whose surfaces are embellished with molded designs (figure 9.1), a technique previously uncommon in Moche pottery.

Significant change also occurred in the thematic content of Moche elite ceramic imagery. Various scholars have noted the replacement of numerous iconographic themes at this time by a restricted number of new examples whose significance I shall discuss below. Most striking is the abrupt disappearance of the portrait vessel from the Moche V ceramic inventory of the central valleys where this form had flourished during the heyday of the southern polity. The elimination of a form that symbolized the extreme individualization of power in the southern sector of the region during the Middle Period cannot be ascribed to simple stylistic evolution. This change goes beyond modification of existing style and reflects rejection of a most prominent thematic concept and the meaning that it conferred. In short, it reflects major adjustment in the structure of social

Figure 9.1 Late Moche (Moche V) blackware press-molded vessels from Galindo, Moche Valley.

integration in the Moche V period and the rejection of the prevailing political order of the southern polity as a consequence of the late Moche IV disruptions. We shall see more profound examples of change in other material expressions of political authority.

There was also significant change in the content of mythical representation in Late Moche art. It appears that in some instances, even where traditional themes persisted, their content was altered, a development probably accompanied by change in meaning. One interesting example of this type of change emerged from the Galindo investigations of the 1970s. Here a rare fragment of textile, one of the few examples of iconography of traditional form found at the site, was recovered from an elite residential context. The piece was analyzed by William Conklin who showed it to contain iconographic elements that had been present in earlier Moche symbolism but were here portrayed in very different form. Thus a common pair of supernatural combatants – a human and an anthropomorphized crab – are depicted in combat. However, as Conklin explains, whereas in previous Moche images the combatants are shown of the same size and with characteristic profile heads (figure 9.2), in the Moche V Galindo example the crab-like figure is of gigantic size relative to its antagonist and is portrayed in full front aspect, a very different composition (figure 9.3). It is tempting to interpret the major change in proportion between the protagonists as a manifestation of the southern Moche V ideological transformation, the small size of the human figure being a graphic reflection of the reduced power of traditional mythical heroes or deities. It should be noted that the frontal crab-like figure is of quite similar form to what have been regarded as the later, and possibly Wari-influenced, murals of the Huaca de la Luna at the Cerro Blanco site that I discuss later (see also figure 8.1). This iconographic similarity reflects not only Moche V stylistic convention in the Moche Valley but is also a local manifestation of the more general phenomenon of ideological modification that characterized this period.

More apparent in the record is iconographic replacement. Thus a new series of themes are associated with the enduring Sacrifice Ceremony (figure 4.3). These include the so-called Revolt of the Objects (figure 9.4), the Burial Theme (figure 9.5),

Figure 9.2 Fine-line drawing of confrontation between mythical figure and anthropomorphic crab-like being. (After Squier 1877: 186)

and the Tule Boat Theme (figure 9.6). This complete thematic cycle may well have been employed only in the northern part of the region. On the basis of his analyses, Luis Jaime Castillo, co-excavator of the late Moche component at the site of San José de Moro in the Jequetepeque Valley, believes that all extant examples of the Burial Theme were created in this valley and may not have had region-wide distribution, certainly not in the central or southern valleys. Generally supporting this view are the Late Period Moche Valley data where quite considerable samples of elite decorated pottery have revealed little evidence of the themes of this mythic cycle. We must assume that the new cycle had its chief significance in the northern part of the region and that even here there may have been local variation.

In attempting to understand this late development we must again look at the nature of myth and its role in maintaining social coherence. I have previously remarked that myth, through metaphor and sacred story, represents the origins and

Figure 9.3 Late Moche (Moche V) textile fragment from Galindo, Moche Valley, depicting confrontation between a small figure garbed as a warrior and a giant crab-like being. (Drawn by William Conklin)

internal structures that provide order for a human group. In serving this primary need for stability, myth is basically conservative and resistant to change. However, it is not timeless and immutable. Myth is humanly constructed to serve the fundamental structural needs of a particular society with its own history and cultural conceptions. Myth can be modified by human agency to meet the changing demands of history. There is abundant testimony of the ability of Andean myths to represent and incorporate foreign elements introduced by European conquest, and thereby regularize them in terms of local community needs. By so doing, the effects of the disruptive events associated with conquest, which would otherwise cause intolerable social and psychological stress to individuals and groups

Figure 9.4 Fine-line drawing of the Revolt of the Objects, from the Munich Vase. (After Kutscher 1983, figure 267)

Figure 9.5 Fine-line drawing of Burial Theme. (Redrawn from Donnan and McClelland 1979, figure 6)

Figure 9.6 Fine-line drawing of Tule Boat Theme. (After Kutscher
            1955: 29)

alike, are mitigated by incorporation into a traditional and
familiar frame of conceptual reference that rationalizes them
and often predicts their passing. Further, the appearance of
vitalizing religions as the focus of resistance to the European
conquerors also represents the intentional human modification
of traditional beliefs in response to major historical pressures.

Given the demonstrated capacity of Andean mythic structure
to accommodate change in recent periods, we can confidently
assume that the same quality obtained earlier and can be traced
in the symbolic manifestations of indigenous Andean societies
like the Moche. When examined from this viewpoint, innovation seen in the content of Moche V narrative art can most
validly be interpreted as adjustment in mythic emphasis, undertaken to confront the wide disruptions of the later Moche IV
Phase. It is in this context of profound challenge and response
that the nature of Late Moche ideological development and its
accompanying symbolic manifestation can be best understood.

The Moche V Phase mythic cycle has been discussed by
various scholars (e.g. Berezkin 1980, 1983; Castillo 1991;
Donnan and McClelland 1979; Golte 1994; Quilter 1990).

Even though their specific interpretations of the themes differ to some extent, they all conclude that there were narrative connections between them that embody deeper mythic coherence. Incorporating this thinking with my own, I suggest that the ordered sequence of Revolt–Burial–Sacrifice–Tule Boat represents the mythic foundation of a ritual cycle of renewal created in response to social and political disruption. Motivating this mythic adjustment was the bid by the leaders of Late Moche society to maintain their political preeminence at this difficult juncture. They achieved this to a large extent by identifying themselves and their reconstituted political order with an ideological base that replaced, or at least seriously modified, the earlier discredited system. The fact that the Moche V response varied throughout the region suggests that local leaders differed both in the strategies that they used to consolidate their new power base and in their success.

In the fullest form of the Moche V mythic cycle, the central Sacrifice Ceremony served the vital role of representing historical continuity by linking the unstable present with the enduring structure of North Coast society. It also symbolized triumph over the disorder portrayed in the Revolt Theme (figures 5.6, 9.4), perhaps a visual metaphor for the troubled times of the late sixth century AD. In this theme, which Jeffrey Quilter (1990) has persuasively described as the depiction of chaos, many familiar objects of ceremonial, military, and domestic activity take on lives of their own. Moreover, they battle with, and in some instances vanquish, their human opponents. However, on the famous Munich Vase (figure 9.4), the dominant Warrior Priest – also the central officiant of the Sacrifice Ceremony – appears to be subduing participants in the revolt. This element forecasts the end of disorder, an end that was accomplished through the process of transformation and sacrifice depicted in the subsequent elements of the cycle.

The Burial Theme depicts a transformational event in which death and funerary ritual is the agent (figures 4.12, 9.5; Donnan and McClelland 1979). The central scene is a burial ceremony of an elite individual in an elaborate casket surmounted by a mask of precious metal, a theme that replicates in narrative art the material reality of the Royal Tombs of Sipán. Elsewhere the related sacrifice and exposure of a female victim underlines the transformative nature of the scene while the assembly of various mythic figures and the transportation of ritual items accompanies the series of events surrounding the burial. This complex theme portrays a ceremony in which the central participant moves from the physical to the supernatural realm of human experience, facilitated by ritual violence. In this separated state he supervises the events of the Sacrifice Ceremony, in which the life essence of the subdued forces of chaos was used to mobilize the supernatural in re-establishing social stability through the transformative process of sacrifice.

Finally, in the Tule Boat Theme heroic figures arrive from the sea (figure 9.6; McClelland 1990). The most conspicuous of these individuals is surrounded by a circle of anthropomorphized rays identical to those that encircle the victorious Warrior Priest of the Munich Vase (figure 9.4). I suggest that this correspondence symbolically relates the two figures, possibly identifying them as versions of the same individual. In several examples of this scene the tule boat bears valued wares, the most important of which are bound prisoners, the objects of the sacrificial event which revitalized society. I believe that this theme symbolizes the restoration of order with the arrival in the physical realm of central figures of Moche mythology bearing the economic commodities and sacrificial offerings vital for the complementary aspects of mundane and sacred renewal. This new emphasis on the sea-borne source of social order may foreshadow the very similar myths concerning the origins of later Chimú ruling order as related in the Taycanamo Legend (Rowe 1948). If so, the Tule Boat Theme illustrates not only mythic and ideological readjustment but also the persistence of important mythic themes in the ideological structure of North Coast society. In any case at this juncture the move from chaos to order through the cathartic media of sacrifice, death, and reemergence is accomplished and the cycle is complete.

The Late Moche mythic cycle forcefully recapitulated on the symbolic plane the Moche IV–V transition and proclaimed the restorative role of myth. Moreover, associated ritual enactment brought this restorative function into the physical world and asserted the political power of myth. By ritually entering the sacred space and time of myth, elite officiants effected the reconstitution of society. At the climax of the cycle the transformative power of sacrificial blood provided the officiants with the supernatural force which allowed them to re-establish order from chaos. Through the transitional phases of the final rituals, the sacralized principals re-entered the social sphere imbued with renewing spiritual power. In this way the ritual cycle vitalized society and ideologically established the right of its officiants to political authority.

Late Moche settlement

Late Period settlement survey suggests that, with the critical exception of withdrawal from the southern valleys, the overall Moche settlement distribution remained much the same. In the Moche, Chicama, and Jequetepeque valleys Moche occupation probably encompassed the entire valley. Further north in the valleys of the greater Lambayeque complex, Moche domination of the middle segments was accompanied by non-Moche occupation both inland and along the coast where societies of the Gallinazo tradition still persisted. However, Izumi Shimada suggests that, following the Moche recovery from the effects of the Phase IV disruptions in the Lambayeque Valley, rulers at the Late Moche center of Pampa Grande conquered their Gallinazo neighbors (figure 7.1; Shimada 1994b), forcing the subjugated population to construct the greatest monument to their revived power. In the far north, Moche occupation also continued in the Upper Piura drainage. Apart from surface survey that outlines the general picture of Late Moche settlement, more specific site investigation at the towns of Galindo in the Moche Valley and Pampa Grande in the Lambayeque Valley (figure 1.1), both established inland at the necks of their respective valleys, and the smaller Jequetepeque Valley settlement of Jose de Moró with its spectacular elite burials, provide much information regarding the nature of both continuity and change in the Late Moche Period.

The Moche Valley The greater part of the Cerro Blanco site, including the Huaca del Sol and much of the residential area located on the adjacent plain, was abandoned at the end of the Middle Period in the context of environmental and social disruptions. However, there was one exception to this pattern of abandonment. Active use of the Huaca de la Luna as a focus of ceremonial activity may have continued without a break into the Late Period, while some limited residential occupation may have persisted along the nearby slopes of Cerro Blanco (Uceda et al. 1994). The higher elevation of these sites would have afforded greater protection from the water damage that affected the remainder of the settlement, thus ameliorating the environmental component of the Moche IV disruptions. While there is some disagreement on the matter, it is possible that the later murals of the Huaca de la Luna incorporated Wari imagery from outside the region (figure 8.1; Bonavia 1985; Mackey and Hastings 1982; but see Uceda et al. 1994 for a dissenting view), a development that suggests attempts by the Moche Valley rulers to transfer their ideological authority to a new foundation, attempts that I believe were unsuccessful.

The former political capital of the southern Moche polity was thus largely transformed into a specialized ceremonial site with a much restricted resident population. The center of residential occupation and political administration moved to a new location. Galindo (figure 1.1; Bawden 1977, 1978, 1982a, 1982b), located on the north side of the Moche Valley at the junction of the broad coastal plain and the narrow upper reaches almost 20 miles from the sea, was the largest settlement in the Moche Valley in the Late Period. Occupying the slopes of Cerro Galindo and the plain at its foot, the town at its greatest extent covered an area of almost 6 square kilometers (figure 9.7). While there had been earlier Moche settlement at the site in the form of a small village, Moche V Galindo was essentially a new Late Period establishment. The town stood adjacent to the main trunk canal, in an ideal situation to control its flow and the watering of fields to the north of the Moche River.

As the dominant center of the Moche Valley, Galindo was a very different type of settlement from its earlier southern counterparts with their dominant platforms and specialized populations of administrators and retainers. The town displayed an urban quality that was only matched by its northern Moche V counterpart, Pampa Grande. It contained a population of several thousand individuals housed in residential areas which in size and density surpassed any previous Moche Valley

Figure 9.7 Oblique air photo of the Late Moche city of Galindo, Moche Valley, as it appeared in the 1930s. Note the large wall running along the base of Cerro Galindo (A–A), separating low status residential areas (B) from the rest of the site; walls (C) isolating elaborate residential architecture (D) located on the quebrada terrace at center; burial platform and associated compound enclosure in bottom right corner (E) with a small platform of traditional form directly above (F); innovative cercadura *complexes on the ridge at center left and center (G). Corporate storage terraces with restricted access are located on the hillside in the distance (H). (Courtesy Department of Library Services, American Museum of Natural History, negative number 334935. Photo: Shippee-Johnson)*

settlement. Residential occupation was strictly segregated by location, by size and architectural elaboration, and by the quality of subsistence and material possessions of the occupants, a strong indication of status inequality. This suggestion is reinforced by the fact that the occupants of lowest-status homes, standing on the steep slopes of Cerro Galindo, were barred by a substantial wall from ready access to water sources and their fellow residents (figure 9.7). Moreover, analysis of the content of cooking refuse demonstrates that these lower-status residents consumed a considerably smaller amount of protein through llama meat than their counterparts. Interestingly, the homes of some of the higher elite were also secluded from the rest of the population by high walls. However, in their case these walls enclosed the principal locations of government, symbolizing and physically asserting their position at the apex of authority.

The physical centers of authority at Galindo also differed greatly from their predecessors. While platforms of similar form to those of the Huaca del Sol were constructed at the new town, they were of minuscule size and located at the periphery of the site, changes that suggest major modification in the social role of this form. Replacing the platform as the dominant symbol of power at the center of the settlement was an architectural structure – the *cercadura* – whose innovative features indicate that it was the site of activities of quite different aspect from those centered at the great platforms of the Middle Period. Most significantly, *cercaduras* eschewed visual access for seclusion. Whereas the ramps, terraces, and summits of the platform comprised large open stage-like surfaces for ceremonies that were fully visible to the surrounding world, the high perimeter walls of *cercaduras* enclosed smaller, compartmentalized spaces that were hidden from public view. In general, then, the rulers of Galindo no longer used public ritual centered on the platform with its earlier powerful supernatural connotations as the central tool of political control, an indication of profound change in the strategy of power and its ideological base.

One other major architectural innovation appeared at Galindo as a manifestation of the Moche V transition. A complex that may have housed the paramount ruler of Galindo contained not only a large domestic component but also a large burial platform, now severely looted (figure 9.8). Both of these units were enclosed within a high wall, pierced by a single elaborate but baffled gateway, whose interior surface was adorned by a polychrome mural. This configuration clearly differs from earlier practice as seen at Sipán, where the burial platform was associated solely with structures of high ceremonial rather than residential status. I and others (Bawden 1982a: Conrad 1974; Kolata 1978; see McEwen 1990 for a dissenting view) have suggested that this complex is a prototype for the much more elaborate palace structures of the later Chimú leaders. The Chimú capital at Chan Chan contains a number of such structures, each primarily marking a generation of leadership. If the same association pertains to Galindo, its burial platform may well have housed a single ruler and possibly his retainers, a situation that would indicate that the town was only occupied for a relatively short period. This suggestion is supported by its uniform architectural style and little evidence of remodelling.

The appearance of the burial platform/palace complex was only the most prominent instance of funerary innovation.

Figure 9.8 Burial platform/elite residential complex, Galindo, Moche Valley. (Photo: Garth Bawden 1971)

Nowhere at Galindo is there evidence of extensive cemeteries, the looted remains of which are omnipresent at earlier Moche sites. Instead two new mortuary practices appear. One comprises in-house burial. In this case, individuals were usually interred with only modest accompanying goods in the stone-faced benches that flank the walls of domestic living spaces (figure 9.9). This practice must have inspired a great sense of the immanence of ancestral presence in the families of Galindo, one that fully conforms to Andean belief structure. In addition, small clusters of stone-lined chamber burials were located in open areas between the houses. The quality and size of funerary

Figure 9.9 Adult male burial with body turned to the side and slightly flexed. Located within a Moche V room bench which has been fully excavated apart from front and back walls, Galindo, Moche Valley. (Photo: Garth Bawden 1973)

possessions indicates that individuals interred in these chamber tombs were of higher status than those buried in their homes. The dimension of change relating to burial at Galindo is heightened by the fact that many of the Galindo burials were of individuals lying on their sides in extended or partly-flexed position (figure 9.9). This posture is almost never present in earlier Moche burials and suggests significant modification in religious belief represented by funerary ritual.

Finally, a large area of corporate storage was built on terraces on a spur of Cerro Galindo, protected from general access by flanking gullies and a succession of high walls. This terrace storage contained numerous large ceramic jars with wide mouths, most suitable for the accommodation of subsistence goods. Here for the first time is unassailable evidence of large-scale storage, constructed and controlled by the ruling authority. Thus, at Galindo economic innovation joins transformations in political, religious, and social domains to emphasize the magnitude of cultural change that affected the southern and central valleys in the Moche Late Period.

The Lambayeque Valley   Although at first glance the magnitude of change in the northern valley of Lambayeque appears to have matched that of the Moche Valley, deeper examination reveals a substantial degree of continuity. The city of Pampa Grande, like Galindo, was a large urban settlement established over a short period of time at the neck of its valley without any significant local antecedent (figure 1.1; Anders 1981; Shimada 1976, 1978, 1994a). This town far exceeds Galindo, or any other known Late Moche settlements, in the density of its extensive residential zones, the size of its monumental architecture, and the formal planning that pervades its huge corporate center (figures 9.10, 9.11). Indeed, it is because of these urban qualities that Pampa Grande has often been regarded as the capital of a reconstituted late Moche state, following the decline of the Cerro Blanco site and the loss of the southern valleys.

The core of government at Pampa Grande is a vast corporate precinct which contains several units of elaborate architecture that were the loci of community administration and religious integration (figures 9.10, 9.11). The functional and formal

Figure 9.10 Plan of the Moche V city of Pampa Grande, Lambayeque Valley. A: Huaca Fortaleza standing within its complex of walled enclosures; H and D mark sectors of elite residence and craft production with regulated access; K is an area of dense residential occupation; the Southern Pediment marks the large semi-segregated peripheral sector of the city where the subjected Gallinazo populace was located. (Courtesy Izumi Shimada)

compartmentalization of these architectural units suggests the presence of a highly differentiated and well-integrated managerial structure. Enclosed within the perimeter walls of the central precinct were a number of specialized craft workshops which produced the metal and ceramic symbols of high status. These workshops were of standardized architectural plan and careful

Figure 9.11 Oblique air photo of Huaca Fortaleza, Pampa Grande, Lambayeque Valley. The huge platform stands in the complex of walled enclosures that comprise the central precinct of the city, with dense residential architecture beyond. (Courtesy Izumi Shimada)

construction as befitted the locations of activities important to broader social integration. Given the central role of their products in asserting Moche social order it is not surprising that access to these workshops was indirect and guarded.

Impressive and informative though these sites of specialized craft production are, they do not by themselves reveal the full nature of Late Moche political reconstitution in the Lambayeque Valley. These industrial facilities, together with the rest of Pampa Grande and the nearby valley segments, are dominated by the monumental complex that stands at the heart of the corporate precinct of Pampa Grande. This complex comprises a series of enclosures and platforms dominated by the vast structure variously named the Huaca Grande or Huaca Fortaleza (figures 9.11, 9.12; Haas 1985; Shimada 1994a). Huaca Fortaleza is one of the largest single architectural units erected in the precolumbian New World. This gigantic platform stands 38 meters high, covers an area of 270 by 180 meters, and is approached by a broad central ramp. It is formally associated with other large platforms in a well-planned architectural complex that dominates the surrounding countryside (figures 9.10, 9.11). More significantly it epitomizes the capacity of the rulers of Pampa Grande to mobilize great construction forces and to assert their power publicly.

Izumi Shimada (1994a), one of the investigators of Pampa Grande, believes that Huaca Fortaleza, and the town itself, was constructed over a short period of time. The platforms are uniform in style and do not reveal the numerous construction stages that characterize the Huaca del Sol in the Moche Valley. They were built by the chamber-and-fill construction method, in which the core of the structure comprises a "honeycomb" of rectangular walled cells filled with rubble. This technique eliminates the need for the vast number of adobe bricks and painstaking bricklaying process required by the earlier southern structures and illustrates a northern procedure that permitted the erection of huge monuments in a relatively economical and rapid manner. This architectural configuration suggests that, like Galindo, Pampa Grande was established hastily in response to the pressures that afflicted North Coast societies in the late sixth century AD. We shall see, however, that this northern social reconstitution appears to have been more successful than its Moche Valley counterpart.

On the community level, the urban plan of Pampa Grande suggests a greater degree of stability than at Galindo. The extreme measures taken by the Galindo rulers to separate themselves from the rest of the community and to segregate the bulk of the population into peripheral and walled habitation zones is absent at Pampa Grande. The largest segment of Pampa Grande's occupants, believed by Shimada to be the subjected Gallinazo population of the Lambayeque Valley, were housed in the huge southern sector (figure 9.10). They were not isolated

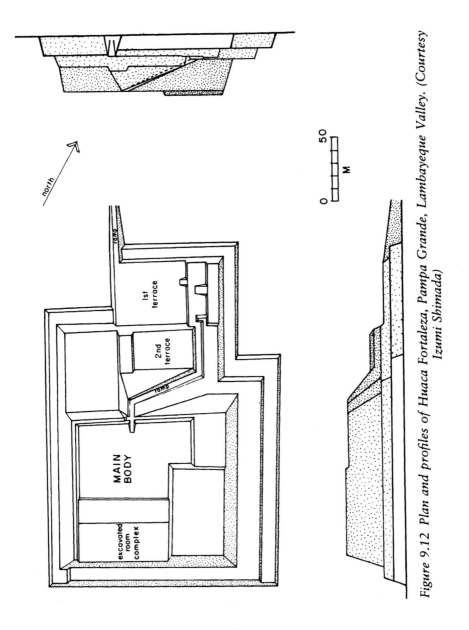

Figure 9.12 Plan and profiles of Huaca Fortaleza, Pampa Grande, Lambayeque Valley. (Courtesy Izumi Shimada)

north

MAIN
BODY

excavated
room
complex

1st
terrace

2nd
terrace

ramp

ramp

0

50

M

by walls or blocked from easy passage into or from the town as was the bulk of Galindo's populace. Moreover, other dense areas of probable non-elite residential occupation spread unhindered across the western sectors of Pampa Grande. Only around the central precinct itself is there clear evidence of architectural exclusivity. This pattern suggests that the leaders of the town felt secure in their authority and that their power was grounded in precepts that were accepted by the population that they ruled. There was thus little overt social tension and no need to use the manmade environment for control to the degree seen at Galindo.

The Jequetepeque Valley The third and, to date, only other Late Moche location that has been intensively investigated is the site of San José de Moro. This site is situated in the northern part of the lower Jequetepeque Valley near the Río Chamán (figure 1.1). Today San José stands adjacent to the main north–south coastal road, the Panamerican Highway, a strategic location now as it was in the Late Moche Period. Moreover, given the fact that the Jequetepeque Valley has always been one of the foremost natural highways to the highlands, San José was well placed to take advantage of the benefits accruing from long-distance traffic. Its location on the northern border of the Jequetepeque Valley offered a further advantage in the Late Moche era. We have seen that the southern banks of the valley, like that of the Moche Valley, were afflicted by sand-dune encroachment late in the Moche IV Phase (Eling 1987). It is probable that the impact of this natural phenomenon, driven as it was by prevailing onshore winds blowing from the southwest, did not extend to the northern reaches of the coastal plain, leaving San José in a choice position to command and utilize the agricultural potentials of its surrounding area.

San José has been the focus of intensive ongoing research by Luis Jaime Castillo of the Pontificia Universidad Católica del Peru and Christopher Donnan of the University of California, Los Angeles (Castillo 1993; Castillo and Donnan 1994; Donnan and Castillo 1992, 1994, 1995). Their investigations reveal that the site was occupied continuously through much of the Moche period. Although residential architecture is not well preserved, the associated domestic remains yielded an abundant ceramic inventory that permitted confirmation of the distinctive nature of Moche stylistic development in the valley. Most significantly, San José was also a major ceremonial, and probably political, center in the Late Moche Period. A complex of adobe brick platforms and associated patios were the site of the important rituals that lay at the heart of Moche political practice. In its composition the Late Moche settlement, while of significant size and undoubted great importance, does not present the appearance of dense urban conglomeration that characterizes its Lambayeque and Moche Valley counterparts, maintaining instead a more traditional form. Nor, of course, was San José a new establishment like the other towns. These formal contrasts at once differentiate San José from Galindo and Pampa Grande and suggest that it largely escaped the most dramatic changes that affected some other areas of the North Coast in the late sixth century AD.

The funerary component of the ceremonial precinct of San José, a later counterpart to the great Sipán tombs, has provided important new data regarding the nature of Late Moche social organization. The large burial inventory at the site indicates a strong correlation between social position of the interred and the quality of their accompanying burial goods, with a range of statuses being represented. This situation generally conforms to the pattern displayed by other Moche settlements of the Middle and Late Periods. However, the highest-status examples, located in the ceremonial precincts and consisting of huge adobe-walled chambers roofed with large timbers, number among the most elaborate ever recovered on the North Coast. More importantly, their contents represent a unique body of Moche social and religious information.

I have previously discussed the importance of the principal occupants of the elaborate tombs at San José de Moro. Two of these individuals in life played the vital ritual role of the priestess in the Sacrifice Ceremony (figure 4.3). In death, like the occupants of the Sipán tombs, they were buried with the symbols of their social status, thereby introjecting their importance into the afterlife (figure 4.4). As sacred repositories of the supernatural power inherent in Moche myth, they served as permanent bulwarks of the political order whose ideology they had ritually manifested during their lives. Generally the San José burials conform to the pattern that we have seen at the Middle Moche tombs of Sipán. However, the difference in form of the later burials and in the identity of their occupants may well denote local ideological variation or temporal change in the focus of Moche ideology, even in those valleys like the Jequetepeque where a significant degree of continuity is apparent.

Other features of the San José burials provide more evidence of the distinctive nature of ideological and social development during the Late Moche Period in the Jequetepeque Valley. As at Pampa Grande, though not at Galindo, the resulting innovations reveal the attempt by a ruling elite to perpetuate traditional strategies of power. However, they also clearly demonstrate that this endeavor was only partially successful and that significant change was necessary to ensure the continuity of Moche power. As I have already intimated, the actual form of change in the Jequetepeque Valley differs from that at Pampa Grande, indicating the operation of local traditions and circumstances.

Castillo and Donnan's work has shown that the San José burials contained an unparalleled concentration of non-Moche ceramic vessels and traits. Nowhere on the North Coast in earlier periods, or in contemporary Moche V sites, is there such evidence for the importation and replication of foreign material symbols of high status. Vessels of the contemporary Teatino, Nievería, and Pachacamac styles of the central coast, of the south coast Pacheco and Atarco traditions (figure 9.13), and of highland Wari and Cajamarca origin, were found in the tombs

---

Figure 9.13 Examples of foreign pottery styles that appeared on the North Coast during and immediately following the Moche V Phase. A: Middle Horizon Period 2 Provincial Wari vessel from Huaca Soledad, Batan Grande, La Leche River Valley. B: Middle Horizon Period 2 Provincial Wari vessel looted from San José de Moro, Jequetepeque Valley. C: Fragment of Middle Horizon Period 2 Provincial Wari Atarco-style vessel looted from San José de Moro. (Courtesy Izumi Shimada)

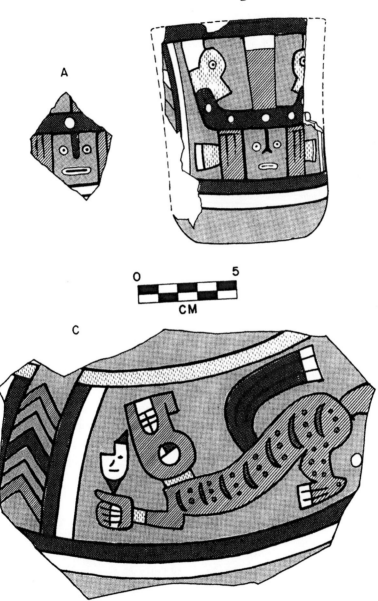

of the highest elite, while less fine local replications occurred in the burials of individuals of lower status. Significantly, these styles were heavily influenced by ideological symbolism associated with the central highland center of Wari, whose influence was affecting much of the Andean world at this juncture. This distribution demonstrates two important points. First, it shows that the rulers of the Jequetepeque Valley had created effective and independent long-distance connections for the procurement of foreign status items. Second, the use of such items as part of funerary ritual shows a ruling group incorporating foreign elements into the continuing local ideological complex.

This latter point reveals that the San José leaders, in common with other Moche V rulers, were effecting ideological adjustment in order to maintain their power. Like the rulers at Pampa Grande they attempted this adjustment within the context of traditional concepts of authority and their public symbolism, anchoring their innovations in a core element of North Coast mythic belief as embodied in the Sacrifice Ceremony. Nevertheless, it appears that significant change did occur at San José. Here, as elsewhere, traditional Moche ideology was partially discredited, forcing a resort to new concepts. I suggest that by utilizing outside symbols of transcendent and pan-Andean religious import to support a threatened ideology, Jequetepeque Valley elites emulated their predecessors of the Chavín Horizon. However, such a recourse brought its own danger. Castillo has stressed the ultimate negative impact of the introduction of foreign objects into the ideological system. For the first time Moche leaders let the production and circulation of material ideology slip from their own grasp. They became increasingly dependent on foreign producers for the symbols of highest significance, while local replicators produced those of lesser status. I suggest that this loss of control would tend to weaken the potency of an ideological complex that had for centuries reproduced itself from the cultural beliefs of North Coast peoples, thus countering the short-term recovery that it undoubtedly generated. Consequently, although the Jequetepeque Valley appears to have suffered the least amount of Late Moche disruption, it shared in the regional structural crisis that in the long run took its toll on the vitality of Moche civilization.

Reconstitution in the Late Moche Period

It is always tempting to confine history within manageable categories with defining characteristics that can be easily described and with boundaries neatly delineated by events and calendrical dates. In practice human social change does not conform to such orderly structures. So it is with the Late Moche. Although the events and pressures that caused regional change on the North Coast in the late sixth and early seventh centuries AD can be identified as general phenomena, we have seen that their impact was far from uniform. Similarly, the response by local Moche rulers to threats to their power resulting from these pressures was directed by the specific contingencies of their particular physical, social, and historical circumstances, and varied accordingly. In the final section of this chapter I will explore in greater detail the final phase of Moche civilization, one of reconstitution and recovery following the difficult times of the late sixth century. I will examine the precise reasons for the differential nature of this reconstitution and its meaning in the context of the continuing history of North Coast societies.

The limits of Late Moche recovery were set by the ability of Late Moche elites to control the conflicting forces of continuity and change to their own advantage in a context of social tension from within and economic and political pressures from without. One can of course see broadly shared qualities in the Late Moche recovery. On the most general level, ideological adjustment was the central element of the Moche V developments. A new mythic cycle emerged to mediate the past disruption through ritual transformation and vitalization. However, in its most complete form this cycle may only have been fully adopted in the north with its center in the Jequetepeque Valley, undoubtedly a continuing focus for the important Sacrifice Ceremony and the area that Castillo has posited as the chief origin for representations of the Late Moche Period Burial Theme. Even within the northern valleys there appears to have been considerable variation in the precise nature of local ideological innovation, with the most drastic change occurring in the Moche Valley. The distinct local courses of social and political development that characterized the earlier period persisted in the latest Moche phase.

The most extreme effects of Moche IV Phase decline were felt in the southern part of the region. First, the political impact is evident. This was the area in which Middle Moche leaders ruled supreme from their great political and religious center at the Cerro Blanco site in the Moche Valley. The most dramatic change of the period occurred in this area with the Moche loss of the southern valleys and the accompanying collapse of the multi-valley polity of which they had composed the greatest part. I have suggested that Moche political structure, with its lack of complex administrative and coercive infrastructure and consequent reliance on the ideologically constructed status of ruling individuals, was ill-prepared to maintain such a large territorial hegemony in the face of major pressure. A combination of environmental disruption and outside political pressure in the late sixth century AD would therefore have prepared the way for the ejection of the Moche from the southern valleys and their replacement by an autonomous polity, in all probability hostile to its former northern rulers.

The economic disruptions in the south were much greater than elsewhere. Prior to the collapse of its political hinterland, the small Moche Valley was able to draw on the subsistence resources of the subject valleys in addition to its own limited resources. The exploitation of settlement and agricultural land in the Santa Valley during the Middle Moche occupation which David Wilson (1988) has detailed clearly demonstrates this manipulation of economic resources. With the disruptions of the late Moche IV Phase, not only was this entire economic sphere lost, but the southern part of the Moche Valley itself fell out of production due to the effects of sand encroachment. This massive blow was probably magnified by the resulting need to support displaced Moche settlers ejected from the southern valleys. This shock was not felt further north where Moche polities were relatively small in size, where no political collapse occurred, and where the only land reduction was that due to limited sand encroachment.

Thus the status of the Moche Valley changed dramatically as

a consequence of these major changes in the political and economic domains. With the loss of its role as the hub of a large territorial polity, it was transformed into a peripheral zone on the southern border of a region still dominated by Moche societies. Moreover, it was probably threatened by its erstwhile subjects to the south and beset by considerable internal pressure resulting from inflated population and loss of agricultural land. It was therefore inevitable that such widespread disturbances on the material plane would be integrally associated with profound change in the ideological sphere that had promoted and justified the successes of the Middle Moche southern polity and formed the basis of its central political power.

It was in the Moche Valley that individualizing ideology reached the zenith of its effectiveness in the Middle Moche period. Lacking a complex administrative system, leaders ritually manipulated Andean structural principles of ancestry, spiritual continuity, and shamanism to create personal power. However, in their very success lay weakness. By focusing social integration on their own persons, leaders qualitatively separated themselves from the society that they ruled, creating a deep structural contradiction. Furthermore, they raised the dangerous possibility that, in the absence of a broader infrastructure, failure would be solely ascribed to them and the political ideology with which they established and maintained power. It appears that the late Moche IV Phase breakdown brought this potential danger to reality. Ensuing structural crisis was so great that the traditional ideological fabric was irreparably torn. Attempting to regain control, leaders rejected the discredited traditional ideology and the symbols that proclaimed and actively constructed it in the social realm. Although many specific features of traditional Moche iconography and architecture were used in the Late Moche Period at Galindo, they appeared as part of different symbolic systems in new social contexts. The codified signs that comprised the "words" of the Moche symbolic language were now recombined and supplemented with new examples to form a new text with a very different meaning.

At Galindo, the manifestations of the attempt by the leaders of the central valleys to reconstitute order are dramatic. Ceramic analysis suggests that iconographic changes are even more extreme than further north. Little evidence of the Moche

V mythic cycle is found there. Religious change radically transformed burial practice. However, it is in the Galindo settlement
plan that the form of Moche V transformation in the central
valleys is most evident. In the architecture of social domination,
cercaduras possessing little historical basis or traditional meaning replaced the platforms as dominant symbols of the new
order. Likewise, a single innovative burial mound suggests the
presence of a paramount ruler without obvious predecessors or
successors. But it is the overwhelming use of spatial enclosure
that best describes the changes in these new architectural forms.
Whereas earlier Moche centers were dominated by great platforms whose overall forms were built to be seen and whose
various activity spaces consisted of open ramps, terraces, and
platform summits, the loci of ceremonial, religious, and administrative activity at Galindo were surrounded and hidden by tall
walls.

The same emphasis on compartmentalization and enclosure
characterizes the town as a whole. Long walls both segregated
the extensive low-status population of Galindo and protected
the residences of the elite from ready access. The movement
of the inhabitants of Galindo was constantly controlled by these
architectural barriers. Whether they ranked among the privileged minority who directed the affairs of the community from
behind the walls of the *cercaduras*, which were themselves
internally compartmentalized, or were members of the vastly
larger lower-status population, the daily lives of the occupants
of Galindo were dominated by the physical manifestations of
control and separation. The contrast of Galindo spatial planning with that of earlier and contemporary settlements is much
too great to be explained by any evolutionary scheme of linear
change. Rather it represents the conscious attempt of a threatened ruling group to impose control by radical physical innovation when traditional ideological methods had failed. The
extreme degree of social segregation reflected by the residential
occupation indicates that these changes occurred in the context
of social stress and structural change.

It appears, then, that in the context of profound political
stress Galindo rulers rejected traditional forms of power to a
degree not seen further north. The very establishment of a large
town broke the tradition of specialized administrative-religious

centers. Urbanism in this context must be seen as a radical response to social crisis, not as the result of smooth evolutionary change. The picture suggests that the resulting society existed in a state of instability in which an embattled elite ruled a highly differentiated population largely through coercion detached from Andean structural sanction. I assume that in this situation the military group within the elite now became the enforcers of the new order. While warriors in Moche culture were always associated with religious ritual, there had been greater emphasis on military coercion in the south than in the northern polities since the conquests of the Moche III Phase. With the removal of its historical religious basis this military resource was now utilized to further a secularized and purely coercive purpose at Galindo. But with power no longer masked by ideology and the foundations of society eroded, structural stress became progressively more explicit. The Galindo polity was vulnerable to complete collapse at the next major crisis. Ironically, with the final removal of structural constraints on power in the context of what can superficially be construed as the triumph of individualizing ideology, Moche Valley society was at its weakest and ripe for the dissolution that occurred within a few decades.

Elsewhere the nature of Late Moche change was substantially different. Although the northern valleys shared the climatic disruptions that afflicted the entire region, they did not experience the catastrophic blows that destroyed the southern polity. None of the northern Moche societies suffered the type of political collapse that transformed the Moche Valley from the center of an eight-valley dominion into a threatened frontier zone which appears to have had significant problems controlling its own political destiny. In fact Izumi Shimada proposes that, following the consolidation of the town of Pampa Grande, Moche V political influence in the Lambayeque Valley actually expanded to include Gallinazo-derived communities that had previously maintained their autonomy (1994a:175–6). Disruption in the Jequetepeque Valley appears in general to have been even less severe; there is no evidence for major demographic realignment like that which occurred elsewhere. In the absence of any permanent loss of major production zones like that which afflicted the south, northern areas were able to surmount the economic depression resulting from prolonged environmental stress without recourse to the profound transformation that characterized the brief existence of Galindo.

In fact, Late Moche developments in the central valleys are best described in terms of transformation while those to the north emphasized a large degree of continuity. Whereas at Galindo most material expressions of earlier political ideology were repudiated, the rulers of Pampa Grande and San José de Moro asserted their authority through symbols that possessed profound meaning and considerable time depth within the historical framework of traditional Moche ideology. The built environment at Galindo proclaimed an abrupt break with the past but the omnipresent platforms of the northern communities, even when built in a new urban settlement as at Pampa Grande, carried the continuity of past Moche culture into the changing world of the seventh century AD. In the south a rejected ideological system was replaced by the overt enforcement of social control in all aspects of community life. By contrast, the northern societies continued to use the ritual enactment of traditional myth as a vital component of their power with the stabilizing constancy that this entailed.

The northern reliance on continuity is probably most visible in the awesome presence at Pampa Grande of the Huaca Fortaleza. Here, Late Moche rulers of the Lambayeque Valley created an organizational system which incorporated an urban settlement of unprecedented size and complexity. In light of the holistic world-view of Andean peoples of the North Coast, this concentration of power may have laid the foundations for future social tension. However, in the short term it effectively sustained political cohesion. The basis of recovery is revealed by Huaca Fortaleza, the central symbol of power, erected in the center of the settlement and dominating the surrounding landscape for miles. Bearing murals that proclaimed the ideological core of power, this huge platform manifested the ability of local elites to reconstruct power by harnessing the force of cultural continuity embodied in symbolic form. By using this powerful symbol of traditional, undifferentiated, North Coast authority as the integrative focus of a complex urban system, the Late Moche rulers at Pampa Grande effected a structural transformation and appropriated exceptional political control, both ends that at best were only partially achieved at Galindo.

However, we cannot simply regard Late Moche reconstitution in the north as a unitary phenomenon to be understood through comparison with the southern situation or in terms of a general northern Moche strategy of statecraft. The archaeological record suggests otherwise. While the underlying currents of continuity in the presence of change connect the Late Moche societies of the Jequetepeque and Lambayeque valleys and set them apart from that of the Moche Valley, in the details of their attempts to bring about reconstitution they differ significantly. The inhabitants of the Jequetepeque Valley were not forced to abandon their settlements like their counterparts in other valleys. Without having to confront the dissatisfaction and hardship entailed by such displacement, it was easier for the leaders of San José de Moro to maintain a more traditional basis of power. This involved preserving the focal status of the Sacrifice Ceremony, albeit with a possible change of emphasis toward the role of the Priestess, at the center of a modified mythic and ritual cycle. The chief innovation in the Jequetepeque Valley was adoption of foreign elements infused with pan-Andean symbolic value to bolster the threatened authority. Apart from this incorporation of Wari-derived elements, continuity of Moche ideology was largely maintained. The situation at Pampa Grande reveals a different solution in the context of greater demographic disruption. Here, in a very new organizational context, foreign features were not utilized. The ruling elite used the construction of the great architectural symbol Huaca Fortaleza both as a focus for social cohesion, and to endow their changes with the aura of ideological continuity. Thus while the strategy used was similar in the two northern areas, the methods were different.

I suggest that these varied responses were historically shaped. First, the societies of the three valleys, though sharing a general cultural tradition, evolved distinct ideological strategies to serve different political goals during the long Moche epoch. Thus the extensive territorial expansion of the southern polity inspired an ideology of power that is unique in its degree of personalized focus, a factor reflected in its related symbolism. Conversely the

However, while each particular society took its own course toward recovery, a common theme was manipulation of the ideological basis of authority. This occurred whether in the dramatic context of political collapse and population disruption in the south, of economic re-organization and urban formation in the Lambayeque Valley, or in the relative demographic and settlement stability seen elsewhere. It is this widespread development in the domain of political structure that, more than any other development no matter how strikingly documented in the archaeological record, heralded the final decline of the Moche political systems.

Two important features characterize Late Moche political decline. The first is that the extent of transformation at the end of the Late Period was directly related to the degree with which various Moche societies maintained their connection to traditional ideological structure. Thus the greatest degree of reconstitution and stability occurred in the northern societies. Here we see Moche belief and symbolism reconstituted at the great Huaca Fortaleza at Pampa Grande and projected into the changed circumstances of the Late Period. Even greater continuity is suggested by the prominence of the Sacrifice Ceremony at San José de Moro. By contrast, the southern rejection of the basic forms of earlier Moche religious and political control accompanied extreme internal stress and social breakdown. Here, in the Moche Valley, leaders could no longer call on the unifying qualities of shared religious belief to bridge the growing gap between holistic and individualizing ideologies and mask the deep southern Moche social contradiction. Rejection of the conceptual base of political authority caused a disjuncture that could not be healed by recourse to wider ideological systems. Only coercion and physical control remained to the leaders at Galindo as the fragile basis of authority. Consequently, collapse when it ultimately occurred was far more complete than in the northern societies.

The second factor involved in the final Moche decline lay in the precise source of ideological innovation. In two of the valleys – Moche and Jequetepeque – there is evidence in the Late Period of the adoption of features derived from beyond the North Coast. In the Lambayeque Valley, this only occurred following the abandonment of the great Late Moche center of

Pampa Grande. There were, thus, two episodes of foreign influence, one during the Moche V Phase and one following its end. The first of these phases of foreign influence was marked by the importation and replication of foreign vessels and adoption of stylistic motifs and decorative techniques that had originated in the religious art of the Wari polity and had been brought to the Central Coast as a consequence of its expansion. The second phase, which followed the end of the Late Period, saw the use of complex Wari religious imagery in the previous centers of Moche power and a more widespread occurrence of elite Wari-related ceramic material.

The Late Moche Period temporally spans the first two phases of the Middle Horizon period of Andean chronology (figure 1.3). It was during the second part of Middle Horizon 1 (Middle Horizon 1B), dating to the seventh century AD, that the first wave of Wari expansion occurred. This correlation probably indicates the source and time-frame of Wari features that were incorporated into northern coastal culture by local Moche V societies of the Late Period. Following a pause, a second phase of Wari expansion probably commenced during the terminal decades of the Late Moche period and continued into the subsequent Middle Horizon 2B Phase. This accompanied the more prominent replacement of Moche by Wari-related religious art in the great ceremonial centers of the North Coast.

The Moche Valley   The situation in the Moche Valley is a little unclear at present. At Galindo itself the chief evidence for outside influence lies in the realm of ceramics. While the great majority of fineware pottery remained solidly within the Moche painted tradition, a smaller range of new forms incorporated innovative surface treatment (Bawden 1987, 1994b). They eschew the traditional bichrome painting technique that is a hallmark of Moche ceramic art in favor of plain black surface which is usually rather roughly polished. Significantly, several of the new forms bear registers of molded decoration whose component motifs are drawn from traditional North Coast imagery (figure 9.1). These images are almost entirely of geometric content. Absent are the depictions of ritual that characterize more conventional Moche pottery of earlier periods. Thus while the formal qualities of the shapes are new, the actual decoration is not, indicating the selective borrowing of technical traits rather than wholesale adoption of foreign vessels. Moreover, the innovative forms were used almost entirely in contexts of religious or ceremonial importance such as elaborate burials and non-residential centers of government, indicating that they realized their meaning as elite ideological symbols. It thus appears that the elite of Galindo emphasized formal and decorative imagery both from outside and within the Moche tradition for symbolic use in the activities of social integration and funerary ritual that asserted their status as rulers.

These innovative traits possessed multiple origins. As I have already stated, the actual decorative motifs were drawn principally from the North Coast artistic heritage. However, their formal arrangement in parallel registers on the bodies of vessels is new, as is the technique with which they were executed. Press molding, which enters the North Coast tradition at this time, is also a prominent presence in the artistic inventory of the Central Coast, an area strongly affected by Wari influence in the Middle Horizon 1 Phase (which corresponds to Moche V). In addition, the custom of flexed burial that we have seen in some burials at Galindo was adopted by Central Coast societies at this time. Thus, while confirmation must await further chronological refinement, it is reasonable to propose that the origin of the innovative Galindo features lay in Central Coast and ultimately Wari religious and ceremonial antecedents. Their introduction into the residual Moche cultural inventory at Galindo could well reflect the attempt by an embattled elite to consolidate its position by embracing for its exclusive use the widely respected symbols and practices of a powerful pan-Andean ideological system.

Elsewhere in the Moche Valley, the Cerro Blanco site, though largely deserted at the end of the Moche IV Phase, continued to be used in a more specialized capacity throughout the Late Period and subsequent centuries. The archaeological information from this later occupation clearly reveals that its chief function was religious and ceremonial. The Huaca del Sol, after a period of disuse in the Late Period, regained importance as a Wari-related religious center following the end of the Moche hegemony. By contrast, it now appears that the Huaca de la Luna continued to be used as a site of religious ceremonial and possibly elite residence (Uceda et al. 1994) through the latest Moche phase and possibly later.

It has long been believed that the later murals that graced the walls of the Huaca de la Luna displayed strong Wari influence in their iconographic content (figure 8.1) and a checker-board organization that closely resembles Wari textile decoration (Bonavia 1985). While recent work at this important complex has cast some doubt on this cultural association on the basis of associated Moche IV burials (Uceda et al. 1994), this revision must be regarded as tentative in the absence of confirming stylistic research. At this juncture the possibility must be accepted that Late Moche Period elite use of the Huaca de la Luna and its immediate environs blended aspects of Wari and traditional Moche religious symbolism.

I suggest that such a fusion would have accompanied a bid by Late Period Moche Valley rulers to construct a new ideological base. To this end they selectively adopted elements of an influential foreign belief system in order to strengthen their own threatened position with its prestige. This endeavor was intended to bring stability to a social situation that is clearly revealed at Galindo to have been charged with intra-group tension and related governmental coercion. There is, however, no indication in the archaeological record that, in the absence of the integrating role played by the now-discredited traditional Moche belief system, the attempt at anchoring the political system in a new ideological foundation met with any success. At Galindo no architectural structure exists with plan, decorative organization, or associated symbolic content resembling that of the Huaca de la Luna. There is no evidence to show that the Huaca de la Luna complex, or its presumed Wari-associated ideological complex, exerted any significant influence at the major population center where all semblances of traditional religious architecture are vestigial in size and consigned to the perimeter of the site and where authority depended instead on the effective exercise of physical control. This suggests that Wari-influenced ideology remained at best an exclusive possession of the elite during the occupation of Galindo, with little meaning to the population at large.

In the absence of any renewed benefit to the populace it is clear that such an extreme state of social instability could not continue without the entire corporate structure giving way. We have seen that the archaeological record indicates a much poorer diet for the large lower-status group at Galindo, a situation that, together with the existence of tightly controlled storage, reflects continuing economic distress. It is easy to imagine a population growing increasingly restive in this context of deprivation while their rulers, protected by their walled enclaves and progressively isolated by their alien ideology, strove to safeguard their privileges and position of authority. It is not entirely clear what triggered the end. There are suggestions that the large wall which segregated the hillside *barrio* and its lower status population (figure 9.7) was actively used as a fortification (Topic 1991). This would suggest actual warfare between rulers and ruled and a violent end to the Late Moche Period. Elsewhere localized areas of burning are scattered around the town without any evidence of directed destruction, a pattern that could indicate a situation of disorganized violence of the type characteristic of social collapse.

At any rate, some time around AD 700 the short and troubled history of Galindo came to an end with the abandonment of most of the residential area, the construction of squatters' shacks in the large administrative centers and spacious homes of the rulers, and the disappearance of all vestiges of urban organization. Galindo's desertion signalled the end of a half-millennium of Moche domination of this valley and the reversion of its population to a rural way of life. While the great Moche center at Cerro Blanco continued to be a center of religious activity through the subsequent period, it played this role in a very different social and political context. There was little structural connection between this later meaning and the long tradition of Moche statecraft whose symbols and rituals had lost their meaning in this part of the North Coast.

The northern valleys   The decline of Late Moche society in the northern valleys, unlike the situation in the central valleys, occurred within the context of marked continuity. We have seen in the Lambayeque Valley that the founders of the Moche V town of Pampa Grande used the traditional religious symbol of the Huaca Fortaleza as the focus of their move to reconstitute power. They achieved this in the short term with such success that Pampa Grande appears to have been the center of renewed Moche political expansion in the Lambayeque area, with previously autonomous Gallinazo societies being brought under its control. Further south, in the Jequetepeque Valley, where the negative consequences of the terminal Moche IV disruptions were relatively minor, continuity was even more marked. There was less demographic adjustment in this valley than elsewhere, with the Moche settlements at Pacatnamú and San José de Moro persisting through the Late Period. This strong thread of continuity is attended in the political domain by the undiminished importance of ceremonial endowed with the prestige of deep history. Most significantly, the sacred ritual of the Sacrifice Ceremony continued to offer the central setting for rulers to constitute and assert their power, as had their predecessors for centuries. Thus, in their distinctive ways, the northern Moche societies appear initially to have weathered the storm which irrevocably damaged their southern neighbors. However, decline soon began to accelerate and in about a century these impressive polities also disappeared as functioning entities, although their end did not precipitate the major disjunction that occurred in the Moche Valley.

Luis Jaime Castillo's work in the Jequetepeque Valley suggests that decline was marked by the progressive loss of control by the ruling elite of the production and manipulation of the symbols of power. The items that made up what I have termed the language of power – those that bore the thematic iconography of the system of Moche political power – were made by specialist potters, metallurgists, and weavers under strict control of the ruling elite. These items embodied meaning that was infused with the power of myth reproduced in ritual. They manifested the mandate of the rulers in the social domain, affirming and sustaining the tenets of Moche political ideology. It is thus not surprising that through the entire history of Moche society elite art comprised a limited range of forms, imagery, and decorative techniques with an unmistakable North Coast affiliation. Elite art emphatically excluded all outside influence by locating its inspiration and meaning solidly within Moche political structure. Indeed, it is this precise definition that characterizes Moche "culture" primarily as an ideology of power.

Such vital symbols of authority could only be effective when under strict control of the ruling group. This control is clearly seen in their distributional pattern. Thus, the most elaborate and potent were confined to the central settings of power – the religious rituals and great funerary monuments in which rulers affirmed their sacred prowess and the timeless sanctity of their social order. By contrast, elaborate pottery emblazoned with the formal imagery of Moche ideology never appears in the homes or tombs of the lower-status majority population of the North Coast during the period of Moche dominance.

This picture of symbolic and ideological stability under the command of unthreatened Moche leadership lasted until the final phase, when the situation irrevocably changed. We have seen how in the Moche Valley, leaders rejected their discredited political system and its symbols and tried to replace it with substitutes derived from the Central Coast, to no avail. While the Jequetepeque Valley escaped this major transformation, it nonetheless suffered impact that provoked somewhat similar response and initiated inexorable, though less dramatic, decline. At the end of the Middle Period elite foreign objects began to be imported into the Jequetepeque Valley by the rulers of San José de Moro for the first time. Fine decorated vessels from the Central Coast valleys 450 miles away began to be placed in the most elaborate San José burials (figure 9.13). This unprecedented development not only introduced a foreign element into one of the most important ideological contexts of Moche society but also suggests that elites were beginning to reach outside of Moche structure for political support.

This trend continued and expanded in the Late Period. The relatively small quantities of foreign ceramics available through long-distance trade were joined by copies and local vessels that combined features of both Central Coastal and Moche cultural traditions (Castillo 1993). These imports not only featured decorative innovations but included specific images of Wari-derived religious origin as modified and utilized in the so-called Pachacamac style of the Central Coast. Castillo has demonstrated that the imported items appear exclusively in the burials of individuals who had played a major role in the Sacrifice Ceremony, specifically that of the Priestess (see chapter 9). Local reproductions and hybrid vessels were confined to lower-status burials. This cultural synthesis in the domain of political ideology has profound implications. The unprecedented incorporation of outside concepts into the prevailing ideological system clearly marks a change at the core of Moche political doctrine.

Change of this magnitude indicates two interconnected factors. First, the previously inviolate Moche structure was undergoing internal transformation at the hands of the elite, a development that clearly indicates the loss of confidence at the center of political authority. Second, by partially transferring the conceptual structure of authority to foreign foundations, the Jequetepeque Valley elite significantly weakened their grasp on leadership by relinquishing exclusive control of the symbols and attendant rituals of authority that lay at the heart of their power. Castillo has argued that the ideological base that had for centuries supported Moche political authority, became a trap that led to dissolution in the Late Period. By overly relying on the untrammelled production of ever more elaborate material symbols both to project power and, through their controlled distribution, to sustain the intergroup relations that composed social order, the elite established a system that could not be modified without loss of stability. When the adverse economic and political circumstances of the late Moche IV Phase hindered their ability to maintain this system, the San José elite had to look beyond the borders of the North Coast region for support for the first time. This shift inevitably eroded absolute elite control, encouraged lower-status groups to share in the production and use of local copies, and promoted the process of decline that in a surprisingly short time resulted in the end of the Moche system.

Further north, at Pampa Grande in the Lambayeque Valley, the process of decline during the Late Period takes yet another form. As in the Jequetepeque Valley, the local Moche V rulers attempted to base their position on the prestige inherent in long-lasting cultural concepts. The Huaca Fortaleza played this role at Pampa Grande, imposing the traditional religious power symbolized by the great platform at the center of the new urban settlement. It appears that this strategy was initially more successful than at San José, for there is no evidence for adoption of foreign religious traits. Only the relatively modest increase in the production of blackware and press-molding may indicate outside influence at the technical level.

The Lambayeque Valley response to disruption, as in the Moche Valley, involved new and increasingly complex social reorganization in the context of population displacement. The earlier demographic pattern was replaced in the Late Period by concentration of much of the population in a single town, located at the neck of the valley so as to ensure access to the temporarily restricted water supply and associated agricultural land. Izumi Shimada, in his recent study of Pampa Grande (1994a), believes that this urban innovation encompassed not only people who had previously been subject to Moche government, but also some newly incorporated Gallinazo groups. Clearly this unprecedented urban concentration would have posed formidable organizational challenges to the political structure. However, while Galindo, far to the south, never came close to solving similar challenges, at Pampa Grande Moche V rulers did achieve a large measure of stability by grounding their new system of urban control in the continuing power of Moche ideology centered on the symbolism and ritual of the Huaca Forteleza.

Shimada points out that urban reorganization and subsequent management at Pampa Grande, in common with all such increases of social complexity, must have involved progressive segmentation and specialization of the agencies of political control. While this development may well have been effective as a response to the compelling economic and environmental problems of the late Moche IV Phase, its ultimate results were less beneficial. The varied groups who were concentrated at Pampa Grande, some of them only recently subjected to Moche rule, naturally possessed a tendency to fragment into their component parts. As I have previously mentioned, adherence to communal autonomy is especially strong in Andean societies because of their fundamentally holistic social conception and kinship-based organizational structure.

Erection of the huge Huaca Fortaleza and concurrent population nucleation inevitably required creation of new agencies of administration. In the new urban setting these institutions would have placed significant burdens on the previously rural inhabitants of Pampa Grande in terms of transfer from agriculture to construction activity, more intensive labor requirements, reduction of freedom of movement, and loss of autonomy by Gallinazo groups. Moreover, this situation would have been exacerbated by the potential for competition between the increased number of administrators created by the new political structure. Together, these inevitable accompaniments of urbanism would have placed pressures on the leadership. Such pressures would have been difficult to address once the immediate problems that had precipitated the establishment of Pampa Grande had disappeared with the return of adequate rainfall in the early eighth century. From this point, Pampa Grande may well have become a society under increasing social pressure from the organizational innovations that had proved so successful a few decades earlier.

Shimada concludes, on the grounds of this reasoning and the absence of evidence for any significant foreign influence at Pampa Grande, or indeed in the Lambayeque Valley as a whole, that the ultimate demise of the town was the result of growing forces from within society. The end was accompanied by violence. Most structures located in the corporate center which contained the centers of administration, elite residence, and the complex of platforms dominated by the Huaca Fortaleza, were burnt. These structures were, of course, those that housed the institutions of political leadership and religious order. The remainder of the town, where the large majority of its inhabitants lived, was untouched. Such selective destruction indicates the explosion of unrestrained revolt against the established order. Significantly, buildings atop the Huaca Fortaleza suffered the most intense conflagration. Shimada suggests that this marks a process of secularization at Pampa Grande which transformed the great edifice into a symbol of naked political domination stripped of its erstwhile religious power. I would suggest alternatively that it may have been this very importance that led the Huaca Fortaleza to bear the brunt of the revolt against the order that it symbolized. At any rate its destruction vividly reveals that neither the immense religious prominence of the vast edifice nor the ideological system of which it was part, could permanently overcome the growing pressures for change. With the flames that swept through the last and greatest center of Moche power, Moche civilization passed into history.

Aftermath: The Time of Transition

In the period which followed the abandonment of the towns of Galindo and Pampa Grande and the collapse of the San José polity, we see the emergence of various avenues through which the Moche legacy passed into the ongoing cultural heritage of the North Coast region. In this historical process, the various cultural forms that had distinguished the Moche period blended with other North Coast traditions and a strong Wari religious element. The merger of broad new foreign concepts with the persisting North Coast cultural legacy in the period immediately following the end of Moche hegemony shaped the subsequent history of the region. Understandably, subsequent history was distinguished by an even stronger element of diversity than had been the case during the Moche period, locally varied though the form of its hegemony had been. While the actual history of this time of transition can be only dimly glimpsed at present, its chief threads are emerging from the archaeological past and allow us to trace the ongoing influence of Moche civilization.

Foreign impact on the North Coast After the decline of the Late Moche societies around AD 700, we see a second, more intensive phase of foreign impact on the North Coast. Like the first, its origins can be attributed to the Wari polity of the south-central highlands. Following the initial Middle Horizon 1B expansion into the central coast and highlands, there was a period of quiescence. However, at the end of Middle Horizon 1B and the subsequent Middle Horizon 2A in the early eighth century, Wari expansion resumed. This second advance occurred at a time of political transition on the North Coast immediately following the dissolution of the Moche V polities and the virtual abandonment of their urban settlements. In this unsettled situation, Wari forces naturally found a more fertile field for direct intrusion than in the previous century. However, I must reiterate that even in this favorable political situation there is very little evidence to indicate direct political domination. Again, the bulk of available information suggests impact in the realms of religious belief and observance.

The specific expressions of Wari influence were varied in content and context, as was the nature of their relationship with residual Moche culture. However, two important attributes link them and indicate that the symbols (and presumably the related dogma) of Wari-derived religion were accepted to a much more complete degree than had been the case in the Late Moche Period. First, in the earlier period, the imported features from Wari-characterized regions to the south were dominated by technical and artistic attributes which were largely modified to conform to Moche norms. Only the San José de Moro cultural inventory strongly suggests religious infusion. By contrast the iconography of the subsequent Middle Horizon 2A period on the North Coast often contains precise and complex foreign religious themes. These compositions were derived from the religious imagery of such Middle Horizon Central Coast societies as Atarco and Pachacamac and ultimately to a significant degree from that of the highland Wari homeland (figure 9.13; see Shimada 1994a:249–52 for a good summary of this development).

The second quality that characterizes the heightened importance of Wari-related religion during Middle Horizon 2A on the North Coast is its social context. Wari imagery was affixed to some of the architectural centers of North Coast social integration, while small-scale articles of like affiliation were used in these settings as integral elements of religious activity. Thus throughout the region, extending from as far south as Pañamarca on the long-abandoned borders of the old southern polity, through the Moche and Chicama valleys, and north to the Lambayeque Valley, previous centers of Moche political ideology incorporated strong elements of Wari religion. Clearly the prestige of the old centers attracted the founders of the subsequent hybrid religion and led to their transformation into the physical foci for the new beliefs. While their meaning changed, their role at the core of social integration persisted.

Moving from south to north, the great complex of Pañamarca in the Nepeña Valley, possibly the southernmost provincial center of political control for the southern Moche polity, was probably abandoned at the end of the Middle Period. This imposing expression of Moche domination over the peoples of the southern valleys had asserted the established political order through its huge mural depiction of the Sacrifice Ceremony. Following their abandonment by the Moche, the valleys from Virú south may well have constituted an independent multi-valley polity (Wilson 1988) in which there is considerable evidence of Wari religious influence. It is in this context that the re-use of Pañamarca must be understood. It appears that in its modified role as center of a new religious ideology, Pañamarca underwent considerable reconstruction (Schaedel 1951b). As part of this construction, ramps and walls were added, some of which hid the older and now superseded mural symbolism of vanished Moche power.

In the Moche Valley the great Cerro Blanco site also occupied a special position in the changed order. Largely abandoned during the Moche V Phase, the Huaca del Sol regained importance at the end of Middle Horizon 1B when its huge Southern Platform again became the site for religious activities (Menzel 1977:37–41). A large number of ceremonial items including ceramic trumpets and whistles, fine-painted vessels bearing intricate Wari religious themes, and llama bones, attest to the performance of rituals involving animal sacrifice attended by offerings and musical accompaniment. This activity, which continued throughout Middle Horizon 2, denotes the restoration to the Huaca del Sol of its eminence as the focus of Moche Valley social integration at a time when earlier political cohesion had irretrievably broken down and the erstwhile urban population of Galindo had scattered through the valley into small rural settlements. There is ongoing disagreement regarding the role of the other great Cerro Blanco site monument – the Huaca de la Luna – in the post-Moche period. However, some authorities (e.g. Bonavia 1985) believe that it too continued to be used as a shrine and that its final murals were painted in the Middle Horizon as a public statement of the new religious complex that incorporated Moche features into a strongly Wari symbolic composition. The persistent significance of two of the most prestigious centers in the entire Moche realm testifies to the continuing, though modified, impact of Moche religious locations on the history of the North Coast.

In the northern valleys, the Huaca La Mayanga, part of the Batán Grande complex in the La Leche Valley, offers the most vivid example of the syncretism of Moche and Wari religious imagery in a public setting. This small adobe structure was probably built in the latest Moche phase during the pre-eminence of Pampa Grande in the greater Lambayeque area and continued in use through the immediately succeeding era (Bonavia 1985:99–104; Donnan 1972). Its period of use thus spans the critical transition from Moche to the subsequent consolidation of the Sicán culture of the northern valleys. The general plan of Huaca La Mayanga comprises a broad U-shaped walled enclosure. The main wall painted in red and yellow, faces the open side of the structure across a large court, and originally contained at least two rows of niches, only the bottom of which has survived.

A series of 20 polychrome murals, colored so as to affect maximum contrast with the background, adorn the back walls of these niches. Each mural depicts in profile a running, winged figure (figure 10.1) who represents the anthropomorphic version of the common Moche club and shield emblem. The figures are arranged in two groups of ten, each facing the center. The

Figure 10.1 Drawing of an anthropomorphized weapon-shield figure from the Huaca La Mayanga, Lambayeque Valley, probably dating from the late Moche V Phase or the immediately succeeding period. (Redrawn from Bonavia 1985, figure 73)

two figures that meet in the center of the wall are embellished with two human legs and feet, unlike the others, which only possess one. The content of the work is thus drawn solidly from the local tradition. However, the composition of the murals and their color scheme suggest Wari concepts. The compartmentalization of the figures into individual niche panels and their marked color contrast are characteristic Wari features which differ noticeably from the more open Moche narrative mural style. In fact the arrangement of the component figures into registers facing a central more complex and highly embellished entity, mirrors that of a focal theme of Wari religion. This theme is best illustrated by the Gateway of the Sun at Tiahuanaco, which also contains rows of winged, running figures facing a central deity. It thus appears that the Mayanga murals reinterpret distinctly Moche ideological symbols within a Wari religious framework in a more graphic example of the syncretism that we saw in the valleys to the south.

In addition to its vital role in the new centers of social integration, the Moche-Wari syncretism of this transitional period exerted authority in other contexts of religious import. Thus pottery items adorned with the precise iconography of Wari religion were part of the funerary paraphernalia of elite burials and of exclusive offerings throughout the region. Examples have been found at the Cerro Blanco site in the Moche Valley (Menzel 1977), at Suasal in the Chicama Valley (Donnan 1968), at San José de Moro in the Jequetepeque Valley (Shimada 1994a:250), and at the Huacas Lucía and Soledad in the Batan Grande complex of the La Leche Valley (figure 10.2; see also figure 9.13; Shimada 1990:315–16). Most of these Wari manifestations contain the characteristic imagery of the Provincial Wari style of Middle Horizon 2 and in some cases are accompanied in the same context by vessels of distinctly Moche inspiration. Significantly, some burials of this type contained individuals resting in the flexed position that first appeared at Moche V Galindo, breaking with the earlier tradition of extended interment (figure 10.2). The increased acceptance of this custom is another important manifestation of change in fundamental aspects of religious custom in the post-Moche era and heralds the full adoption of flexed burial in subsequent North Coast history.

Figure 10.2 Tightly flexed burial of the terminal Moche V Phase, Huaca Lucía, Lambayeque Valley. Note the mixture of modified Moche V and Provincial Wari pottery associated with the burial. (Courtesy Izumi Shimada)

A further notable component of the archaeological record of this period may reflect other significant inter-regional interactions. This is the great increase of Cajamarca cultural influence on the North Coast, as represented by the Middle Cajamarca B style, better known as Floral Cursive, together with locally-manufactured variants (Kroeber 1925; Shimada 1994a:250–4). The distinctive kaolin wares of the highland societies that adjoined the Moche immediately to the east filtered down to the coastal valleys throughout much of the Early Intermediate Period. However their quantities were usually small, feasibly denoting informal interaction between neighbors. The single major exception to this pattern occurred when, in the Middle and Late Moche societies of the Jequetepeque Valley, the creation of formal long-distance exchange networks became an important element of political strategy. One of the results of this economic expansion was a great increase in the acquisition of fine Cajamarca ceramics via the natural route that followed the course of the Rio Jequetepeque connecting the highlands and coastal plain. Following the final collapse of Moche dominion, this more intensive flow of highland pottery accompanied by large-scale local production of related Coastal Cajamarca wares became the rule rather than the exception throughout the region.

This ceramic dispersion probably marks the expansion of a relatively cohesive cultural entity into a political vacuum. However, it is difficult to discern whether the intrusion represents political encroachment or whether it was the outcome of peaceful exchange. Shimada (1994a:249–54) points out that the production of considerable quantities of Coastal Cajamarca pottery in the region may well indicate the physical presence of highland communities, a development that would certainly suggest some appropriation of political control from the native societies. He also raises the troublesome question of the relationship between the Cajamarca expansion and contemporary Wari incursion. Shimada tentatively proposes that Cajamarca acted as an agent of dominant Wari power in the north, although he properly concedes that in the context of our current inadequate understanding of the complexities of Wari history, this must remain an open question. The interaction of the North Coast with neighboring regions had ranged from peaceful trade to overt conquest during the Moche period. However, during this unsettled time the North Coast was itself strongly affected by foreign influences.

The end of urbanism   A vital component of Late Moche daily life also disappeared in the period directly following the end of the Moche polities. The urban configuration that most dramatically characterized the Late Moche Period vanished from the region. Neither the impressive Late Intermediate Period centers of the Sicán culture nor the great Chimú city of Chan Chan displayed the pattern of dense, functionally and residentially variegated urban structure of Galindo and Pampa Grande. Rather they follow a more characteristic pre-European Andean "oikos" pattern (Kolata 1983) in which principal settlements were planned and built for the exclusive use of rulers and their retainers. Ironically, urban structure similar to that of the Late Moche Period reappeared on the North Coast as a function of European invasion with the founding of Trujillo by Francisco Pizarro eight centuries later.

Just as the change that accompanied the emergence of the Late Moche Period was most extreme in the Moche Valley, so was that attending its end. Galindo ceased to exist as the center of a valley-wide polity. The town was largely deserted, with only a few areas showing evidence of continued occupation. Poignantly, these areas include the large, walled compounds where the rulers of Galindo, inheritors of centuries of Moche power, had secluded themselves from their subjects as they futilely sought to prolong their supremacy. Sometime in the early eighth century they departed and Galindo began its bleak transformation to the huge adobe ruin that we see today with only scattered remains of great walls and the ravaged hulk of its solitary burial platform to echo a former existence. With the end of Moche social order, a few poor families moved into the great empty compounds and built modest houses of cane and mud in the shadow of the now-meaningless monumental architecture. Most people assumed a rural life in small villages scattered throughout the valley plain, abandoning a way of life that must always have been alien to them.

However, while this picture at first glance appears to be one of dissolution, further examination reveals another very different component, one that emphasizes the vitality of North Coast peoples. I indicated in the first chapter of this book that Andean society is sustained by a holistic concept of group organization in which kinship principles are paramount. In this social order, a person's social position is determined by relationships within the community rather than by personal aspiration and achievement. Moreover, Andean social relationships are delineated by wider structures of genealogy. Thus, individual identity and its social roles are merged with those of lineage ancestors in a collective universe peopled by the entire group, past and present. This conceptual pattern always promotes communal interest over that of any single individual.

Within this holistic framework, Andean social structure embodies two features that have constituted central themes of this book and that are relevant to understanding post-Moche developments. First, the priority of collective conception creates an holistic ideology of social organization which innately counters the formation of individual power. We have seen that it was this contradiction between holistic and individualizing ideology in the Early Intermediate Period of North Coast history that constituted the dynamic that shaped political growth and ultimately was a major factor in the demise of the Moche system.

The second quality concerns the nature of extensive Andean social formations. The cohesion of large social entities in the pre-European Andean epoch depended on the ability of leadership to hold together discrete local communities. Each of these social groups possessed its own kin-based conceptual system which continued to promote group solidarity within the larger unit. This is probably best seen in the Inka Empire, where the central government comprised an administrative superstructure with ideologies and institutions of power directly derived from kinship principles. This superstructure was imposed over a diverse group of largely intact subject societies. We have seen that the Moche system similarly utilized principles of ancestry, myth, and shamanistic ritual to create a political ideology that fostered the growth of individualizing power, removed from communal sanction. It follows that when this system dissolved at the end of the Late Period, the impact fell almost exclusively at the level of the political superstructure. With this removed, the basic strength and tenacity of the component groups which had comprised the various Moche polities reasserted itself and they again assumed the autonomous statuses from which they had been drawn by Moche political expansion and the later establishment of urbanism.

It was natural that the Moche V towns, the artificial creations of a rejected social order, should be abandoned and that the population should disperse through the coastal valleys in a rural occupation based on the traditional allegiance of particular communities to their ancestral homes and the sacred geography that defined them. After all, urbanism had never been the product of long-term social evolution and was never universally established in the region. Thus it lacked the structural stability that derives from centuries of accumulated development. The

Moche towns were merely a desperate response by a threatened political order to major disruption. Moreover, we have seen at both Galindo and Pampa Grande that internal tension was an integral part of urban formation. Consequently, it is easy to understand that in the context of the disruptions that brought the Moche V Phase to an end, the radical experiment would have been rejected together with the towns that it had created.

I have already noted that the shift away from urbanism was accompanied by the widespread introduction of foreign religious elements into the North Coast tradition. These concurrent developments had unequal impact in various parts of the region. The move to a more traditional rural way of life was, of course, most pronounced in the Moche and Lambayeque Valleys, the sites of the Moche V towns. This was especially so in the Moche Valley, the area that had borne the brunt of disruption both at the end of the Middle Period and at the end of the Late Period. Here it appears that the Moche ideological system had lost its meaning so completely that there was little room left for continuity at this level in the local cultural tradition. Thus, the sole focus of ideological integration beyond the basic community level for a considerable period of time came from the revived use of the Huaca del Sol as the center for Wari-related religious observance. There is no indication that this renewed importance derived from Moche religious tenets. Rather it stemmed from the historical role of the *huaca* as a place of supernatural reverence. The dissolution of the Moche system of social integration was so complete in this valley that it would be some two centuries before the rural pattern of small autonomous communities was again augmented by the rise of a new valley-wide political center and the southern valleys were again embraced by regional unity.

In the Lambayeque Valley, traditional cultural threads were more in evidence, even though this had been the location of the largest Moche town. In this regard we must remember that the crisis of the later Moche periods had never been so great here and that Moche religious principles manifested by the Huaca Fortaleza persisted at the heart of political ideology throughout the life of Pampa Grande. This may explain why, in the period immediately following the abandonment of Pampa Grande, now termed the Early Sicán by Izumi Shimada (1990), the roots of a powerful integrative structure were formed from the convergence of Moche and outside concepts. The combination of local and foreign religious iconography at Huaca La Mayanga augur the consolidation of an influential system of social cohesion that drew its potency equally from the historical prestige of the Moche tradition and the wider influence of pan-regional Wari ideology. It is not surprising, then, that within a relatively short time in the Lambayeque Valley the physical manifestations of a new order – traditionally called the Lambayeque Culture, now termed the Sicán – emerged.

Lasting from the early eighth century AD until well into the fourteenth century, this long period of North Coast cultural history mirrored that of the Moche, not only in significant aspects of its religious imagery but also in its system of political control. In the earliest period, corresponding to the Middle Horizon 2 period, the Sicán culture is best known for its fine Wari-influenced pottery. However, evidence from the Batan Grande architectural complex suggests the contemporaneous construction of platform mounds as important foci of social cohesion. This little-known period inaugurated a return to the traditional administrative pattern in which specialized centers of government dominated by great platforms replaced the fleeting urban phase and set the stage for future development in the northern valleys. Indeed, during the succeeding florescent Middle Sicán Period, the influence of this resurgent northern society spread through much of the North Coast. We can suppose that the people of the Chicama and Jequetepeque Valleys, where urbanism had never really consolidated and where there had been considerable cultural continuity, would have been quite receptive to this native cultural expansion. Certainly the re-use of such major Moche centers as Huaca El Brujo, San José de Moro, and Pacatnamú as Sicán centers accords well with historic regional patterns of social development. In many respects, then, the Sicán Culture stands solidly with the Moche as an expression of the North Coast tradition.

In conclusion, while the circumstances were distinctive, the changes that distinguish North Coast society in the late seventh and eighth centuries transcended any single cultural phase. Rather, as expressions of a particular historical course they recurred at times of stress as dynamic structural forces. Even

trace unchanged through the centuries. At a slightly deeper level are the rituals and myths that, while modified by time according to the needs and pressures of history, reflect the persistence of a distinctive cultural legacy associated with the North Coast population. Most significant is the fundamental social structure which gave meaning to the two other levels. It is by means of this tripartite framework that the Moche legacy can be explored.

The Cultural Tradition of Moche

At the most superficial level we see specific Moche traits transmitted into later phases of North Coast culture. Most apparent in the archaeological record are the technological and iconographic features that were adopted by the succeeding societies of the pre-European North Coast. A variety of Moche ceramic attributes appears in Sicán and Chimú styles even though several centuries intervened between the florescence of the latter and the end of Moche. This situation must be attributed to the persisting esteem accorded the earlier civilization whose great monuments continued to overshadow the fields and villages of the coastal valleys. Thus the blackwares of the Late Moche became dominant in all later periods. Likewise press-molding, an innovative feature in the Late Moche Period, persisted in the Chimú ceramic style together with traditional forms like the stirrup-spout vessel. Many specific iconographic features such as the Moche fanged beings, the "Moon Animal" that long ago had been adopted by the Moche from their Recuay neighbors, the embellishment of stirrups with animal adornos, and the depiction of marine themes, all enriched the elite art of the successors of the Moche. While their context and meaning changed, their presence remained to attest to the persisting influence of Moche culture.

Transcending the rise and fall of rulers and the polities they create are customs that possess remarkable longevity and which link the Moche with the present-day north coast. The Moche tule boats fashioned from bundles of coastal cane propelled by split cane paddles have modern counterparts in the sharp-prowed fishing crafts of the northern coast (figure 2.3). The pervasive use of coca to combat fatigue in daily life and as a ritual offering in the religious sphere, endures, together with its traditional accessories – gourd lime container, applicator, and decorated bag. Potters at Mórrope in the Lambayeque Valley still shape large utilitarian pots by paddling the unfired surface against an oval cobble placed inside the vessel (Shimada 1994a:197) and fire the vessels in open pits like those used at Galindo. The traditional manufacture of textile from indigenous cotton on back-strap looms survives unchanged into the present (figure 3.7; Shimada 1994a: 208). Finally, a variety of other implements retain their Moche form almost unchanged. These include many ceramic forms, agricultural and fishing implements, and musical instruments – pan pipes, ceramic whistles, shell trumpets, drums, and rattles. Their use in rituals of elite power may have changed, but they still retain a role in the supernatural domain of shamanism.

At a second level of continuity are myths that often had powerful meaning within the Moche ideological system and which were enacted by the rulers as an integral component of power. Some of these continued in modified form as part of the formal ideologies of later North Coast polities. A prominent example of this category lies at the heart of Sicán ideological structure. This society, which we have already noted as possessing a strong degree of continuity with its Moche antecedents, placed a prominent human being, or human-like divinity, at the center of its formal iconography. The so-called Sicán Lord has been characterized by Izumi Shimada and earlier scholars (Menzel 1977:61–2) as embodying the Moche concept of multiple paramount mythic lords. The Sicán Lord is probably derived from Wari symbolism. This iconographic syncretism suggests that, albeit in modified form, important elements of Moche ideological doctrine entered the structure of Sicán political doctrine.

Other examples of the persistence of Moche mythical belief in the later political sphere appear in the Chimú setting of the early second millennium AD. In this category we can place the Tule Boat Theme, an element of the Late Moche mythic cycle. Late Moche iconographic emphasis on maritime themes like the Tule

Boat Theme and the Anthropomorphized Wave (McClelland 1990), a symbolic ocean wave with a human deity head, reappear in Chimú elite art. A final example of this category is the Moche fanged deity which, deriving from remote Andean origins, also appears in Chimú material symbolism. Given the temporal gap that separated the abandonment of Galindo and the rise of Chan Chan, we must presume that the meaning of these symbolic forms had changed. Nevertheless, their continued use strongly suggests that powerful concepts from the formal Moche ideological domain were adapted by its successors to the changed political and social needs of North Coast statecraft in later centuries.

Other myths that had been used by Moche leaders as part of their political structure re-entered the realm of broader cultural experience which had been, of course, their ultimate origin. We are indebted to Father Antonio de la Calancha, an Augustinian monk who lived on the north coast of Peru in the early seventeenth century, for the local accounts of mythic stories, without which it would be impossible to detect the long historical continuities that link Moche symbolism with its enduring structural base (see chapter 1). Father Calancha wrote of the beliefs and customs of the people of the North Coast during the Colonial Period and the origins of these customs in times before the coming of the Europeans. At the time he wrote, the local people had already been subjugated to the Spanish Crown for a century. Their tradition of autonomous political achievement was quickly fading into the past. Nevertheless, the mythical stories persisted as part of the cultural heritage. Not surprisingly, several of these deal with aspects of shamanism, a fundamental feature of Andean social structure. Here I use three examples to demonstrate the enduring quality of North Coast mythic structure in the face of internal disruption and foreign invasion.

An important theme of Father Calancha's work concerns the nature of local witchcraft and curing. As part of his discussion he lists individuals whom we would term shamans from various parts of the region and offers specific descriptions of their activities. One especially colorful and popular witch was a particularly dirty man called Mollep (The Lousy) who lived in the Jequetepeque Valley (Rowe 1948:51). According to Calancha, his claim to fame was that he told the people that they would multiply in proportion to his lice! Christopher Donnan (1978:90) has noted the existence of several elite Moche stirrup-spout vessels that depict individuals with the fanged mouths which denote supernatural attributes carrying small insects that may well be lice. Given the similarity between the Colonial account and the Moche representation, Donnan feasibly suggests that a myth of this type may well have existed throughout the time-span separating them.

A second such example of a mythic component of Moche political ideology persisting in deep cultural structure is the Burial Theme, one of the best-described constituents of the Late Moche mythic cycle (Donnan and McClelland 1979). The numerous fine-line painted examples of the representation of the burial ceremony of an elite individual are so similar in detail as to suggest that a specific event with known actors is being depicted (figure 9.5). One of the elements of the scene shows a naked woman who has apparently been killed and is being consumed by birds. While we cannot know the identities of these characters or the event that they enact, we can confidently assume that these were well known to the viewers and communicated important social meaning as part of the mythic symbolism of Moche political ideology.

Significantly, this myth persisted in the cultural awareness of North Coast people long after the passing of the Moche epoch. One thousand years later, Father Calancha reports that local lore asserted that curers had possessed high public status in the Chimú period and continued to do so in his time, though in changed circumstances. His informants related that in pre-European times, if a patient were lost because of negligence, the curer was killed (Calancha [1638] 1976:556). He or she was then tied to the patient's corpse. When the victim was buried the curer's body was left above ground to be eaten by birds. This, of course in a more general sense, perfectly describes the content of the Late Moche Burial Theme. Again, the correlation of mythic representation in seventh-century graphic symbolism and seventeenth-century North Coast oral narrative is too close to be coincidental. Rather, it appears that a central component of Late Moche ideological mythology has resumed its more basic role as part of the substratum of cultural perception which brought order to the often unpredictable lives of North Coast people.

A third and final example is visible in the long-lasting Andean conviction that order in the cosmos emerged from primordial chaos. In Colonial times people still believed that at some time in the distant past the relationships that maintained balance in the world had been overturned. This momentous disorder was explained in Andean mythology by the so-called Revolt of the Objects, a prominent component of the Moche V mythic cycle. (figures 5.6, 9.4). In the Huarochirí Manuscript, this myth relates how rocks came alive, mortars and grinding stones ate their human owners, and llamas herded men (Salomon and Urioste 1991:53). The regular state of the universe is reversed. Jeffrey Quilter (1990) has analysed the Moche theme and related it to the mythological memories of the Colonial Period. Again, a fundamental element of Andean, indeed of wider indigenous American mythical belief, was for a time incorporated into Moche political ideology and upon its passing re-entered its structural substratum.

The curer as steward of cultural continuity

It remains to discuss the third and most tenacious facet of cultural continuity, one that embraces all North Coast societies including those of the Moche and modern periods. This is a deep structure whose innate principles at once define a long-lasting cultural tradition and give meaning to its specific social constructions, their component customs and material symbols. We have seen that shamans and their rites figure prominently in both of the more superficial levels of continuity. Moreover, I have stressed throughout this book that the exercise of shamanistic authority was the most essential constituent of political power in Moche society. Indeed Moche rulers were themselves shamans and as such conducted the rites that focused the various dimensions of human social experience to further the interests of their people and sustain their own power. Thus, structural principles that are manifested in the social arena through the practice of shamanism lie at the core of the cultural tradition which shaped Moche political strategy.

The peoples of coastal Peru have been much more affected by European domination than their counterparts in the more remote villages of the Andes. The populous and fertile valleys that flank the Pacific Ocean offered the new arrivals the promise of agreeable climate, abundant harvests, and a readily available native work force. It is thus no surprise that the burden of foreign rule fell heavily on the inhabitants of the North Coast in the generations that followed Pizarro's arrival and that their traditional beliefs and customs were much altered by the imposition of European traditions. Most seriously affected were systems of social organization and religion, the twin pillars of indigenous political structure. Through population relocation, replacement of Andean political institutions by those of Colonial Spain, prohibition of native religious practice, and the compulsory adoption of the Roman Catholic religion, the new masters sought to replicate European traditions and to consolidate their dominion in the conquered lands of Peru.

Consequently, the old myths and rituals disappeared as the ideational cores of powerful political organizations, together with the ruling hierarchies which had so effectively manipulated them in order to control the material and cultural wealth of their lands. In their place the common people of the Andes became the sole inheritors of thousands of years of a rich cultural legacy. As the substratum to a succession of native dominions they had long nurtured the kin-based structural foundations of Andean social life despite the endeavors of systems like that of the Moche to subordinate this to a more hierarchical and exclusive political system. Ultimately, the commoners with their primary conception of social order outlasted all of the imposed political systems. After 1532 the common people continued to play the same role in the era initiated by the Spanish conquerors that they did under the Moche. However, the new order brought unprecedented challenges. No longer could people openly congregate in the places made sacred by the transcendental history of ancestral reverence and natural cosmology. These sites were now damned as the haunts of the devil and his minions. Also condemned were the rites that symbolized the associated beliefs as vital forces in the daily lives of the people. With the banning of traditional practice the alien Roman Catholic creed took its place at the center of religious life.

However, with the tenacity that is a central part of the Andean cultural inheritance, North Coast peoples, like their counterparts elsewhere, shaped the Colonial order to their benefit as far as the new circumstances would allow. While superficially adhering to the state religion, they significantly adjusted its meaning to accommodate ancient Andean precepts. Christian saints adopted attributes of native divinities and Christian festivals marked important stages in the ancient agricultural cycles. Conversely, traditional religious elements assumed different meaning in the new synthesis. Some precolumbian personages and divinities were identified with destructive spiritual forces while the ruined cities, cemeteries, and ceremonial centers of the Moche, Sicán, and Chimú became identified as the abodes of dangerous spirits, their stone and ceramic images identified with supernatural power. Importantly, whether expressed through Christian or pre-Christian precepts, religion retained a close connection to all aspects of the natural and supernatural Andean world.

While the persistence of indigenous conceptions of the world is a vital quality of Andean religious syncretism, on the North Coast as elsewhere, these conceptions are necessarily expressed within the liturgical confines of the imposed Catholic Church. However, in the absence of an authorized institutional forum for expression of traditional religious concepts, there is another, ostensibly secular, context in which continuity is much more explicit. This is the sphere of the traditional curer. Here the roles are reversed and Catholic religious precepts are merged into a distinctly indigenous Andean rite, grounded in shamanistic belief. Consequently, the practice of curing can be examined in its context of political domination, religious syncretism, and a world-view suffused with the immediate presence of the supernatural, as a powerful agency through which Andean North Coast structural meaning has been transmitted into the modern world.

The North Coast curer has increasingly become the focus of recent anthropological study (Joralemon and Sharon 1993; Sharon 1978). I draw heavily on this work in this section. The curer is a traditional medical practitioner, usually male in contemporary North Coast society, who uses a profound understanding of natural remedies to bring relief to the sick. As in all occupations that require a specialized knowledge, the curer usually undergoes an extensive learning period, working with more senior curers to master the qualities and properties of a wide range of healing herbs, minerals, and their physical applications.

There is a fundamental aspect of the curer's skill that sets it apart from mere knowledge of herbs. This is the exceptional and deeply personal ability to identify the cause of sickness through divination and to effect healing in the setting of direct spiritual engagement. In many cases the curer's commitment to his vocation follows growing awareness as a youth of his special ability to experience the spiritual realms. However, the event that seals the commitment is usually a vision in which the curer rejects the devil's offer to give him unusual powers in return for subjection to his desires. By rejecting the satanic overtures the dreamer becomes aware of his ability to subdue the beings that cause sickness and he becomes a true shaman, committed to a lifetime of healing in his community.

Several qualities of the curing practice clearly reveal its shamanistic character and deep structural roots in Andean society. First, although the patient is certainly a chief focus of the healing, the broader community is also deeply involved. The effect of the sickness not only impacts the sufferer. The patient's symptoms also manifest dysfunctional social relations whereby such divisive mechanisms as revenge, jealousy, or disloyalty threaten the wider community. The curer strives to heal sickness so as to allow patients and their acquaintances to confront its wider causes. Consequently the curing ritual, in reality a process that promotes resolution of communal danger, takes place in a group setting. This pattern conforms to the concepts and related practices that Victor Turner describes in his classic work on ritual (Turner 1969). Here sickness is seen as a manifestation of the alienating and divisive forces inherent in hierarchical social formation, in the Andean context the modern Republican state. The ritual process detaches patient, officiants, and attendants from their normal social roles and allows them to enter the sacred state of "liminality." Here, in a narrow sense, the shamanistic curer balances the opposing forces of good and ill to effect healing. However, there is broader significance to the process. In the separated space of ritual community members evoke the essential and generic human bond without which there can be no society. It is in this sense that they bring back an element of sacredness into the real world to support and sustain community cohesion. It is thus very understandable that this social role of the North Coast curer has been especially important during the European centuries in the face of massive pressures on indigenous social structure.

A second important feature of present-day North Coast healing is that it is conducted within the formal structure of a religious ceremony. A preparation phase activates the participants and the ritual table. During this phase the curer invokes spiritual help through prayer, song, or special rites, to first vitalize the powerful dualistic forces of the two sides of his ritual table, then, usually through the taking of an hallucinogen, to prepare the entire participating group. In the succeeding healing phase the principal officiant, the curer, divines the cause of sickness and engages spiritual forces for the purpose of healing. The event concludes with the ritual cleansing of all participants. Within this formal structure there are many other standard features. Thus the healing ceremony incorporates ritual chants, dances, and music performed on traditional instruments. Invariably the participants drink a mixture of the hallucinogenic San Pedro cactus to invoke the sacred world. Finally, each step of healing and spiritual cleansing involves use of the ritual table.

The most fundamental shamanistic quality of curing lies in the essential nature of the curer himself. Through the powerful agency of the San Pedro cactus, he enters the time and space of the spiritual world where he experiences his encounters with the supernatural on behalf of his threatened community. Central to this spiritual journey and its success is the ritual table (figure 11.1; see also figure 5.2). The organization of the table and its content symbolically evokes the deep cultural experience of the community, while its active manipulation directs the vital force that enables the curer to succeed in his supernatural quest.

Briefly, each curer's table, while expressing the specific character and approach of its user, manifests a shared conceptual origin. The table contains an inventory of objects that fall primarily into two opposing categories – or fields. A group of therapeutic herbs and items of Christian affiliation comprises the right field, representing positive, healing force. Precolumbian artifacts, weapons, and objects from places of danger such as ancient sites, mountains, and highland lagoons

Figure 11.1 The Moche Valley curandero *Eduardo Calderón sitting in front of his* mesa. *(Courtesy Douglas Sharon)*

are to the left, the field that represents supernatural threat and confrontation. The opposing fields are often separated by a small middle one whose contents, such as the San Pedro cactus, activate and mediate the entire ritual.

Here the collective Christian–precolumbian religious heritage, regulated in the Church through synthesis, is separated into two opposing entities, representing the forces of good and evil. This conforms to the dualistic principle that is fundamental to Andean social structure. In this context duality implies the harnessing of energy that flows from the dynamic conflict of opposing forces for the benefit of the community. The curer activates the dual sources of power inherent in the contents of his table and regulates the resulting force through confronting the supernatural causes of sickness. Thus he embodies the basic shamanistic qualities of spiritual mediation within the sacred context of ritual time and space.

Many traits link modern North Coast curers and their Moche predecessors. These are clearly depicted in elite art (Donnan

1978:102–58). The famous ceramic representation of a Moche curer (figure 5.3) illustrates a variety of herbs and objects that are still in use today. Through her owl identity this curer assumes supernatural authority that continues to be associated with this bird in modern curing ritual. The continued use of the San Pedro cactus from the Moche period to the present has been clearly documented in precolumbian art and Colonial written accounts. Numerous Moche shamanistic scenes are located in mountains, settings regarded by modern curers as charged with supernatural force and the homes of powerful spirits. Modern curers commonly utilize staffs crowned with animal and birds heads (figure 11.1), objects of shamanistic significance that have also been found in elite Moche burials. Panpipes, drums, and rattles are a feature of Moche shamanistic ceremonial depictions and modern healing rituals. Most eloquently, actual Moche objects appear an the tables of modern curers, giving immediacy to the historic continuum.

In conclusion I return to the significance of shamanistic structure for understanding Moche society. In this final chapter I have sought to establish both that shamanistic principles were a central part of Moche political ideology and that the underlying structure from which this ideology emerged continues to form the social conception of North Coast peoples. The frequent depiction of curers in elite Moche ceramic art reveals the social importance of this profession. Great rulers like the Warrior Priest of Sipán were extreme practitioners of the shaman's art in the political sphere. Through the ritual of sacrifice they mediated a spiritual balance in the paradoxical tension between holistic and individualizing ideology that they themselves had generated in their quest for power. When they could no longer balance these forces, they fell, and with them fell the great civilization which they had created. In the end ordinary curer-shamans, simple heirs of the Moche curers we know through ceramic art and mythic symbolism, of Mollep of Jequetepeque and his fellows, became responsible for the preservation of a structural balance in the lives of their fellows and thereby perpetuated North Coast society in the face of the great changes that it has experienced through the centuries.

Thus, in the character and performance of the shaman we see

the fundamental legacy of the Moche and other authors of North Coast civilization. The legacy and its enfolding tradition has two faces, both central to North Coast peoples. On one hand is the gloriously attired Moche ruler of long ago. In the full glare of public spectacle, he evokes the awesome power of myth, through sacred rituals conducted high on great artificial mountains like the Huaca del Sol. On the other hand is the impoverished villager in his bare earthen patio adjoining a rude adobe house, conducting a healing ceremony for a few poorly dressed patients in the raw, dark night. These vastly dissimilar beings both draw on the power of a single belief system which embodies the vitality of an enduring people. One uses this power to effect social unity in the interests of political gain, the other to achieve physical healing and communal cohesion in the face of overwhelming outside pressure. They employ a common holistic experience to direct opposing cosmic forces toward the balance that assures social order and explains the human universe. Both, then, are representatives of a human cultural tradition that transcends calendrical time and shapes the thought of its members, the specific customs that they develop, and the material residue that is the window through which some, like the Moche, can be seen.

The Moche, then, are still with us in the urban dwellers of Trujillo and Chiclayo, in the fishers of Huanchaco, the traditional potters of Mórrope, and the rural farmers of coastal cooperatives. People of the same occupations have lived for millennia in these locations ever since their forebears first moved inland in the search for a better life. Through the vast precolumbian epoch, small groups of these people manipulated their kinship structure to elevate themselves in power. After a time they departed, leaving some of the most splendid monuments ever created by human hands as the legacy of their struggle for domination over their fellows. At last the native rulers withdrew entirely from the stage, to be replaced by new masters from distant Europe who created their own sequence of triumphs together with a very different set of material memorials to their fleeting eminence. Through this history of success and failure the common people exist, largely unseen in history, but ultimately triumphant over it. Their ability to transcend the drama of history is affirmed by their constant success in molding new beliefs to a familiar form, to direct the forces of change, and to maintain their customs and world-view. The Moche legacy, then, lies in the ultimately universal capacity of the human spirit to surmount the vicissitudes of time and space.

Bibliography

Alva, W. 1990. New Tomb of Royal Splendor. *National Geographic Magazine* 177, 2–15.

Alva, W. and C.B. Donnan. 1993. *Royal Tombs of Sipán.* Los Angeles: Fowler Museum of Cultural History, University of California, Los Angeles.

Amaro Bullon, I. 1995. Reconstruyendo la Identitad de un Pueblo. In K. Makowski, C.B. Donnan, I. Amaro Bullon, L.J. Castillo, M. Diez Canseco, O. Eléspuru Revoredo, and J.A. Murro Mena (eds), *Vicús,* Lima: Banco de Crédito del Peru, 23–82.

Anders, M.B. 1981. Investigation of State Storage Facilities in Pampa Grande, Peru. *Journal of Field Archaeology* 8, 391–404.

Arntz, W. 1984. El Niño and Peru: Positive Aspects. *Oceanus* 27, 36–9.

Bastien, J.W. 1985. *Mountain of the Condor: Metaphor and Ritual in an Andean Ayllu.* Prospect Heights, IL: Waveland Press.

—— 1989. A Shamanistic Curing Ritual of the Bolivian Aymara. *Journal of Latin American Lore* 15(1), 73–94.

Bauer, B.S. 1992. *The Development of the Inca State.* Austin: University of Texas Press.

Bawden, G. 1977. Galindo and the Nature of the Middle Horizon on the North Coast of Peru. Unpublished Ph.D. dissertation, Department of Anthropology, Harvard University, Cambridge, MA.

—— 1978. Life in the Pre-Columbian Town of Galindo. *Field Museum of Natural History Bulletin* 3, 16–23.

—— 1982a. Galindo: A Study in Cultural Transition During the Middle Horizon. In M. Moseley and K. Day (eds), *Chan Chan: Andean Desert City,* Albuquerque: University of New Mexico Press, 285–320.

—— 1982b. Community Organization Reflected by the Household: A

Study of pre-Columbian Social Dynamics. *Journal of Field Archaeology* 9, 165–83.

——1987. Early Middle Horizon Ceramic Innovations from the Moche Valley on the Peruvian North Coast. Greeley, CO: University of Northern Colorado, *Occasional Publications in Anthropology, Archaeological Series* 42, 60–94.

——1990. Domestic Space and Social Structure in Pre-Columbian Northern Peru. In S. Kent (ed.), *Domestic Architecture and the Use of Space: An Interdisciplinary Cross-Cultural Study*. Cambridge, England: Cambridge University Press, 153–71.

——1994a. La Paradoja Estructural: la Cultura Moche como Ideología Política. In S. Uceda and E. Mujica (eds), *Moche: Propuestas y Perspectivas*, Lima: Travaux de l'Institut Francais d'Etudes Andines 79, 389–414.

——1994b. Nuevas Formas de Ceramica Moche V Procedentes de Galindo. In S. Uceda and E. Mujica (eds), *Moche: Propuestas y Perspectivas*, Lima: Travaux de l'Institut Francais d'Etudes Andines 79, 207–22.

——1995. The Structural Paradox: Moche Culture as Political Ideology. *Latin American Antiquity* 6(3), 255–73.

Bell, C. 1992. *Ritual Theory, Ritual Practice*. New York: Oxford University Press.

Bennett, W.C. 1939. *Archaeology of the North Coast of Peru: An Account of Explorations and Excavation in Virú and Lambayeque Valleys*. New York: American Museum of Natural History, Anthropological Papers 37, Part 1.

——1950. *The Gallinazo Group, Virú Valley, Peru*. New Haven: Yale University Publications in Anthropology 43.

Benson, E.P. 1974. *A Man and a Feline in Mochica Art*. Washington DC, Dumbarton Oaks: Studies in Pre-Columbian Art and Archaeology 14.

——1985. The Moche Moon. In D.P. Kvieok and D.H. Sandweiss (eds), *Recent Studies in Andean Prehistory and History*, Papers from the Second Annual Northeast Conference on Andean Archaeology and Ethnohistory, Ithaca, NY: Cornell University Latin American Studies Program, 121–36.

Berezkin, Y.E. 1980. An Identification of Anthropomorphic Mythological Personages in Moche Representations. *Ñawpa Pacha* 18, 1–26.

——1983. *Mochika*. Leningrad: USSR Academy of Sciences.

Bird, J. 1962. Art and Life in Old Peru, An Exhibition. *American Museum of Natural History Quarterly* 2(3): 147–210.

Bird, R. McK. 1987. A Postulated Tsunami and its Effects on Cultural

348 *Bibliography*

Development in the Peruvian Early Horizon. *American Antiquity* 52, 285–303.

Bloch, M. 1992. *Prey into Hunter: The Politics of Religious Experience.* Cambridge, England: Cambridge University Press.

Bode, B. 1989. *No Bells to Toll.* New York: Scribner.

Bonavia, D. 1985. *Mural Painting in Ancient Peru.* Bloomington: Indiana University Press.

Brennan, C.T. 1980. Cerro Arena: Early Cultural Complexity and Nucleation in North Coastal Peru. *Journal of Field Archaeology* 7, 1–22.

Burger, R.L. 1988. Unity and Heterogeneity within the Chavín Horizon. In R.W. Keatinge (ed.), *Peruvian Prehistory*, Cambridge, England: Cambridge University Press, 99–144.

—— 1992. *Chavín and the Origins of Andean Civilization.* London: Thames and Hudson.

Cabello Balboa, M. [1586] 1951. *Miscelánea Antártica.* Lima: Universidad Nacional Mayor de San Marcos.

Calancha, A. de la [1638] 1976. *Corónica Moralizada del Orden de San Agustín en el Peru con Sucesos Ejemplares Vistos en Esta Monarquía.* Barcelona: P. Lacavallería.

Carrera, F. de la [1644] 1939. *Arte de la Lengua Yunga.* Ed. R.A. Altieri. Tucumán, Argentina: Universidad Nacional de Tucumán, Publicaciones Especial del Instituto de Antropología 3.

Casas, B. de las [1555] 1948. De las Antiguas Gentes del Peru. In F.A. Loayza (ed.), *Los Pequeños Grandes Libros de Historia Americana*, Lima: Editorial de Domingo Miranda, 1–152.

Castillo, J.C. 1989. *Personajes Míticos, Escenas y Narraciones en la Iconografía Mochica.* Lima: Pontificia Universidad Catolica del Peru, Fondo Editorial.

—— 1991. Narrations in Moche Iconography. Unpublished M.A. Paper. University of California, Los Angeles.

—— 1993. Prácticas Funerarias, Poder e Ideología en la Sociedad Moche Tardía. *Gaceta Arqueológica Andina* 7(7), 67–82.

Castillo, J.C. and C.B. Donnan. 1994. La Ocupación Moche de San José de Moro, Jequetepeque. In S. Uceda and E. Mujica (eds), *Moche: Propuestas y Perspectivas*, Lima: Travaux de l'Institut Francais d'Etudes Andines 79, 93–146.

—— 1995. Los Mochica del Norte y Los Mochica del Sur. In K. Makowski, C.B. Donnan, I. Amaro Bullon, L.J. Castillo, M. Diez Canseco, O. Eléspuru Revoredo, and J.A. Murro Mena (eds), *Vicús*, Lima: Banco de Crédito del Perú, 143–76.

Chang, K.C. 1983. *Art, Myth, and Ritual.* Cambridge, MA: Harvard University Press.

Collier, D. 1955. *Cultural Chronology and Change as Reflected in the Ceramics of the Viru Valley, Peru.* Chicago: Field Museum of Natural History, Fieldiana: Anthropology 43.

Collier, G.A., R.I. Rosaldo, and J.D. Wirth. 1982. *The Inca and Aztec States, 1400–1800: Anthropology and History.* New York: Academic Press.

Conklin, W.J. 1990. Architecture of the Chimú: Memory, Function, and Image. In M.E. Moseley and A. Cordy-Collins (eds), *The Northern Dynasties: Kingship and Statecraft in Chimor,* Washington, DC: Dumbarton Oaks, 43–74.

Conrad, G.W. 1974. Burial Platforms and Related Structures on the North Coast of Peru: Some Social and Political Implications. Unpublished Ph.D. dissertation, Department of Anthropology, Harvard University, Cambridge, MA.

——1981. Cultural Materialism, Split Inheritance, and the Expansion of Ancient Peruvian Empires. *American Antiquity* 46, 3–26.

——1982. The Burial Platforms of Chan Chan: Some Social and Political Implications. In M.E. Moseley and K.C. Day (eds), *Chan Chan: Andean Desert City,* Albuquerque: University of New Mexico Press, 87–118.

——1990. Farfán, General Pacatnamú, and the Dynastic History of Chimor. In M.E. Moseley and A. Cordy-Collins (eds), *The Northern Dynasties: Kingship and Statecraft in Chimor,* Washington, DC: Dumbarton Oaks, 227–42.

Conrad, G.W. and A.A. Demarest. 1984. *Religion and Empire.* Cambridge, England: Cambridge University Press.

Cordy-Collins, A. 1990. Fonga Sigde, Shell Purveyor to the Chimú Kings. In M.E. Moseley and A. Cordy-Collins (eds), *The Northern Dynasties: Kingship and Statecraft in Chimor,* Washington, DC: Dumbarton Oaks, 393–418.

——1992. Archaism or Tradition? The Decapitation Theme in Cupisnique and Moche Iconography. *Latin American Antiquity* 3(3), 206–20.

Currie, E.J. 1995. Archaeology, Ethnohistory and Exchange along the Coast of Ecuador. *Antiquity* 69(264): 511–26.

Darwin, C. 1839. *Narrative of the Surveying Voyages of His Majesty's Ships Adventure and Beagle, Between the Years 1826 and 1836, Describing Their Examination of the Southern Shores of South America, and the Beagle's Circumnavigation of the Globe.* Volume III. London: Henry Colburn.

Demarest, A.A. 1981. *Viracocha: The Nature and Antiquity of the Andean High God.* Monographs of the Peabody Museum 6. Cambridge, MA: Peabody Museum Press.

Diez Canseco, M. 1995. La Sabuduría de los Orfebres. In K. Makowski, C.B. Donnan, I. Amaro Bullon, L.J. Castillo, M. Diez Canseco, O. Eléspuru Revoredo, and J.A. Murro Mena (eds), *Vicús*, Lima: Banco de Crédito de Perú.

Disselhoff, H.D. 1972. Metallschmuck aus der Loma Negra (Vicús), Nord Peru. *Antike Welt, Zeitschrift für Archäologie und Urgeschichte* 3, 43–53. Zurich: Raggi-Verlag, Küsnacht.

Disselhoff, H.D. and H. Linné. 1961. *The Art of Ancient America.* New York: Crown.

Donnan, C.B. 1965. Moche Ceramic Technology. *Ñawpa Pacha* 3, 115–38.

—— 1968. An Association of Middle Horizon Epoch 2A Specimens from the Chicama Valley. *Ñawpa Pacha* 6, 15–18.

—— 1972. Moche-Huari Murals from Northern Peru. *Archaeology* 25(2): 85–95.

—— 1973. *Moche Occupation of the Santa Valley, Peru.* Los Angeles: UCLA Latin American Center Publications.

—— 1976. *Moche Art and Iconography.* Los Angeles: Latin American Studies Publications, University of California, Los Angeles.

—— 1978. *Moche Art of Peru.* Los Angeles: Museum of Culture History, University of California, Los Angeles.

—— 1986. Introduction. In C.B. Donnan and G.A. Cock (eds), *The Pacatnamú Papers*, Volume 1. Los Angeles: Museum of Culture History, University of California, Los Angeles, 19–26.

—— 1995. Moche Funerary Practice. In T.D. Dillehay (ed.), *Tombs for the Living: Andean Mortuary Practices*, Washington, DC: Dumbarton Oaks, 111–60.

Donnan, C.B. and L.J. Castillo. 1992. Finding the Tomb of a Moche Priestess. *Archaeology* 45, 38–42.

—— 1994. Excavaciones de Tumbas de Sacerdotisas Moche en San José de Moro, Jequetepeque. In S. Uceda and E. Mujica (eds), *Moche: Propuestas y Perspectivas*, Lima: Travaux de l'Institut Francais d'Etudes Andines 79, 415–24.

Donnan, C.B. and C.J. Mackey. 1978. *Ancient Burial Patterns of the Moche Valley, Peru.* Austin, University of Texas Press.

Donnan, C.B. and D. McClelland. 1979. *The Burial Theme in Moche Iconography.* Studies in Pre-Columbian Art and Archaeology 21. Washington, DC: Dumbarton Oaks.

Dumont, L. 1980. *Homo Hierarchicus: The Caste System and Its Implications.* Chicago: University of Chicago Press.

—— 1986. *Essays on Individualism: Modern Ideology in Anthropological Perspective.* Chicago: University of Chicago Press.

Eagleton, T. 1991. *Ideology.* New York: Verso.

Eling, H. 1987. *The Role of Irrigation Networks in Emerging Societal*

Complexity During Late Prehispanic Times. Ph.D. dissertation, Department of Anthropology, University of Texas, Austin. Ann Arbor, MI: University Microfilms International.

Farrington, I.S. 1974. Irrigation and Settlement Pattern: Preliminary Research Results from the North Coast of Peru. In T.E. Downing and M. Gibson (eds), *Irrigation's Impact on Society*, Tucson: Anthropological Papers of the University of Arizona 25, 83–94.

Feldman, R.A. 1985. Preceramic Corporate Architecture: Evidence for the Development of Non-Egalitarian Social Systems in Peru. In C.B. Donnan (ed.), *Early Ceremonial Architecture in the Andes*, Washington, DC: Dumbarton Oaks, 71–92.

Fogel, H. 1993. *Settlements in Time: A Study of Social and Political Development during the Gallinazo Occupation of the North Coast of Peru.* Ph.D. dissertation, Yale University. Ann Arbor, MI: University Microfilms International.

Ford, J.A. 1949. *Cultural Dating of Prehistoric Sites in Virú Valley, Peru.* New York: Anthropological Papers of the American Museum of Natural History 43(1).

Franco, R., C. Gálvez, and S. Vásquez. 1994. Arquitectura y Decoración Mochica en la Huaca Cao Viejo, Complejo El Brujo: Resultados Preliminares. In S. Uceda and E. Mujica (eds), *Moche: Propuestas y Perspectivas*, Lima: Travaux de l'Institut Francais d'Etudes Andines 79, 147–80.

Furst, P.T. 1968. The Olmec Were-Jaguar Motif in the Light of Ethnographic Reality. In E.P. Benson (ed.), *Dumbarton Oaks Conference on Olmec*, Washington, DC: Dumbarton Oaks, 143–78.

Garcilaso de la Vega, El Inca. [1609] 1987. *Royal Commentaries of the Incas and General History of Peru.* Translated by H.V. Livermore. Austin: University of Texas Press.

Gero, J. 1988. Early Administrative Centers in the Callejón de Huaylas, Peru. Paper presented at the 53rd Annual Meeting of the Society for American Archaeology, Phoenix, AZ.

——1990. Pottery, Power and Parties! *Archaeology* 53(2), 52–6.

Giddens, A. 1984. *The Constitution of Society.* Berkeley: University of California Press.

——1990 [1979] *Central Problems in Social Theory.* Berkeley: University of California Press.

Golte, J. 1994. *Iconos y Narraciones: La Reconstrucción de una Secuencia de Imágenes Moche.* Lima: Instituto de Estudios Peruanos Ediciones.

Grieder, T. 1978. *The Art and Archaeology of Pashash.* Austin: University of Texas Press.

Guaman Poma de Ayala, F. [1614] 1980. *El Primer Nueva Corónica y Buen Gobierno.* Translated by J.I. Urioste. Mexico City: Siglo Vientiuno.

Guffroy, J. 1989. Un Centro Ceremonial Formativo en el Alto Piura. *Bulletin de l'Institut Francais d'Etudes Andines* 18(2), 161–208.

Guffroy, J., P. Kaulicke, and K. Makowski. 1989. La Prehistoria del Departmento de Piura: Estado de los Conocimientos y Problemática. *Bulletin de l'Institut Francais d'Etudes Andines* 18(2), 117–42.

Haas, J. 1985. Excavations on Huaca Grande: An Initial View of the Elite at Pampa Grande. *Journal of Field Archaeology* 12, 391–409.

—— 1987. The Exercise of Power in Early Andean State Development. In J. Haas, S. Pozorki, and T. Pozorski (eds), *The Origins and Development of the Andean State*, Cambridge, England: Cambridge University Press, 31–5.

Haas, J., S. Pozorski, and T. Pozorski (eds). 1987. *The Origins and Development of the Andean State.* Cambridge, England: Cambridge University Press.

Hastings, C.M. and M.E. Moseley. 1975. The Adobes of the Huaca del Sol and the Huaca de la Luna. *American Antiquity* 40, 196–203.

Heyerdahl, T. 1995. Túcume and the Maritime Heritage of Peru's North Coast. In T. Heyerdahl, D.H. Sandweiss, and A. Narvaez (eds), *Pyramids of Túcume: The Quest for Peru's Forgotten City,* New York: Thames and Hudson, 9–37.

Hill, J.D. (ed.). 1988. *Rethinking History and Myth: Indigenous South American Perspectives on the Past.* Urbana: University of Illinois Press.

Hocquenghem, A.M. 1979. *L'iconographie Mochica et les Rites de Purification.* Baessler-Archiv 27, 127–57.

—— 1981. Les Mouches et les Mortes dans l'Iconographie Mochica. *Ñawpa Pacha* 19, 63–70.

—— 1987. *Iconografía Mochica.* Lima: Fondo Editorial de la Universidad Catolica de Peru.

—— 1991. Frontera Entre Areas Culturales Nor y Centroandinas en los Valles y la Costa del Extremo Norte Peruano. *Bulletin de l'Institut Francais de Etudes Andines* 29(2), 309–48.

Humboldt, A. von. 1814. *Researches Concerning the Institutions and Monuments of the Ancient Inhabitants of America.* Translated by H.M. Williams. London: Longmans.

Isbell, W.H. 1986. Emergence of the City and State at Wari, Ayacucho, Peru, During the Middle Horizon. In R. Matos, S.A. Turpin, and H.H. Eling Jr. (eds), *Andean Archaeology; Papers in Memory of Clifford Evans,* Los Angeles: Institute of Archaeology, University of Calfornia, Los Angeles, Monograph 27, 189–201.

Bibliography   353

——1988. City and State in Middle Horizon Huari. In R. Keatinge (ed.), *Peruvian Prehistory*, Cambridge, England: Cambridge University Press, 164–89.

Jones, J. 1979. Mochica Works of Art in Metal: A Review. In E.P. Benson (ed.), *Pre-Columbian Metallurgy of South America*. Washington, DC: Dumbarton Oaks, 53–104.

Joralemon, D. and D. Sharon. 1993. *Sorcery and Shamanism: Curanderos and Clients in Northern Peru*. Salt Lake City: University of Utah Press.

Kauffman Doig, F. 1973. *Manual de Arqueología Peruana*. Lima: Ediciones Peisa.

Kaulicke, P. 1991. El Período Intermedio Temprano en Alto Piura: Avances del Proyecto Arqueológico "Alto Piura (1987–1990)." *Bulletin de l'Institut Francais d'Etudes Andines* 20(2), 381–422.

——1992. Moche, Vicús Moche y el Mochica Temprano. *Bulletin de l'Institut Francais d'Etudes Andines* 21(3), 853–903.

——1993. Evidencias Paleoclimáticas en el Alto Piura durante el Periódico Intermedio Temprano. In J. Macharé and L. Ortlieb (eds), *Registro de Fenómeno El Niño y de Eventos ENSO en América del Sur*. Lima: Bulletin de l'Institut Francais d'Etudes Andines 22(1), 283–311.

——1994. La Presencia Mochica en el Alto Piura: Problemática y Propuestas. In S. Uceda and E. Mujica (eds), *Moche: Propuestas y Perspectivas*, Lima: Travaux de l'Institut Francais d'Etudes Andines 79, 327–58.

Klein, O. 1967. *La Cerámica Mochica: Carácteres Estílicos y Conceptos*. Valparaíso: Universidad Técnica "Féderico Santa María," Scientia, 131.

Kolata, A. 1978. Chan Chan: The Form of the City in Time. Unpublished Ph.D. dissertation, Department of Anthropology, Harvard University, Cambridge, MA.

——1983. Chan Chan and Cuzco: On the Nature of the Ancient Andean City. In R.M. Leventhal and A.L. Kolata (eds), *Civilization in the Ancient Americas: Essays in Honor of Gordon R. Willey*, Albuquerque and Cambridge, MA: University of New Mexico Press and Peabody Museum of Archaeology and Ethnology, Harvard University, 345–72.

Kosok, P. 1965. *Life, Land and Water in Ancient Peru*. New York: Long Island University Press.

Kroeber, A.L. 1925. *The Uhle Pottery Collections from Moche*. Berkeley: University of California Publications in American Archaeology and Ethnology 21(5), 191–234.

——1926. *Archaeological Explorations in Peru, Part I: Ancient Pot-

tery from Trujillo. Chicago: Field Museum of Natural History, Anthropology Memoirs 2(1).

——1930. *Archaeological Explorations in Peru, Part II: The Northern Coast.* Chicago: Field Museum of Natural History, Anthropology Memoirs 2(2).

Kubler, G. 1948. Towards Absolute Time: Guano Archaeology. In W.C. Bennett (ed.), *A Reappraisal of Peruvian Archaeology,* Menasha, WI: Society for American Archaeology and Institute of Andean Research, Memoirs of the Society for American Archaeology 4: 29–50.

Kus, J.S. 1972. *Selected Aspects of Irrigation Agriculture in the Chimu Heartland, Peru.* Ph.D. dissertation, Department of Geography, University of California, Los Angeles. Ann Arbor, MI: University Microfilms International.

Kutscher, G. 1954. *Nordperuanische Keramic.* Monumenta Americana, I. Berlin: Gebr Mann.

——1955. *Ancient Art of the Peruvian North Coast.* Berlin: Gebr Mann.

——1983. *Nordperuanische Gefässmalereien des Moche-Stils.* Munich: Verlag C.H. Beck.

La Industria. 1995. Article on the Recent Discovery of the Skeletal Remains of Sacrificial Victims at the Huaca de la Luna. July 12: page 1, Trujillo, Peru.

Larco Hoyle, R. 1938. *Los Mochicas, Tomo 1.* Lima: La Crónica y Variedades.

——1939. *Los Mochicas, Tomo 2.* Lima, Rimac.

——1941. *Los Cupisniques.* Lima: La Crónica y Variedades.

——1944. *La Cultura Salinar.* Buenos Aires: Sociedad Geográfica Americana.

——1945. *La Cultura Virú.* Buenos Aires: Sociedad Geográfica Americana.

——1946. A Culture Sequence for the North Coast of Peru. In J. Steward (ed.), *Handbook of South American Indians,* Vol. 2, Washington, DC: Smithsonian Institution, Bureau of American Ethnology Bulletin 143.

——1948. *Cronología Arqueológica del Norte del Perú.* Buenos Aires: Sociedad Geográfica Americana.

——1965. *La Cerámica Vicús.* Lima: Santiago Valverde.

——1967. *La Cerámica de Vicús y sus Nexos con las Demás Culturas.* Lima: Santiago Valverde.

Lechtman, H. 1979. Issues in Andean Metallurgy. In E.P. Benson (ed.), *Pre-Columbian Metallurgy of South America,* Washington, DC: Dumbarton Oaks, 1–40.

——1980. The Central Andes: Metallurgy without Iron. In T.A. Wertime and J.D. Muhly (eds), *The Coming of the Age of Iron*, New Haven: Yale University Press, 267–334.

Lizárraga, R. de. [1560–1602] 1916. *Descripción Colonial*, 2 vols. Buenos Aires: Biblioteca Argentina 13, 14.

Lumbreras, L.G. 1979. *El Arte y la Vida Vicús*. Lima: Banco Popular del Perú.

——1987. *Vicús: Colección Arqueológica*. Lima: Museo Banco Central de Reserva del Perú.

Mackey, C.J. and C.M. Hastings. 1982. Moche murals from the Huaca de la Luna. In A. Cordy-Collins (ed.), *Pre-Columbian Art History: Selected Readings*, Palo Alto, CA: Peek Publications, 293–312.

Makowski, K. 1995. Los Señores de Loma Negra. In K. Makowski, C.B. Donnan, I. Amaro Bullon, L.J. Castillo, M. Diez Canseco, O. Eléspuru Revoredo, and J.A. Murro Mena (eds), *Vicús*, Lima: Banco de Crédito del Perú, 83–135.

Makowski, K., I. Amaro Bullon, and O. Eléspuru Revoredo. 1995. Historia de una Conquista. In K. Makowski, C.B. Donnan, I. Amaro Bullon, L.J. Castillo, M. Diez Canseco, O. Eléspuru Revoredo, and J.A. Murro Mena (eds), *Vicús*, Lima: Banco de Crédito del Perú, 211–81.

Martínez de Compañón y Bujando, B.J. [1782–1788] 1978–1991. *Trujillo del Perú a fines del Siglo XVIII*, 9 vols. Madrid: Ediciones Cultura Hispanica.

Masuda, S., I. Shimada, and C. Morris (eds). 1985. *Andean Ecology and Civilization*. Tokyo: University of Tokyo Press.

Matos, R. 1965–6. Algunas Consideraciones sobre el Estilo de Vicús. Lima: *Revista del Museo Nacional* 34, 89–130.

McClelland, D. 1990. A Maritime Passage from Moche to Chimu. In M.E. Moseley and A. Cordy-Collins (eds), *The Northern Dynasties: Kingship and Statecraft in Chimor*, Washington, DC: Dumbarton Oaks, 75–106.

McEwen, G.F. 1990. Some Formal Correspondences Between the Imperial Architecture of the Wari and Chimu Cultures of Ancient Peru. *Latin American Antiquity* 1(2), 97–106.

Means, P.A. 1931. *Ancient Civilizations of the Andes*. New York: Charles Scribner's Sons.

Menzel, D. 1964. Style and Time in the Middle Horizon. *Ñawpa Pacha* 2, 1–105.

——1969. New Data on the Huari Empire in Middle Horizon 2A. *Ñawpa Pacha* 6, 47–114.

——1977. *The Archaeology of Ancient Peru and the Work of Max*

Uhle. Berkeley: R.H. Lowie Museum of Anthropology, University of California.

Moore, J.D. 1995. The Archaeology of Dual Organization in Andean South America: A Theoretical Review and Case Study. *Latin American Antiquity* 6(2): 165–81.

Moorehead, A. 1969. *Darwin and the Beagle*. Harmondsworth, England: Penguin Books.

Moseley, M.E. 1975a. *The Maritime Foundations of Andean Civilization*. Menlo Park, CA: Cummings Publishing Company.

——1975b. Prehistoric Principles of Labor Organization in the Moche Valley, Peru. *American Antiquity* 40, 191–6.

——1978. An Empirical Approach to Prehistoric Agrarian Collapse: The Case of the Moche Valley. In N. Gonzalez (ed.), *Social and Technological Management in Dry Lands*, AAAS Selected Symposium, Boulder, CO: Westview Press, 9–43.

——1983. The Good Old Days *Were* Better: Agrarian Collapse and Tectonics. *American Anthropologist* 85(4), 773–99.

——1987. Punctuated Equilibrium: Searching the Ancient Record for El Niño. *The Quarterly Review of Anthropology* 8(3), 7–10.

——1992a. *The Incas and Their Ancestors*. London: Thames and Hudson.

——1992b. Maritime Foundations and Multilinear Evolution: Retrospect and Prospect. *Andean Past* 4, 5–42.

Moseley, M.E. and K.C. Day (eds). 1982. *Chan Chan: Andean Desert City*. Albuquerque: University of New Mexico Press.

Moseley, M.E. and E. Deeds. 1982. The Land in Front of Chan Chan: Agrarian Expansion, Reform, and Collapse in the Moche Valley. In M.E. Moseley and K.C. Day (eds), *Chan Chan: Andean Desert City*, Albuquerque: University of New Mexico Press, 25–53.

Moseley, M.E., R.A. Feldman, and C.R. Ortloff. 1981. Living With Crisis: Human Perception of Process and Time. In M. Nitecki (ed.), *Biotic Crises in Ecological and Evolutionary Time*, New York: Academic Press, 231–67.

Moseley, M.E. and C.J. Mackey. 1972. Peruvian Settlement Pattern Studies and Small Site Methodology. *American Antiquity* 37, 67–81.

——1974. *Twenty-Four Architectural Plans of Chan Chan, Peru*. Cambridge, MA: Peabody Museum Press, Harvard University.

Moseley, M.E. and L. Watanabe. 1974. The Adobe Sculpture of Huaca de los Reyes: Imposing Artwork from Coastal Peru. *Archaeology* 27(3), 154–61.

Murra, J.V. 1968. An Aymara Kingdom in 1567. *Ethnohistory* 15, 115–51.

——1980. *The Economic Organization of the Inka State.* Greenwich, CT: JAI Press.

Narváez, A. 1994. La Mina: una Tumba Moche I en el Valle de Jequetepeque. In S. Uceda and E. Mujica (eds), *Moche: Propuestas y Perspectivas,* Lima: Travaux de l'Institut Francais d'Etudes Andines 79, 59–92.

Netherly, P. 1977. *Local Level Lords on the North Coast of Peru.* Ph.D. dissertation, Department of Anthropology, Cornell University, Ithaca, NY. Ann Arbor, MI: University Microfilms International.

——1984. The Management of Late Andean Irrigation Systems on the North Coast of Peru. *American Antiquity* 49, 227–54.

——1990. Out of Many, One: The Organization of Rule in the North Coast Polities. In M.E. Moseley and A. Cordy-Collins (eds), *The Northern Dynasties: Kingship and Statecraft in Chimor,* Washington, DC: Dumbarton Oaks, 461–87.

Nials, F.L., E.E. Deeds, M.E. Moseley, S.G. Pozorski, T.G. Pozorski, and R.A. Feldman. 1979. El Niño: The Catastrophic Flooding of Coastal Peru. *Field Museum of Natural History Bulletin* 50(7), 4–14; (8), 4–10.

Nolan, J.L. 1980. *Prehispanic Irrigation and Polity in the Lambayeque Sphere, Peru.* Ph.D. dissertation, Department of Anthropology, Columbia University, New York. Ann Arbor, MI: University Microfilms International.

Obeyesekere, G. 1992. *The Apotheosis of Captain Cook.* Princeton, NJ: Princeton University Press.

Ortloff, C.R., R.A. Feldman, and M.E. Moseley. 1985. Hydraulic Engineering and Historical Aspects of the Pre-Columbian Intervalley Canal Systems of the Moche Valley, Peru. *Journal of Field Archaeology* 12, 77–98.

Ortloff, C.R., M.E. Moseley, and R.A. Feldman. 1983. The Chicama-Moche Intervalley Canal: Social Explanations and Physical Paradigms. *American Antiquity* 48, 375–89.

Patterson, T.C. 1991. *The Inca Empire: The Formation and Disintegration of a Pre-Capitalist State.* Oxford, England: Berg.

Paz Maldonado, J. [1582] 1965. Relación y Descripción de los Pueblos del Partido de Otavalo. In Marco Jiménez de la Espada (ed.), *Relaciones Geográficas de Indias,* tomo. 2, Madrid: Ediciones Atlas, 261–4.

Pozorski, S. and T. Pozorski. 1987. *Early Settlement and Subsistence in the Casma Valley, Peru.* Iowa City: University of Iowa Press.

Proulx, D.A. 1968. *An Archaeological Survey of the Nepeña Valley,*

Peru. Amherst: University of Massachussetts Department of Anthropology, Research Report 2.

—— 1982. Territoriality in the Early Intermediate Period: The Case of Moche and Recuay. *Ñawpa Pacha* 20, 83–96.

—— 1985. *An Analysis of the Early Cultural Sequence in the Nepeña Valley, Peru*. Amherst: University of Massachussetts Department of Anthropology, Research Report 25.

—— 1994. Stylistic Variation in Proliferous Nasca Pottery. *Andean Past* 4, 91–107.

Quilter, J. 1990. The Moche Revolt of the Objects. *Latin American Antiquity* 1, 42–65.

Rabinowitz, J. 1983. La Lengua Pescadora. In D.H. Sandweiss (ed.), *Investigations of the Andean Past*, Papers from the First Annual Northeast Conference on Andean Archaeology and Ethnology, Ithaca, NY: Cornell University Latin American Studies Program, 243–67.

Rappaport, J. 1990. *The Politics of Memory: Native Historical Interpretation in the Colombian Andes*. Cambridge, England: Cambridge University Press.

—— 1994. *Cumbe Reborn: An Andean Ethnography of History*. Chicago: University of Chicago Press.

Ravines, R. 1985. Early Monumental Architecture of the Jequetepeque Valley, Peru. In C.B. Donnan (ed.), *Early Ceremonial Architecture in the Andes*, Washington, DC: Dumbarton Oaks, 209–26.

Reinhard, J. 1991. *Machu Picchu the Sacred Center*. Lima: Nuevas Imagenes S.A.

—— 1993. *The Nazca Lines: A New Perspective on their Origin and Meaning*. Lima: Editorial Los Pinos E.I.R.L.

Richardson, J.B. III. 1987. The Chronology and Affiliations of the Ceramic Periods of the Departments of Piura and Tumbes. Paper presented at the 51st Annual Meeting of the Society for American Archaeology, Toronto.

Richardson, J.B. III, and Heaps de Peña, A. 1974. The Emergence of the State in the Chira Region of Northwest Peru. Paper Presented at the 39th Annual Meeting of the Society for American Archaeology, Washington, DC.

Rivero, M. and J.J. von Tschudi. 1855. *Peruvian Antiquities*. Translated by F.L. Hawkes. New York: A.S. Barnes and Company.

Roe, P.G. 1974. *A Further Exploration of the Rowe Chavín Seriation and its Implications for North Central Coast Chronology*. Washington, DC: Dumbarton Oaks Studies in Pre-Columbian Art and Archaeology 13.

——1982. *The Cosmic Zygote: Cosmology in the Amazon Basin.* New Brunswick, NJ: Rutgers University Press.

Rostworowski de Diez Canseco, M. 1975. Pescadores, Artesanos y Mercaderes Costeños en el Peru Prehispanico. Lima: *Revista del Museo Nacional* 41, 311–49.

——1977. Coastal Fishermen, Merchants, and Artisans in Prehispanic Peru. In E.P. Benson (ed.), *The Sea in the Pre-Columbian World*, Washington, DC: Dumbarton Oaks, 167–86.

——1981. *Recursos Naturales Renovables y Pesca, Siglos XVI y XVII.* Lima: Instituto de Estudios Peruanos.

Rowe, J.H. 1946. Inca Culture at the Time of the Spanish Conquest. In J.H. Steward (ed.), *Handbook of South American Indians*, Vol. 2, Washington, DC: Bureau of American Ethnology Bulletin 143(2).

——1948. The Kingdom of Chimor. *Acta Americana* 6, 26–59.

——1962a. *Chavín Art: An Inquiry into its Form and Meaning.* New York: The Museum of Primitive Man.

——1962b. Stages and Periods in Archaeological Interpretation. *Southwestern Journal of Anthropology* 18(1), 40–54.

Russell, G.S., B.L. Leonard, and J. Briceño. 1994. Cerro Mayal: Nuevos Datos Sobre Producción de Ceramica Moche en el Valle de Chicama. In S. Uceda and E. Mujica (eds), *Moche: Propuestas y Perpectivas*, Lima: Travaux de l'Institut Francais d'Etudes Andines 79, 181–206.

Sallnow, M.J. 1987. *Pilgrims of the Andes: Regional Cults in Cusco.* Washington, DC: Smithsonian Institution.

——1989. Precious Metals in the Andean Moral Economy. In J. Parry and M. Bloch (eds), *Money and the Morality of Exchange*, Cambridge, England: Cambridge University Press, 209–31.

Salomon, F. 1986. *Native Lords of Quito in the Age of the Incas: The Political Economy of North Andean Chiefdoms.* Cambridge, England: Cambridge University Press.

Salomon, F. and G.L. Urioste. 1991. *The Huarochirí Manuscript: A Testament of Ancient and Colonial Andean Religion.* Translated by F. Salomon and G.L. Urioste. Austin: University of Texas Press.

Schaedel, R.P. 1951a. Major Ceremonial and Population Centers in Northern Peru. In S. Tax (ed.), *The Civilizations of Ancient America: Selected Papers of the 29th International Congress of Americanists*, Chicago: University of Chicago Press, 232–43.

——1951b. Mochica Murals at Pañamarca. *Archaeology* 4(3), 145–54.

——1966. Urban Growth and Ekistics on the Peruvian Coast. *Proceedings of the 36th International Congress of Americanists.* Buenos Aires, Vol. 2, 531–9.

——1985. The Transition from Chiefdom to State in Northern Peru. In H.J.M. Claessen, P. van der Velde, and E. Smith (eds), *Development and Decline: The Evolution of Sociopolitical Organization*, South Hadley, MA: Bergin and Garvey, 156–69.

Schele, L. and M.E. Miller. 1986. *The Blood of Kings: Dynasty and Ritual in Maya Art*. Fort Worth, TX: Kimbell Art Museum.

Seler, E. 1912. Archaologische Reise in Sud- und Mittel-Amerika. *Zeitschrift für Ethnologie* 44, Heft 1, 201–42, Berlin: Berliner Gesellschaft für Anthropologie, Ethnologie und Urgeschichte.

Sharon, D. 1978. *Wizard of the Four Winds: A Shaman's Story*. New York: Free Press.

Sherbondy, J. 1982. *The Canal Systems of Hanan Cuzco*. Ph.D dissertation, Department of Anthropology, University of Illinois, Urbana.

Shimada, I. 1976. *Socioeconomic Organization at Moche V Pampa Grande, Peru: Prelude to a Major Transformation to Come*. Ph.D. dissertation, Department of Anthropology, University of Arizona. Ann Arbor, MI: University Microfilms International.

——1978. Economy of Prehistoric Urban Context: Commodity and Labor Flow in Moche V Pampa Grande, Peru. *American Antiquity* 43, 569–92.

——1987. Horizontal and Vertical Dimensions of Prehistoric States in Northern Peru. In J. Haas, S. Pozorski, and T. Pozorski (eds), *The Origins and Development of the Andean State*, Cambridge, England: Cambridge University Press, 130–44.

——1990. Cultural Continuities and Discontinuities on the Northern North Coast, Middle-Late Horizons. In M.E. Moseley and A. Cordy-Collins (eds), *The Northern Dynasties: Kingship and Statecraft in Chimor*, Washington, DC: Dumbarton Oaks, 297–392.

——1991. *Pachacamac Archaeology: Retrospect and Prospect*. Part I: A New Introduction to Max Uhle's *Pachacamac*. Philadelphia: The University Museum of Archaeology and Anthropology.

——1994a. *Pampa Grande and the Mochica Culture*. Austin: University of Texas Press.

——1994b. Los Modelos de Organización Sociopolítica de la Cultura Moche: Nuevos Datos y Perspectiva. In S. Uceda and E. Mujica (eds), *Moche: Propuestas y Perspectivas*, Lima, Travaux de l'Institut Francais d'Etudes Andines 79, 359–87.

Shimada, I. and R. Cavallaro. 1986. Monumental Adobe Architecture of the Late Pre-Hispanic Northern North Coast of Peru. *Journal de la Société des Américanistes* 71, 41–78.

Shimada, I. and A. Maguña. 1994. Nueva Visión sobre la Cultura Gallinazo y su Relación con la Cultura Moche. In S. Uceda and E.

Mujica (eds), *Moche: Propuestas y Perspectivas*, Lima: Travaux de l'Institut Francais d'Etudes Andines 79, 31–58.

Shimada, I. and J.F. Merkel. 1991. Copper Alloy Metallurgy in Ancient Peru. *Scientific American* 265, 80–6.

Shimada, I., C.B. Schaaf, L.G. Thompson, and E. Mosley-Thompson. 1991. Cultural Impacts of Severe Droughts in the Prehistoric Andes: Application of a 1500-year Ice Core Precipitation Record. *World Archaeology* 22(3), 247–70.

Shimada, M.J. and I. Shimada. 1985. Prehistoric Llama Breeding and Herding on the North Coast of Peru. *American Antiquity* 50, 3–26.

Squier, E.G. 1852. *Nicaragua: Its People, Scenery, Monuments.* 2 vols. New York: Harper.

—— 1877. *Peru: Incidents of Travel and Exploration in the Land of the Incas.* New York: AMS Press.

Squier, E.G. and E.H. Davis. 1848. *Ancient Monuments of the Mississippi Valley.* Washington, DC: Smithsonion Contributions to Knowledge, 1.

Stothert, K.E. 1992. Early Economies of Coastal Ecuador and the Foundations of Andean Civilization. *Andean Past* 3, 43–54.

Strong, W.D. and C. Evans 1952. *Cultural Stratigraphy in the Virú Valley, Northern Peru.* New York: Columbia University Studies in Archaeology and Ethnology, 4.

Tello, J.C. 1942. *Origen y Desarollo de las Civilizaciones Prehistóricas Andinas.* Lima: Actas del XXVII Congreso de Americanistes, 1939, Librería e Imprenta Gil.

Topic, T.L. 1977. Excavations at Moche. Unpublished Ph.D. dissertation, Department of Anthropology, Harvard University, Cambridge, MA.

—— 1982. The Early Intermediate Period and Its Legacy. In M. Moseley and K.C. Day (eds), *Chan Chan: Andean Desert City.* Albuquerque: University of New Mexico Press, 255–84.

—— 1991. The Middle Horizon in Northern Peru. In W.H. Isbell and G.F. McEwan (eds), *Huari Administrative Structure: Prehistoric Monumental Architecture and State Government.* Washington, DC: Dumbarton Oaks, 233–46.

Topic, J. and T. Topic. 1987. The Archaeological Investigation of Andean Militarism: Some Cautionary Observations. In J. Haas, S. Pozorski, and T. Pozorski (eds), *The Origins and Development of the Andean State.* Cambridge, England: Cambridge University Press, 47–55.

Torero, A. 1987. Deslindes Lingüísticos en la Costa Norte Peruana. In L. Muelle and H. Rodriguez (eds), *1ro y 2do Seminario de*

Investigaciones Sociales en la Región Norte (Cajamarca 1984 y 1986), Lima: Consejo Nacional de Ciencia y Tecnología, 111–35.

Turner, V. 1969. *The Ritual Process: Structure and Anti-Structure*. Chicago: Aldine.

Ubbelohde-Doering, H. 1967. *On the Royal Highways of the Inca*. London: Thames and Hudson.

——1983. *Vorspanische Graber von Pacatnamú, NordPeru*. Materialen zur Allegmeinen und Vergleichenden Archaologie, Band 26. Berlin: Verlag C.H. Beck.

Uceda, S. 1995. Proyecto Huaca de la Luna: Evaluacion y Perspectivas. *MASA: Revista Cultural del Indies*, Año VII, 09, 35–40.

Uceda, S. and J.C. Amico. 1993. Evidencias de Grandes Precipitaciones en Diversas Etapas Constructivas de la Huaca de la Luna, Costa Norte del Perú. *Bulletin de l'Institut Francais Etudes Andines* 22(1), 313–43.

Uceda, S., R. Morales, J. Canziani, and M. Montoya. 1994. Investigaciones Sobre la Arquitectura y Relieves Polícromos en la Huaca de la Luna, Valle de Moche In S. Uceda and E. Mujica (eds), *Moche: Propuestas y Perspectivas*, Lima: Travaux de l'Institut Francais d'Etudes Andines 79, 251–306.

Uhle, F.M. 1913. Die Ruinen von Moche. *Journal de la Société des Américanistes de Paris* n.s.10, 95–117.

——1915. Las Ruinas de Moche. *Boletín de la Sociedad Geográfica de Lima* 30(3–4), 57–71.

UNESCO. 1980. *Proceedings of the Workshop on the Phenomenon Known as El Niño*. Paris: United Nations Educational, Scientific, and Cultural Organization.

Urton, G. 1981. *At the Crossroads of the Earth and the Sky: An Andean Cosmology*. Austin: University of Texas Press.

——1990. *The History of a Myth: Pacariqtambo and the Origin of the Inkas*. Austin: University of Texas Press.

Willey, G.R. 1953. *Prehistoric Settlement Patterns in the Virú Valley, Peru*. Washington, DC: Smithsonian Institution, Bureau of American Ethnology Bulletin 155.

Williams, Carlos. 1985. A Scheme for the Early Monumental Architecture of the Central Coast of Peru. In C.B. Donnan (ed.), *Early Ceremonial Architecture in the Andes*, Washington, DC: Dumbarton Oaks, 227–40.

Wilson, D.L. 1988. *Prehispanic Settlement Patterns in the Lower Santa Valley, Peru: A Regional Perspective on the Origins and Development of Complex North Coast Society*. Washington, DC: Smithsonian Institution Press.

.

—— 1991. Prehispanic Settlement Patterns in the Casma Valley, North Peru: Preliminary Results of the 1989–1990 Seasons in the Casma Branch of the Valley. Second Report to the Committee for Research and Exploration. Washington, DC: National Geographic Society.

Wolf, E. 1982. *Europe and the People Without History*. Berkeley: University of California Press.

Zuidema, R.T. 1990. *Inca Civilization in Cuzco*. Austin: University of Texas Press.

Index

Printed in the United States
84888LV00008BB/1-6/A

9 780631 218630